Ca... BEYOND ANY
REASONABLE
DOUBT?

Class No. 345, 02523   Acc No. C/35,722
Author: DEALE, K.   Loc: 1 3 APR 1997

**LEABHARLANN
CHONDAE AN CHABHAIN**

1. **This book may be kept three weeks.
   It is to be returned on / before the last date
   stamped below.**
2. **A fine of 20p will be charged for every week
   or part of week a book is overdue.**

BEYOND ANY REASONABLE DOUBT?

A BOOK OF IRISH MURDER TRIALS

KENNETH E.L. DEALE

Gill and Macmillan

Published in Ireland by
Gill and Macmillan Ltd
Goldenbridge
Dublin 8
with associated companies in
Auckland, Delhi, Gaborone, Hāmburg, Harare,
Hong Kong, Johannesburg, Kuala Lumpur, Lagos, London,
Manzini, Melbourne, Mexico City, Nairobi,
New York, Singapore, Tokyo
© The Estate of the late Kenneth E.L. Deale 1960, 1971, 1990
0 7171 1811 8
Print origination by
Seton Music Graphics Ltd, Bantry, Co. Cork
Printed by
The Guernsey Press

Contents

Foreword

I am happy to write this foreword on the occasion of the republication of my late father's book, *Beyond any Reasonable Doubt.* Indeed, not only does this edition contain all the material from the first edition of 1971, it also includes three cases taken from the earlier work, *Memorable Irish Trials.*

I am sure that the time is ripe for the republication of these cases. I remember vividly that when my father's books first appeared there was considerable interest among lawyers and general public alike. Then, as now, so little had been written on Irish legal trials that there was an eager and enthusiastic readership at hand. I am sure that as with the first edition so with the second.

All these trials are thoroughly researched and lucidly written. They deal with and throw light upon some extremely interesting aspects of Irish life. All of them are cases which have post-dated the foundation of the state and, for a lawyer at least, that gives the book a certain piquant flavour, as it traces the gradual development of our independent system of jurisprudence. Most important of all, however, I believe that it brings the law alive for the layman with a vitality and immediacy that is hard to match.

I note that the publishers have retained the original format and have not updated the work in any way and I think that that enhances its appeal. Obviously many of the legal personnel referred to as being extant are no longer alive. Certain descriptions are perhaps now anachronistic, particularly my father's description of Corbawn Lane in 'Danse Macabre'. His description of it as it was then and as it was when he wrote the book bears no relationship to today's Corbawn Lane — a busy thriving residential area built up the whole way down from the main road to the sea.

However, I think it is right to retain the original format; otherwise it would require complete redrafting which would not convey the same sense of period which I think has been done very well by my late father.

I wish the publishers well with this new edition and I have no doubt that it will be a best seller! Certainly, my father would have been delighted to think that his work was destined to have such a long life in print. He laboured long and hard on the research; trawling through the records, obtaining transcripts of evidence and witnesses' testimony. Indeed, the thought occurs to me that the time may well be right for the publication of a further book, dealing with the many famous and infamous cases that have been tried since the first publication of *Beyond Any Reasonable Doubt*. However, I had better write no more on that point, for the ways of publishers are sometimes even more inscrutable than those of lawyers!

Julian Deale
Dublin
July 1990

Preface

The Nature of Circumstantial Evidence

A friend once remarked to me, 'I would never convict a man on circumstantial evidence', showing that, like many people, he misunderstood the nature of this kind of evidence. Since criminal wrongdoers usually take care not to be seen committing their crimes and criminal trials nearly always depend on circumstantial evidence, a short explanation of the nature of circumstantial evidence may be helpful.

Circumstantial evidence is contrasted with direct evidence. If you see A putting his hand into B's pocket, taking out B's wallet, and running away with it, and you swear at A's trial, you will be giving direct evidence. You have seen the event, and no inference is needed to show that A is the thief. But suppose that you only see A standing beside B, and having looked away for a moment, you look again and see A running. You pursue and catch him and find B's wallet in his hand. If all this is sworn to at A's trial, it will be circumstantial evidence that A picked B's pocket. Nobody saw him do it, but the only rational inference from the circumstances is that he is the thief.

So far, so good. But the circumstances may point to more than one inference. Suppose this time that A and B, strangers to each other, are staying at the same hotel. On Monday B's wallet is stolen, the thief being unknown. On Wednesday the wallet is found in a drawer in A's room, and that is the only evidence against A. It cannot now be safely inferred that A is the thief, for the presence of the wallet in his bedroom may equally well mean that someone else stole it, and either gave it to A, who put it in the drawer, or hid it there unknown to A — a reasonable probability, since a hotel room may be accessible to several people besides the occupier. So, more than one inference being equally open, A cannot be convicted of the theft. The foregoing are simple examples designed

1

to show the nature of circumstantial evidence, but, of course, in a trial the facts are far more numerous and, because of contradictions, difficult to determine.

Circumstantial evidence has its limits, but is frequently more reliable than direct testimony, for it is not subject to human frailty. If a witness swears that he saw the accused, a stranger to him, at the scene of a crime fifty yards away on a dark night, he may be convinced he is right, yet he may be wrong. The bad light, a defect in his vision, or a simple mistake in identification such as is often made even in daylight, may vitiate his testimony. Suppose, though, that no one sees the accused, but a footprint identifiable with one of his shoes is found at the scene, or some threads which match a tear in his coat, or even a personal belonging such as a ring or cigarette case — that evidence may be much safer proof that he was in fact there.

It is said that circumstantial evidence cannot lie, and in one sense this is true. Its weakness is not in its nature, but in the inference which the tribunal chooses to draw from it. If more than one inference is open, the rule of law is that the accused may not be convicted unless the inferences point conclusively to his guilt, and to no other rational conclusion. When this rule is properly applied, circumstantial evidence is by far the most reliable evidence.

K.E.L.D.

Beyond Any Reasonable Doubt?

(Attorney-General v. David O'Shea, 1931)

THE COUNTY CORK HORROR was the newspapers' description of the murder in 1931 of Ellen O'Sullivan, aged 24. It was a clear case of murder; less clear was the identity of the murderers. Ellen O'Sullivan lived with her parents, brothers and sisters outside Rathmore, a village in County Kerry, near the border between Counties Cork and Kerry. She was a strong, handsome girl, the daughter of a small farmer, and at the time of her death was unofficially engaged to Jeremiah Cronin, farmer and garage owner. She used to cycle daily to her work at the creamery on a machine, the back mudguard of which was loose and made a distinctive rattle — a point of importance.

On Sunday 8 February 1931, after attending morning Mass, she and her father went to two funerals in Rathmore, returning home in the afternoon. Ellen went out at about 4 p.m. on her bicycle to call on her cousin Kathleen Moynihan, who lived at the far end of the village, and after she left the house her father never saw her alive again. She stayed with her cousin until about 6.30, when the two left the house, Ellen carrying a novel *The Gamblers*, borrowed from Kathleen, and they walked down the village street to where Cronin was waiting. The girls parted then, and Ellen and Cronin walked off together along the dark unlit road. It was now about 6.45 p.m.

Cronin had come into Rathmore earlier in the day in his car with two friends, to one of whom — Kelleher — he lent his car while he was with Ellen. Kelleher brought the car to a crossroads called Shinagh Cross, a short distance outside Rathmore, and there waited while Cronin and his fiancée strolled, she wheeling her bicycle, towards Ellen's home about half-an-hour's walk away. It was a route they had taken at least thirty or forty times in the previous two years, varying it by an occasional visit to Ellen's house. On the way, that night, they passed and greeted several people and finally stopped to talk near the cottage belonging to Timothy Hickey, whom they had met a few minutes earlier. After about fifteen minutes the lovers parted, Cronin walking back to Shinagh Cross, and Ellen O'Sullivan going down the lonely side road to her home, and to her death. These roads were then, and are even today, unlit quiet country roads in a district where the few inhabitants all knew each other. By day and by night passers-by always noticed and greeted each other even if strangers. Cronin reached Shinagh Cross at about 8.35 p.m. and his friends were there with the car, in which he drove to his home seven miles away.

When by midnight Ellen O'Sullivan had not appeared, her parents became alarmed, and alerted some neighbours who made a search, but in the dark it was useless. Next day, as she had neither come home nor gone to work, the Gardaí were notified and a massive search begun. The first discovery was Ellen's bicycle leaning against a ditch beside a house about 250 yards from Shinagh Cross, and visible to all. But there was no sign of the missing girl, and the search continued for five more days, until 14 February when a Mr John Murphy found her dead body near the river which separates the counties of Kerry and Cork. Murphy was searching the ground above the river bank on the Kerry side, when he noticed a mass of hair protruding from under a furze bush. He peered in and saw what looked like a human body, and with the help of two Gardaí he lifted out the dead girl. The body had lain on a bed of growing furze and was covered with broken branches of furze. It was naked from the waist down, save for part of a stocking on one leg and a complete stocking on the other. Above the waist were a piece of overcoat torn down the back, stained with sand and mud, and a pullover, slip, corset and chemise similarly stained.

Soon afterwards other clothing was found nearby, in a field on the Cork side of the river. The girl's hat, covered with gravel, a handkerchief, gaiter, and a belt were all in a pile of stones and gravel in a corner of this field, which was just off the road where Ellen O'Sullivan lived. Three days later one of her shoes was found on top of a hedge along the main road to Shinagh Cross, not very far from the field mentioned already. More than one person passing along that road had noticed the shoe, without disturbing it from its strange position, but on 15 February when a Garda went to recover the shoe it was no longer on the hedge top. It was now on the ground inside the field and covered with furze. The

4

book *The Gamblers* was found in two parts, the title page and cover on the grass margin on the public road, and the rest of the book hidden in another field in the vicinity. There was still some under-clothing unaccounted for, but a vigilant Sergeant of the Gardaí discovered it all, except the knickers, rolled up and stuffed into a hole covered over with grass. The knickers did not come to light until 9 March, when they were found by a Garda at the base of a fence on the land of Denis O'Sullivan, the murdered girl's father. They too were rolled up and concealed. Beside the knickers was a car cushion with some flock (stuffing) attached. These articles were about 260 yards from the house of David O'Shea, whose small holding adjoined O'Sullivans'.

An examination of the area on the Cork side of the river showed tracks leading from the gravel and stones through a gap into the next field and from there to the river, which at this point had no bank but instead a cliff. The distance from the gravel to the cliff edge was 250 yards, and the tracks were strongly suggestive of a body having been dragged. The tracks ended at the cliff top, and the body had been found on the far side of the river. How, if dragged to the cliff, had it been got across? There was a ford below the cliff, and the murderer must have cast or lowered the body down to this, and then dragged it through the waters to the far bank where it had been found. A small island in the middle of the narrow river would have helped this grisly operation, con-ducted as it must have been in black darkness.

The murdered girl had weighed about ten stone, so that the killer must have been strong, and, said the Gardaí, must have been a local man, who knew that field and gap and the cliff, ford, and river, else he could not have known in the dark how to get the body to the cliff, or even known the river was there.

It was now possible for the Gardaí to work out a theory of how the murder had been committed. Anyone knowing Ellen O'Sulli-van's habits would expect her to pass along the lonely road to her home after leaving Cronin, and could have waited for her in the dark. He would either have induced her to come into the field, or pulled her in, and then attacked her, afterwards moving the body as suggested. Who was this person?

Whoever he was, Jeremiah Cronin was under suspicion; although he lived seven miles away and might not have know the field and river as the murdered seemed to, Cronin was the last person known to have been with Ellen O'Sullivan. He was fortunate that his movements were accounted for by independent witnesses. His times of walking down the road with the girl, and returning to Shinagh Cross were proved by several people, yet only by estimates — half an hour, about twenty minutes, about eight o'clock, and so on. Nobody had read any of the times on a watch or clock, and Cronin could have murdered the girl between being last seen on the way back towards Hickey's cottage with her, and next seen on the way back to Shinagh Cross. He had no one to support his statement that Ellen O'Sullivan had left him on her bicycle to go down the road to her home. And if he was the murderer, he could have come back in his car later that night to the field, when all was quiet, taken the body across the river — if he knew the way — and driven home again. So Cronin's position was serious, and although there was really no evidence against him he was arrested on 14 February and kept in custody for nine days.

But later clues caused the finger of suspicion to move towards David O'Shea. He was a neighbour of the O'Sullivans, a labourer aged 33 who owned a few cattle and a small piece of land, and was a man of limited intelligence. He lived with his mother and sister in a cottage at Knockanalamon, close to Rathmore, and of course knew Ellen O'Sullivan, but beyond dancing with her occasionally at the local dance hall and passing the time of day with her when they would meet, he rarely spoke to her.

On the evening of the murder, O'Shea had left home about 6.30 and walked towards Rathmore village. A Mrs Hickey who lived near him was going in the same direction and they walked some of the way together. She asked him if he was going to his father's house, which was a little past the village, and he said he was not, but was going to a shop. O'Shea was perfectly normal as they chatted, and they parted when Mrs Hickey's young son appeared whom she was meeting, O'Shea continuing in the direction of the village. Mrs Hickey had seen O'Shea that morning near Mass time, wearing what she said were his usual Sunday clothes and black polished leggings with black boots. Several other people confirmed that he had been wearing black leggings that morning, but Mrs Hickey did not see if he still wore the leggings that night as it was too dark. No other person so far as was known saw David O'Shea again that night or could say where he had gone after leaving Mrs Hickey. The importance of the leggings was that a single black left legging had been found in a pool on the little island in the river. It had the usual small strap and buckle at the top for securing it to the leg, and at the bottom, a steel piece for the same purpose. Another find was a single grey sock on the Cork side of the river bank, 45 yards downstream from where the body had been found.

The Gardaí interviewed O'Shea in February at his cottage, and asked him to account for his movements on the eighth, and he told them about meeting Mrs Hickey, which they knew already, and going on towards Shinagh Cross, on the way to which he met, coming on towards him, a man and girl, she wheeling a bicycle. He said he did not recognise these people, though they were almost certainly Cronin and Ellen O'Sullivan both of whom he knew, but he gave a greeting which the man returned. At the trial the prosecution suggested that O'Shea, after meeting these two, had doubled back and waylaid the girl when she was alone.

When he reached Shinagh Cross, O'Shea said, at about 7 p.m., nobody was there, nor the car, and he waited for half an hour without person or car appearing. As at least seven people had told the Gardaí of Cronin's car being there, and of five or six different persons being there at O'Shea's time, it was clear that O'Shea was lying, and either he never reached the Cross — this was the prosecution's suggestion — or he had got there much later than he said, and the question was: Where had he been in the meantime? He had left the Cross, he said, at about 8 o'clock and walked home, arriving about 9 o'clock and meeting no one on the way, and especially not Ellen O'Sullivan. His house was in darkness as his mother and sister were already in bed, and he went straight to bed without taking any food.

When the interview ended, the Gardaí made a superficial search of the cottage, and found in O'Shea's bedroom a pair of brown — not black — leggings, not hidden but displayed for all to see on a window ledge. Outside, a manure heap, on being turned over with a fork, yielded up some flock — a material used for stuffing cushions. The brown leggings, according to several people who knew O'Shea well and saw him daily, were worn by him on weekdays, and never on Sundays. He wore black leggings, they said, on Sundays.

––––––––

The Gardaí were not satisfied with O'Shea's account of his movements, and soon afterwards questioned him again. He stuck to what he had said the first time, but added a kind of explanation for his seemingly odd behaviour in standing at the Cross, alone on a cold February night, for half an hour or more: 'I thought I'd take a trip

7

to my father's, but I thought I stopped too long at the Cross.' This really explained nothing, but it revealed itself as a lie, for he had told Mrs Hickey as they walked along that he was not going to his father's house, and obviously had forgotten this. And his father's house was a mere five minutes walk from the Cross, so the wait at the Cross really looked strange. But at a third interview, O'Shea furnished final proof that he was lying about his movements, for he told the Gardaí he had left home *intending* to go to his father's, but had changed his mind, 'probably' when at the Cross, and decided not to go because if he did he would stay there gambling until late.

He was asked about his leggings, and said he had worn no leggings at all on 8 February. He said he sometimes wore brown leggings on Sundays, which he often blackened with black polish though he had not done so that year. He denied positively that he ever had owned any black leggings although (probably unknown to him) a shoe repairer named Humphrey McAuliffe of Rathmore had told the Gardaí of having repaired a black legging for O'Shea in the previous May or June. McAuliffe could not identify the legging found at the river as O'Shea's, but said it had a repair similar to one he had often done on that kind of legging — a lining inserted where legging and boot rubbed together. And he had never repaired the brown leggings. But a neighbour, Timothy Collins, proved convincingly to police (and jury) that the black legging was O'Shea's, for one night when he and O'Shea were at a cottage dance together he saw the protruding steel rib in O'Shea's left legging rip the leather. O'Shea and his partner had had to stop dancing while the legging was secured again, and Collins recognised the river legging by the protruding steel rib, and was sure it was the same one. Asked at the trial how he could be certain that it was O'Shea's *left* legging, he answered with assurance. 'O'Shea was next to the cottage door, and the door was facing to the east, and his left foot was nearest the door.'

Some days later the Gardaí saw O'Shea again, determined to try and get from him what they believed to be the truth. This time the interview was in the nature of a cross-examination of one hundred and four questions altogether, which O'Shea answered surprisingly well, especially considering he was an ignorant labourer up against an experienced and able Garda Superintendent. After he told Superintendent O'Dowd that he had met a young man and two girls on the way to the Cross, and gave them a greeting, and nearer the Cross another young man with one girl, the questioning proceeded:

1. *Q.* Did you meet any other person between there and Shinagh Cross?
   A. I did.
2. *Q.* Who?
   A. Yes, I remember meeting a boy and a girl.
3. *Q.* Who were they?
   A. I did not know them at all; a sure fact.
4. *Q.* Did you speak to them?
   A. Yes, I said good-night.
5. *Q.* Did they reply?
   A. Yes, the man did. They were talking very low and walking easy.
6. *Q.* Had they anything with them?
   A. Yes, they had. The girl had a bicycle.
7. *Q.* Who was that girl?
   A. I can't say. I did not know her.
8. *Q.* Where did you meet the boy and the girl with the bicycle?
   A. I met them about 100 yards after meeting the boy with the two girls.
9. *Q.* How was the girl dressed?
   A. It was a dark night, and they all appeared to me to be wearing dark clothes.

It will be noticed O'Shea's answer to the dangerous question 3 is emphatic — 'a sure fact'— and that is the only place where emphasis occurs. The two people were assuredly Cronin and Ellen O'Sullivan, and it was most unlikely that O'Shea did not recognise them, even in the black dark, for in the small community he would be certain to know his next door neighbour's daughter. But he had twice before told the Gardaí he did not know the pair, and he was obviously determined to maintain this position, and so dissociate himself from any knowledge of the movements of the girl that night. And that could be consistent with innocence, for O'Shea would not want to say anything to suspicious Gardaí which could possibly involve him in the crime; after all, Cronin was already in custody. But O'Shea cannot have realised he was trying to do the impossible — to place himself on the road at the important time to show innocence, and yet dissociate himself from the guilty connotation that he knew Ellen O'Sullivan was there then. And none of the people O'Shea said he met (including Cronin, whom he said he did not know he met) could say that they saw him. How then did O'Shea know that these several people were on the road

9

at that time? If he *was* there, yet not seen, he must have been in hiding. And that was the prosecution's suggestion — that he had lain in wait.

The questioning continued, some of it covering familiar ground, the Superintendent perhaps trying to break his suspect. But he failed, though the repeated denials told him something, as did the emphasis in the answers to the dangerous questions 16 and 17.

10. *Q.* Had you leggings on you that Sunday, 8 February?
    A. No.
11. *Q.* Do you ever wear leggings on Sunday?
    A. Yes. I do, sometimes.
12. *Q.* What sort of leggings are they?
    A. Brown ones.
13. *Q.* Did you ever blacken them?
    A. I did often.
14. *Q.* When did you blacken them last?
    A. Not this year anyway.
15. *Q.* Did you ever go to Mass without blackening the leggings?
    A. Perhaps I did.
16. *Q.* Did you ever get leggings repaired?
    A. No, sure.
17. *Q.* Are you certain of that?
    A. I am, sure.
18. *Q.* Who does your repairs?
    A. Humphrey McAuliffe of Rathmore.
19. *Q.* When did he do repairs for you last?
    A. At the present time he has a pair of boots belonging to me.
20. *Q.* When before did he do repairs for you?
    A. 'Tis two months ago, anyway, he repaired a pair of strong boots for me.
21. *Q.* When did he repair leggings for you last?
    A. Not for me.
22. *Q.* When did you last buy a pair of leggings?
    A. 'Tis six years ago, I got them from Mike Lynch of Rathmore.

The Gardaí made another visit to O'Shea's cottage, and found a single grey sock. And a dramatic incident occurred there, still talked of in the district forty years afterwards and which will be described later. The investigations continued for about two more weeks, and then O'Shea was arrested and charged with the murder.

The Trial

O'Shea's trial began on 9 June 1931, before Mr Justice Hanna and a jury, and took four days. Ellen O'Sullivan had been violently assaulted with blows over the eyes and head, the latter probably by a heavy stone which caused bleeding, unconsciousness, and death soon or immediately afterwards. The murderer had seized her by the throat, but without strangling her, and had brutally raped her. Ellen O'Sullivan had been a virgin, and either the connection had continued after death, or the man had had a fresh connection with her after death, a fact which must have coloured the jury's feelings. There was no controversy on the medical evidence, during which the public were excluded from court, and Mr Thomas O'Donnell, counsel for O'Shea, did not cross-examine.

Horrible though these injuries were, it might have been thought that O'Shea's chances of an acquittal were reasonably good, for the case against him was thin. There were no bloodstains on his clothes, nor seminal stains on his trousers and, whatever the suspicions may have been, nobody had seen him in Ellen O'Sullivan's company that night. Of course, if there had been blood stains, O'Shea had had at least five days to remove them, but that of course was no proof that there had been stains. And it was unlikely that a man of O'Shea's limited intelligence would have known to look for, and remove, seminal stains from his clothing.

The prosecution proved all the facts already narrated, and some new ones. Garda Tormey, one of about a hundred Gardaí who had been engaged in investigating the murder, said that on 18 February he had noticed scratches and small wounds on O'Shea's hands, and asked him about them. He had examined the backs of the hands and saw that the scratches were somewhat dried up, and seemed healed. O'Shea made a statement that on 11 and 12 February he had been cutting furze in a ditch near his cottage, using a reaping hook and a 'goulogue' — a forked instrument to keep the prickly furze away from the worker's hand as he cuts with the hook. According to O'Shea, the furze branches scratched his hands as they fell. Tormey asked him to demonstrate how this had happened, and they went out to the ditch, where O'Shea placed the goulogue against the bottom of the vertical furze branch, and the hook around the top; so, of course, when he cut with the hook the branch fell towards, instead of away from, his right hand. Properly used, the goulogue should be placed at about the middle of the branch, and the cut should be made near

11

the bottom, so that on severance the loose branch is still controlled by the goulogue. Tormey agreed, of course, when asked by Mr O'Donnell, that the scratches on O'Shea's left hand could have been caused by the branches falling on it from the way O'Shea had demonstrated, though this left the right hand cuts unexplained. Still, it had not been a bad performance for a stupid man under suspicion of murder, but Tormey, who knew how the goulogue should be used, added that the area O'Shea said he had cut — 7 or 8 yards long — should have taken about half an hour, and not six hours as O'Shea claimed, the point being that O'Shea had too many scratches on his hands for half an hour's work.

Mr O'Donnell had tried to keep out Tormey's evidence, suggesting that O'Shea had been in no fit condition to make a statement, being bewildered and confused from ceaseless Garda questioning and shadowing daily, and even having to submit to Gardaí living in his cottage. All these suggestions, except the last, were denied by Tormey, and the Judge allowed them in the evidence to be given. But Mr O'Donnell's cross-examination watered down Tormey's evidence somewhat, though Tormey flatly rejected the suggestion that O'Shea was exhausted and desperate when he made the statement and was making mistakes. Then came this question:

Q. When the statement was finished, was he not a little more stupid that he naturally is?
A. No, he didn't betray any signs of stupidity *whatever.*

That was asking a lot of the jury to believe. But Tormey agreed that putting furze in drains, which is one of its uses, must scratch the hands, and that the drains on O'Shea's land were at least 120 yards long and filled with furze. And, indeed, any handling of cut furze must scratch the skin, including, of course, breaking the furze used to conceal Ellen O'Sullivan's body.

Two vital matters in the case were the whereabouts of the fellow of the black legging found in the pool, and of the sock found on the river bank, and whether either pair was owned by O'Shea. The prosecution set about proving these matters with some unusual evidence. Garda John Keane was amongst a party of Gardaí who had visited and searched O'Shea's house on 15 February. They were there about two hours and then departed — all but Keane. Unknown to the O'Sheas, Keane had hidden himself under a bed in the room used by Mrs O'Shea and her daughter Kathy. If the O'Sheas had counted the number of Gardaí who arrived, and the number who left, they would have known that one was still in the house, but they hadn't.

12

Garda Keane's evidence held the courtroom in tense silence. He described how he got under the bed, helped by two other Gardaí, and heard all his companions leaving. The bedroom door was then open. O'Shea came into the cottage from the yard, and Keane heard the following dialogue from the kitchen, the centre room in the building, and adjoining the room where he lay concealed.

Kathy: My God, where is the legging? Did they take it?

O'Shea: See is it behind the box. Look quick. It's here.

Kathy: Rush quick, take it away. Burn it.

David O'Shea then left hurriedly for the yard and returned after a couple of minutes.

O'Shea: It is all right now.

Kathy: Wasn't it the luck of God they did not take it away or we were ruined? That was a nice Garda that was looking at it. We were lucky the others did not see it.

O'Shea: They are looking for clothes. I wonder did they take my trousers? They were looking at them but I told them they got wet digging drains and they went and looked at the drains.

Kathy: Didn't I tell you to brush your clothes when you came in that night? Wasn't it well that we washed the pants? Didn't I tell you not to leave any clay on them — that is what they were looking for.

At this point O'Shea began to brush his clothes but the dialogue went on.

O'Shea: What did you do with the sock?

Kathy: I was looking for it all day and I couldn't find it. My God! I must burn it if I find it. They were looking at the hatchet and the hammer. They must have suspicions of you. I suppose it was Timmy Hickey who told them that he saw you. Do you think they will come for you tonight? They might come in the middle of the night for you.

O'Shea: Let them. Sure they will not prove it for I gave a good account of myself in the statement I gave. I said I was at Shinagh Cross at 8 o'clock. Sure I saw Cronin with Ellen O'Sullivan that night but I did not tell them.

Kathy: If they come again don't tell them another word and don't leave the house this night. Don't go to the wake either.

Keane was under the bed, lying on his side, in a cramped uncomfortable position for half an hour, during which Kathy and the accused came into the room, and lifted up a sack in the corner containing books, but did not see him. When the half hour was

13

up, some of the other Gardaí returned, rescued Keane, and all departed, without the O'Shea having any inkling that they had been overheard. Keane had no writing materials under the bed, but when he got back to the barracks ten minutes later he immediately wrote down from memory what he had learned.

This was remarkable testimony. But was it accurate? The dialogue, which Keane said was not sustained or continuous but was spoken in snatches, revealed some very odd things. One of the articles the Gardaí went to the cottage to find was the missing black leggings, yet Kathy O'Shea said that 'a nice Garda' looked at it, and how lucky they were no other Garda saw it. So, a Garda sees the wanted legging yet does not immediately seize it, or report its presence to a superior. Even stranger, however, Kathy has to ask her brother where is the legging, although she saw the nice Garda look at it, and O'Shea has to ask her if it is behind the box and presumably, from his next words, searches there and finds it.

Although the vital missing legging is in the kitchen, Keane stays under the bed and makes no attempt to retrieve it. The Judge wanted to know why:

1. *Q.* Then why didn't you jump out immediately and look behind the box to see if the legging was there?
   A. Because I thought at the time when the man left the house that we would be in a position to find the legging afterwards, and that by remaining under the bed I could have got further information concerning the crime.
2. *Q.* You thought they would leave the legging about?
   A. Yes. I thought we could find it afterwards.
3. *Q.* But the woman said, 'Rush quick, take it away and burn it.' Did that not show they were about to destroy evidence, and what explanation have you for lying under the bed after that?
   A. I thought the legging could be found afterwards, but had they attempted to burn it I would have undoubtedly left the room. I thought when the man left the room and went out of the house that the legging would be found afterwards.
4. *Q.* Did you not think he was taking it away to burn it.
   A. No, my lord, I did not form that opinion at all.

As Keane did not believe O'Shea was going to burn the legging, one would expect that he might have searched for it immediately on being relieved, or told another Garda to do so, or perhaps

14

informed his superior officer there and then of what he had heard about the legging. But he did none of these things, and simply returned to the barracks where he made his report.

One may wonder, however, how five Gardaí had failed in a two-hour search of a small cottage to find a legging which was behind a box in the kitchen. What kind of a search was that? As Mr O'Donnell put it to the jury, pouring scorn on the whole episode, in two hours the searchers would have poked out everything in the place, even to the cockroaches! One may also wonder why O'Shea and his sister — if she was privy to the murder — had kept the legging instead of hiding or destroying it. Why keep such a dangerous object?

Yet another remarkable thing is that mother and sister were in O'Shea's confidence about the murder, for otherwise the dialogue could never have taken place. But is this credible? Stupid though he was, would O'Shea have told his sister that he had attacked Ellen O'Sullivan? Perhaps his wet clothing — if he had forded the river — and dishevelled appearance called for some explanation if the women had been up when he got home, at whatever hour it was. But if it was late, which seems likely if he were the murderer, it is improbable that either woman would have been up. However, if O'Shea did have to explain his condition, is it likely that he would tell Kathy, and thus provide a witness against himself? It is much more probable that he would tell her some cock and bull story to stop her questions, and that she may have guessed the rest, or some of it. But he would surely keep the truth to himself as long as possible, except in the final resort.

Superintendent O'Dowd was the next witness, and sprang another surprise. He told how, after Keane's return to the barracks, he (O'Dowd) had gone to O'Shea's cottage at about 7.30 p.m. and searched it. He found a grey sock in a disused milk tankard in O'Shea's bedroom which, as Mr O'Donnell pointed out, was very strange indeed since the cottage had been searched that afternoon and no sock had been found. And even stranger, if this was the missing sock, how did Kathy O'Shea not know it was there when she spoke to her brother as Garda Keane lay under the bed?

She was looking for it all day, according to the dialogue, and wanted to burn it. Therefore she had not put the sock into the tankard, for either she would have remembered doing so, or if she had forgotten would have looked there in her day-long search. And O'Shea could not have put it there either, for if he had he would have asked Kathy what she had done with it, which implied, of course, that he did not have it to put there. And Mrs O'Shea can be eliminated from this enquiry, for she was a quiet old woman and would not have interfered in such a matter, but if she had taken the sock she would have told Kathy on being asked. And, finally, the tankard was in a very odd place for one of the O'Sheas to choose to put the sock in. So who put it there? Was it a police 'plant'? Apart from the oddity of the sock only being found on the second search — 'it baffles me,' as the Judge said when he was charging the jury — it was very curious that this other incriminating article had also been kept by the O'Sheas in the house for seven days instead of being destroyed, for the Keane dialogue showed that they knew the sock was incriminatory.

The sock was so important that one might have expected Superintendent O'Dowd to confront O'Shea with it, and ask for his explanation, as had been done when the manure heap was being turned over. O'Shea had been standing by then and had been asked to explain where the flock came from. But the sock was found in his absence (if it was not a 'plant'), removed without his knowledge, and produced to him for the first time at his trial. Fairness alone demanded that he be shown the sock when it was found, and be asked a few more questions after the hundred already asked by the police. Was the omission to question him sinister?

The prosecution had to prove that the river sock and the tankard sock were a pair, and sought to do this through Dr John McGrath, the State pathologist. A textile expert, or an analyst, might have been a better choice for this important task. Dr McGrath told of a microscopic examination which showed that the socks were made of wool, had the same number of stitches at the top, in the body, at the bottom and at the heel, and were equal in height and foot length. The fibres were similar, and grains like oat husks were embedded in each sock. The differences between the two socks were in their colour, the tankard sock being lighter, and their state of repair, that sock having been repaired, whereas the river sock had holes in the toe and top. Dr McGrath's opinion was that the socks were exactly similar save for the colour difference, due, he thought, to one (the river sock) having been exposed and thus become darker, but this opinion was based upon the unproved assumption that the tankard sock had never been exposed like the river sock. There was no evidence, whatever of the history of the tankard sock — there couldn't have been. Dr McGrath said that the grey thread was composed of white fibres and coloured fibres, which together produced the grey colour. Exposure would cause

16

the white fibres to darken, and the coloured ones to lose brilliance. This opinion was based on an experiment of dubious value, with a pair of coloured — not grey — socks which the pathologist had *not* microscopically examined and which might, or might not, have contained cotton, the behaviour of which under exposure might or might not be different from that of wool. And the experimental exposure had not been in water for six days, but on grass in the open air for three weeks. Perhaps the two grey socks were really a pair, but there is an uncomfortable lack of certainty about the proof.

The prosecution case had now closed, and Mr O'Donnell applied to have the case withdrawn from the jury for lack of evidence, but the Judge refused to do this, and so David O'Shea went to the witness box. His evidence followed what he had already told the Gardaí. He had not worn leggings on 8 February. He denied positively that he and his sister had had any of the dialogue as narrated by Garda Keane, or that he had gone out to the yard when Keane was in the house — of which he had of course not known.

The solo black legging was handed to him by Mr O'Donnell, and he said it was not his, and that brown leggings were the only ones he ever owned, which he blackened sometimes and then they would look as black as the single black legging. He said he had worked nearly two weeks at the furze for his ditches, and not half an hour as Garda Tormey had suggested. He denied owning a sock like the tankard one and never wore such, but it is unlikely the jury believed that, for the socks were of the type very commonly worn by men such as O'Shea.

Mr Vincent Rice, K.C., cross-examined O'Shea, who was soon in difficulties. He said he did not know that Cronin had been courting Ellen O'Sullivan, which the jury must have disbelieved, for O'Shea lived in the house next to the girl, and it was inconceivable that in a small place like Rathmore he would not have known her young man. That lie forced him to say that he had never seen the girl on a Sunday in the young man's company during the previous two years, although Cronin had sworn he and she had passed along the road together at least forty or fifty times at night and many times in daylight, but O'Shea was trying to refute the prosecution's suggestion that he knew Ellen O'Sullivan would be on her road home alone that night.

Mr Rice handed O'Shea the brown leggings, and O'Shea had to agree that they had no sign of black polish on them but, he said, it was four months since he had used black polish on them —

i.e. four months before the murder, for the brown leggings had been in the Gardaí possession from February. O'Shea was in a corner, for he was saying in effect that the brown leggings looked brown and not black in February, and it followed, therefore, that those who saw black leggings on him on 8 February had not seen a brown one blackened but a black pair and therefore that the black polishing of the brown leggings was a red herring. He denied that McAuliffe had ever repaired a legging for him.

The next topic was the field with the gap in it, and he was asked if he knew the cliff above the river bank. He said he did, but when the question was repeated in a slightly different form, he said he did not take any notice of it, and then that he did not know the place. The Judge inquired how long he had been living in the area, and O'Shea said all his life, but he still said he did not know the cliff, nor the fords in the river. This was strikingly evasive, but of course the topic was a dangerous one, and he was in another corner when reminded of what he had told Superintendent O'Dowd in February.

Q. Do you know the short cut from Rathmore to your place?
A. I do; I often came and went that way for the past four years.
Q. When did you go that way last?
A. I did not go there for a long time; not this year anyway.
Q. When were you down at the river last?
A. I was not down this year anyway.
Q. Where do you cross the river when using the short cut?
A. I'd cross it near the cliff.
Q. How near the cliff?
A. About forty yards.
Q. Were you ever down there for gravel and stone?
A. No, sure.
Q. Can the river be crossed below the cliff in winter time?
A. No.
Q. Did you ever take off your boots when crossing the river?
A. No. I could not walk in the river with my boots off.

Asked to explain this contradiction he could not, and finally admitted that he knew the place. The river, he said, would be very shallow in the summer and easy to cross but flooded in winter, and impassable both to the island in midstream, and from the island to the opposite bank — i.e. where Ellen O'Sullivan's body had lain. O'Shea agreed he had often gone from the field with the gap in to the Kerry bank in the summer, but not in winter. Then followed a

18

bad bit for him, which, if he was the murderer, must have vividly recalled to him the horror of that night.

Q. When you would be going down that way from Creedon's house to cross the river would you go through the gaps in the field?

A. I would.

Q. And you know the place well?

A. No.

Q. Would you be able to find your way there in the dark?

A. (No answer)

Q. Answer the question sir! Had you gone there so often that you could find these gaps in the dark?

A. No.

Q. You would not?

A. No.

When he was questioned about meeting the man and girl with the bicycle he hedged again, said one of them answered his greeting but he did not know the voice, nor whether it was a salute or not, nor, of course, who the couple were. He stuck to this, and resisted suggestions that he had thought they were Cronin and the girl. He was asked did the girl's bicycle rattle and he said he took no notice of that, his attempt to parry a dangerous question, for a witness had told of being passed by a bicycle, at about 10.15 p.m. on the night of the murder, which rattled like Ellen O'Sullivan's machine. This witness could not see the rider but the bicycle was going towards Rathmore, and the prosecution's suggestion was that O'Shea had ridden the bicycle up towards Shinagh Cross to create a false trail at a time when Ellen O'Sullivan was in fact dead. This would certainly have called for nerve.

O'Shea was asked how he had passed the time from leaving Mrs Hickey, at 6.45 p.m., till about 8 p.m. when, as he now said, he had got to Shinagh Cross, though he had told the Gardaí it was 'at least' 7.30 p.m. The measured distance to the Cross was 2⅔ miles, and he said it would take him an hour and a half to walk it. He had stayed there fifteen minutes (forty-five he had told the Gardaí) and walked home, so he should have been at his house by 9.45 p.m., but he had told the Gardaí 9 p.m., and, of course, he could not explain not seeing the car and all the people who had sworn they were at the Cross.

He was probably at a genuine disadvantage when asked to say which of the two grey socks was his, and after a long pause he

19

pointed to one and said that was it as far as he knew, but the question was unfair, because the sock was like tens of thousands to be found all over the country, and if either sock had been his he could hardly recognise them after a four months' interval. Mr Rice pressed O'Shea to say that *both* were his but he was not sure, and indeed it would be difficult to say how he could be sure. He denied putting a sock into the tankard, and rejected an unrealistic suggestion that the sock was 'hidden' in the tankard. One only had to lift the lid and the sock was exposed — if, of course, it were there.

He did not pretend he had not put the flock in the manure heap, but said he had simply thrown it away there, and not hidden it. But it was from an old car cushion, belonging to his father, he insisted, and his sister gave a plausible corroborating account of this cushion and the flock. He had to explain the scratches on his hands, which he insisted had been new and not dried up when Garda Tormey saw them, and repeated what he had told Tormey, and that the 'goulogue' did not give full protection to the user's hands. He had to agree, of course, that a man's hands would get scratched from breaking furze pieces, but denied that he had ever done that.

'What did you talk about after the Gardaí had left?' asked Mr Rice of the period when Keane was under the bed.

'About tidying up the room,' was O'Shea's answer, and it was true that the searchers had left the place in some disorder. But after more questioning he said he 'did not think' he or Kathy had discussed what the Gardaí were looking for, or why they had come to the house, which cannot have sounded convincing. The trousers forced him into another lie, for he told Mr Rice they did not get wet when he worked on the drains, but he had told Superintendent O'Dowd the opposite, and when Mr Rice asked him more questions about the trousers his answers were noticeably weak.

Q. Did you say to your sister after the Gardaí had left — 'I wonder did they take my trousers. They were looking at it. I told them it got wet digging drains.' Had you that conversation with your sister?

A. I do not think so.

Q. Are you sure you did not say it to her?

A. I do not believe I did.

Q. They were in fact looking at the trousers when you were there?

A. Yes.

Q. And at this time was the trousers hanging up there?

20

away some clothes with them that Sunday.

…see them look at that pair of trousers (produced) the
…g they were in your home on 15 February.

…u say to your sister the Gardaí had been looking at
…rousers?
…' not.

…e, like everyone else, was puzzled by O'Shea's alleged
…o recognise Ellen O'Sullivan as she passed by with Cronin
…ht, and questioned him about it.

. When you passed those two people, the man and the girl,
I suppose you saw they were walking along like lovers?
A. I did not take any notice of them.
Q. Where was the bicycle? Was it next to you or was it on the
far side?
A. I believe it was next to me.
. Q. Which in your opinion was wheeling the bicycle?
A. The girl was next to me.
4. Q. And the man was on the far side?
A. Yes, my lord.
5. Q. Were they close together or fairly apart?
A. They were walking side by side.
6. Q. Was the man a tall man?
A. He appeared to be.
7. Q. Was the man much taller than the girl?
A. I did not take any notice.
8. Q. How near was the girl when you passed her? Could you
touch her?
A. No, my lord.
9. Q. Could you have touched the bicycle?
A. No.
10. Q. Were you as far from the girl as from the front of the
desk here to yourself there? (indicated).
A. I cannot exactly say.

The answer to question 1 should be compared with the following
answers given on three different occasions to Gardaí.

1. They were walking close together.
2. They were going slow as if in conversation . . . I'd say he had
his arm around the girl.
3. They were talking very low and walking easy.

21

And the answer to question 7 is clearly evasive
the man was tall, and saw the figure of the girl, and
been able to say if he was much taller.

O'Shea returned to the dock after answering one
ther questions which showed that he had not joined in t
for Ellen O'Sullivan, 'because I was not asked,' nor go
funeral, a most serious omission in rural Ireland, where
attendance by neighbours is universal, but he had not been
wake. His absence from the funeral, he said, was due to the
being at his house searching, but he had at first said he
reason for not going to the funeral and only gave the other a
on being pressed to explain.

Kathy O'Shea proved to be an intelligent and clear-headed
ness, who ought to have made a good impression with the jury.
said that on 8 February she and her mother went to bed betwee
8 and 8.30 p.m. and heard her brother come in about 9 p.m., an
go to his room without having any food. She denied that the Kea
dialogue ever took place, and said Keane couldn't have heard
was said as, when the Gardaí had left, she went into her mothe
room, tidied it, helped by O'Shea, and went back to the kitche
closing the bedroom door. As the month was February the close
door should have sounded highly probable. When Mr O'Donnell
asked her if she had told her brother to brush his clothes o
8 February because of their state, she replied that she couldn't
have said that because she was in bed when he came in and didn't
see him. This answer reads convincingly in the transcript of the
trial evidence, as does the following one about the black leggings,
which she said O'Shea had never owned or worn.

Q. Then these people are lying when they said he did wear black
polished leggings on Sunday?
A. Well, he is living with me for five years, and I saw him going
out every Sunday, and he did not have them to my knowing.
Nor do I know where he could have got them.

Of course, the spoken word is very different from its written record,
and one must remember that the jury saw and heard the witness,
and she may have made a totally different impression from her
words as they are in print, but the man from whom O'Shea
bought his leggings was never called to prove he had ever sold
O'Shea a black pair. Kathy said that O'Shea used to put black polish
on the brown leggings, the last time being on 8 January, though
O'Shea had said he didn't do so in 1931, and of course there was

22

no sign of black on the brown leggings in Court. 'I saw oil on them' she asserted, 'leather oil'. She contradicted McAuliffe who, she said, had never repaired leggings for her brother that she had ever paid for, and she was the person who paid for all shoe or legging repairs. 'McAuliffe could not repair any black leggings, because David never had any.'

When she was shown the trousers, she said O'Shea had not worn them on 8 February, but had worn a blue pair and matching jacket, both of which were clean and undamaged on the ninth without a trace of dirt on them, and were not brushed that day. If she was lying about all these things she was making a valiant effort to save her brother, unlettered though she was, alone in the alien atmosphere of the city and a criminal court.

As she told about the socks she was listened to in dead silence. She washed the clothes for her own household and her father's and darned the men's socks — her father's, David's, and another brother's, who lived with his father. She said she did not know either of the grey socks but had several pairs like them, and they were all of the same kind which she always bought for the three men. She examined the darns in the tankard sock as she sat there in the witness box, and coolly said they were very like her work, but she could not swear to it — (the other sock was not darned) — and could not account for its having been in the tankard. She thought the sock could have been in that bedroom, because she kept soiled socks there, and it might have been left behind when the clothes were being removed, but she did not put it into the tankard. This theory was as good as, indeed better than, the prosecution's one that O'Shea or Kathy had used the tankard to conceal the sock. The defence accusation of a 'plant' was given a fillip by Kathy's statement that the Gardaí had taken away all the clothes *and socks* in the house, including the suit O'Shea was wearing when they came, and even all his underclothing, leaving nothing behind. This statement was never contradicted, and meant *inter alia* that the Gardaí had lots of socks to choose from if they wanted a 'plant'.

She gave more detail about the flock and cushion cover than O'Shea had. The flock and covers belonged to old cushions used in a cart of her father's, which he had given to her mother and herself and David when they left his house in Rathmore and came to Knocknamalon five years earlier. When they got new cushions with a new cart in 1929 one old cover was destroyed, the other kept in the house where it still was, and the flock kept in a bag and put into the manure heap in January 1931. O'Shea had said he did not know what had become of the old covers, and Kathy said that was probably because she had taken charge of them. This evidence arose because of a dubious suggestion put forward by the prosecution. A Mrs McCarthy had sworn that two cushions had been stolen from her horse-drawn trap in January or February 1931, and identified the cushion covers found on O'Sullivan's land and some adherent flock as hers, and it will be recalled that Ellen O'Sullivan's knickers had been found beside these covers. The prosecution's suggestion, a highly speculative one, was that O'Shea stole the covers (of which there was no evidence whatever), hid them somewhere or other with the knickers, and threw the flock away, but later thought that the best place to put the knickers was beside the car cushions on O'Sullivan's land, 260 yards away from his cottage. The best place for the knickers, one would have thought, was the fire.

As both O'Sheas had denied that the Keane dialogue ever took place, Kathy was asked did she and her brother speak about the murder when Keane was there. She said not, nor did she ask O'Shea what the Gardaí had wanted with him for two hours earlier that day, and she did not even ask him where he had been on the night of the eighth. This was obviously untrue, or at least very unlikely. The questioning continued.

Q. Were you not curious about this matter?
A. I was curious about it.
Q. Did you know this girl well?
A. Yes.
Q. Was she a friend of yours?
A. Yes.
Q. And one of your nearest neighbours? Her father's land is up to yours?
A. Yes.
Q. And you say that on Friday, Saturday and Sunday (13, 14 and 15 February) you never spoke to your brother about where he had been on the previous Sunday night?
A. No.
Q. Or whom he had met or seen?
A. No.
Q. And the first time you knew where he had been was when the Gardaí came to the house and he made a statement?
A. Yes. I heard them in the Court (i.e. the District Court, where the proceedings preliminary to the trial took place).

24

Q. And you never spoke to your brother about what the Gardaí were there about?

A. No.

Q. You took it as an ordinary incident and that it required no comment that a number of Gardaí came to your house?

A. I took it it was the crime they had come about, as it was the general thing that they were to take statements from everybody.

Q. How did you know that?

A. There was a notice posted up in the village asking all men living west of Shinagh to report themselves at the barracks.

Q. Where was that notice posted up?

A. At the public house.

Q. Your brother did not go to the barracks to report his movements that night?

A. No.

Q. When did you see the notice?

A. Coming from Mass in the morning on the fifteenth.

Q. Did you discuss that notice when you got in?

A. No.

Q. Or at your breakfast that Sunday morning?

A. No.

Q. Or with your brother after coming from Mass?

A. No.

Q. Did you say to him after seeing the notice that he should go to the barracks?

A. No.

Q. Did you say to him not to go?

A. No.

Judge: *Q.* Tell me, Miss O'Shea, did your brother read the notice?

A. No, my lord, we were passing in the pony and car. He was driving.

Judge: *Q.* Were you able to read the notice as you went past?

A. I was, as I was sitting next to it.

Judge: *Q.* Had your brother his back to it?

A. My brother was driving the pony and did not see it.

Judge: *Q.* Did you call your brother's attention to this notice?

A. No.

Judge: *Q.* Why didn't you?

A. Well, I didn't take any more notice of it.

Judge: *Q.* Did you think that your brother didn't know about it?

       A. I didn't know about that, my lord. I didn't know whether he saw it or not.

Judge: *Q.* He didn't pass any remarks about it?

       A. No. He didn't pass any remarks about it.

It was almost unbelievable that these two did not talk in some way about the murder, but if they did, Kathy O'Shea was determined not to disclose what they said, and although the questioning went on for another ten minutes she could not be shaken. The information that the Gardaí had asked all men in the area to call to the barracks was new, and the Judge commented unfavourably to the jury on O'Shea's failure to call, but when Mr O'Donnell pointed out that O'Shea had made two of his statements at the barracks the Judge recalled the jury and corrected what he had said.

The last witness was Daniel O'Sullivan, a man of undoubted respectability, who said that he passed Shinagh Cross between 7.45 and 8 p.m. on the eighth, and he did not remember seeing anybody there, nor did he see Cronin's car. Some questions came from the jury about McAuliffe's evidence and he was recalled. One juror asked if he kept accounts or records of repair jobs, and McAuliffe said he didn't; his business was all cash and he was speaking from memory about O'Shea's repair. Another juror asked if the brown leggings could look brown if they had ever been blackened with black polish. They could, said McAuliffe, and pointed out that the top of the leggings was rubbed by the fold of the short trousers usually worn with leggings, and the rubbing would remove any black polish there. The final juror's question elicited the answer that McAuliffe did not charge for repairs and so had never been paid for the O'Shea repair, and thus undermined Kathy's evidence that she had never paid McAuliffe for any repair.

With the ending of the evidence, Mr O'Donnell rose to address the jury on behalf of O'Shea. He attacked what he called 'contemptible and mean' police methods in posting a Garda under the bed, but it is unlikely that the jury were sympathetic to that description of an astute piece of criminal investigation. But when he went on to accuse Garda Keane of perjury and manufacturing a case against O'Shea, he may have made some impression. The Keane dialogue, he urged, was so obviously false that the jury must reject it, for, lo and behold: the two things which the Gardaí need to make any case at all against O'Shea are the very things O'Shea and his sister speak of. Who, asked counsel, could possibly believe that? But even if Keane *did* hear something through the closed door, was his record of it as written up in the barracks accurate? Did he omit from it something which might help the accused? And why not jump out and grab the priceless legging when O'Shea had it in his hand? Perhaps his orders were to stay under the bed until the other Gardaí returned, but Keane had said he thought his duty was to wait and see if the O'Sheas would say anything more about the crime. The supposed discovery of the sock, too, gave valuable ammunition to Mr O'Donnell, and he fired it with spirit, but perhaps uncertain effect. Mr Cecil Lavery S.C. closed for the prosecution, and told the jury that the case against O'Shea was irresistible, which seems rather an overstatement even if the jury believed wholly in the sock and the legging, and there had been no inconsistencies in the case.

The Judge's charge began with a dissertation on necrophilia — the act of connection by a man with the body of a dead woman — a feature of the murder which had perhaps been forgotten since the doctor had described poor Ellen O'Sullivan's injuries, thus bringing back to the jury's minds the revolting brutality of the murder, which the Judge called a lust murder, as though the murder had been committed for the purpose of achieving connection after death. But this was not necessarily true, because the murderer may have thought that when he had his second connection with her she was still alive, albeit unconscious. When dealing with the finding of the sock, which he said baffled him, the Judge said it seemed strange 'that the Gardaí were searching the little room . . . for over two hours and nobody saw or found the sock until the later search. Was the sock found there? Is it one of the socks the accused was wearing that night? Are you satisfied with the explanation that the Gardaí have given that in this little house, as small a house as you have in the country, and in this small bedroom of the accused they were searching for two hours and never found that sock; or was it that perhaps they did not know there was any importance to be attached to the sock until they learnt of the conversation Garda Keane says he heard when he was under the bed? But they had found the sock on the river bank, so they could not say they did not know the importance of finding a sock when they went to O'Shea's house that Sunday.'

The Judge said that if Garda Keane had invented what he heard as he lay under the bed, he was a devil out of hell to lie so, and should be in the dock, and he almost told the jury that he didn't think a Garda would do such a thing. He drew the jury's attention to the naturalness of the dialogue, and said it was a matter for them to decide whether or not to believe Keane, but that if the dialogue was concocted they might think Keane showed some of the gifts of a playwright.

The jury took three hours, and returned to Court at 8.15 p.m. with a verdict of guilty. When it was announced, O'Shea very nearly collapsed, and had to be supported in the dock. When the Judge asked him had he anything to say on why sentence of death should not be passed on him, O'Shea vehemently protested his innocence.

The jury had added a rider that the murder was unpremeditated, and was committed during a period of mental abnormality and recommended that consideration be given to that factor. The Judge said he would pass on the recommendation, but the Government gave no effect to it, and the Court of Criminal Appeal rejected an argument for O'Shea that the verdict was the equivalent of 'guilty, but insane,' and dismissed O'Shea's appeal. He was executed on 4 August 1931.

––––––––––

The verdict might have been different, for although O'Shea may have been guilty, one feels that convincing proof was lacking. If the sock and the legging could have been eliminated from the case, O'Shea could hardly have been convicted, and indeed the Judge would have been constrained to withdraw the case from the jury. Were the jury then entitled to feel convinced about Keane's and O'Dowd's evidence, beyond any reasonable doubt? Even the Judge was baffled about the non-discovery of the sock in the first search. Why did the jury not feel the same way? And the inconsistencies in the O'Shea dialogue, analysed earlier in this narrative, one feels must have made the jury wonder. Doubts by a jury do not necessarily require that they condemn witnesses as liars, but simply mean that the jury do not feel sure enough to accept their evidence, and so the case is not proved beyond a reasonable doubt. Must not the jury have felt uncertain? Surely.

2.

The Quarry
(Attorney-General v. Gerard Toal, 1928)

FAUGHART, a village near Dundalk, Co. Louth, contains little but a church, and the house of the parish priest who, in 1927, was Father James McKeown. His household included two others — the housekeeper, Mary Callan, a spinster of about 36, and the yard boy and servant, Gerard Toal, an orphan, aged 18. On Monday 16 May 1927 the priest had church business to attend to in Dublin, sixty miles south, and told Toal to get his car ready to drive him to Dundalk to catch the midday train. After breakfast he spoke to Mary Callan and gave her some routine instructions. She was in the kitchen preparing to start the weekly washing, and wearing working clothes, which included a checked overall.

At 11.30 Father McKeown was ready, and with Toal beside him drove to Dundalk station some seven miles away. There was little talk on the journey. The priest, a reserved man in his fifties, did not usually say much unless it was to the point. He was a careful, conscientious, and meticulous person who led an orderly and regular life, and required order and tidiness in those who served him. He was not, perhaps, a popular man but was liked and respected. He did not know it then, but that was to be the last day of order and regularity in his life for many months to come. Toal, too, had little to say. He was a quiet youth, likeable and seemingly gentle, and efficient in his work. He was much more intelligent than one of his humble position might be expected to be. At the station Father McKeown told Toal to take the car home, and to meet him again that evening on the 7.40 p.m. train. Toal drove off as instructed, and the priest stepped on board the train for Dublin.

The evening train was on time and Toal was waiting at the station in the car. They drove to Faughart, again little being said on the way. As they came near the parochial house, a neighbour, Mrs McGuinness, came towards them on the road from the direction of the house. 'She has probably been up looking to see if

29

Mary was there,' said Toal. It was an odd remark, as it would be most unusual for the housekeeper not to be at home when her employer returned after having been away all day, but when Father McKeown went in to the house there was no sign of Mary Callan. She usually greeted him when he came in, but as she did not appear Father McKeown went into the kitchen and found, to his surprise, that the door was locked. He said to Toal that Mary was not at home, and Toal replied that she must have gone out. As the evening meal should have been ready Father McKeown was puzzled, but he put his car away, and waited in his study for a while, expecting the woman to come in at any moment. When she still did not appear, he looked into the several rooms in the house, getting into the kitchen by the outside door, but there was no sign of her.

The kitchen fire was out, which was very odd, and the floor had a clean patch as though recently washed or scrubbed. The table in the dining room was laid for the priest's evening meal, but Mary Callan's bicycle was missing, and there seemed to be very few clothes in her bedroom. Father McKeown had to do without food that evening, and when Toal came in at about 10.30 p.m. for the keys, usually given to him by Mary Callan, the priest said that probably Mary's mother was ill and that she would surely be back in the morning. Toal said nothing and went off to lock up for the night.

Next morning Father McKeown went to Mass at 8.45 a.m., telling Toal to light the fire and prepare him a light breakfast. When he came back for the meal he noticed several things missing from the table, still laid from the night before, which was not at all what the priest was accustomed to from his careful methodical housekeeper.

After breakfast Father McKeown asked Toal what one would expect him to have asked the night before, namely, what had happened in the house the day before. Toal, who should have volunteered the information immediately he met his employer at the station, said he had got back at the house at about noon and put the car in the garage. Mary had come out to the yard and told him to come in at 1 o'clock for his midday dinner, as she was going away. She said no more, and he had asked her no questions, which might seem strange, as her departure without warning or notice would be a serious upset for Father McKeown. But Toal and Mary Callan were not on friendly terms and said very little to each other, and this could explain his reticence with her. At 1 o'clock, he

30

continued, she called him in to his meal and gave it to him in the kitchen. She was wearing her best clothes, hatless and without a coat, and when she had served him had gone upstairs, presumably to her bedroom. He did not see her again, and went back to his work outside when he had eaten, about an hour later.

Father McKeown wondered why Mary had been upstairs for so long and Toal suggested she must have been parcelling her clothes, a reasonable surmise if in fact she had gone to her room. Father McKeown thought it peculiar that Toal had not observed Mary leaving, as, if she had cycled home, which the priest assumed as her bicycle was missing, she would have passed the garden and would be visible over the hedge. Toal's explanation was that he had not looked up from his work, and it is true that if he had been stooping or digging at the place where he had been, the hedge would obscure a passer-by, even cycling. In any case, if Mary Callan had not cycled to her home, some miles away, she could have taken another road not visible from the garden.

Father McKeown was curious to know what work Toal had been doing in the garden, for he had always had difficulty in getting the boy to work there. Toal preferred working about the yard, cleaning the car, and that kind of work. But the priest got no satisfactory reply to his question, and not being that kind of man did not press for one. Some time later he asked Toal the same question, and Toal said he could not remember. As it came to light later, a glance in the garden might have given a valuable clue as to what Toal *had* been doing there. However, there the questioning ended, and Father McKeown seemed not to think it peculiar that Toal had had to be asked before saying that he *knew* Mary Callan had left; nor that Toal allowed him to think the night before that she had merely gone out.

The priest then instructed Toal to go to Mary's home, tell her mother she had gone away or disappeared, and find out if she was there. Toal left, and was back at one o'clock to say that Mary had not been home and her mother knew nothing about her. 'This is terrible,' said Father McKeown, shocked and distressed by the news. 'Father,' said Toal, 'there was something wrong with her and she went away.' This cryptic comment was left there, Father McKeown not asking what Toal meant, though he was beginning to think his housekeeper might have committed suicide. He instructed Toal to buy a new lock for the kitchen door, and then the two men searched the stables and loft. They found nothing, but they omitted to search Toal's room, which was in one of the stables.

During the search, Father McKeown spoke of the strange disappearance, but Toal said almost nothing, and showed by his gruff manner that he did not like the subject.

On the following day, 19 May, Father McKeown notified the nearby Garda Síochána Station of the disappearance, giving them the little information he possessed. He would have done this immediately had he not been asked by Mary Callan's brother to wait a day or two. As the Gardaí seemed to show no interest in the affair, he went to them again two days later and repeated what he knew to the Sergeant in charge. Still no move was made by the Gardaí, so on the thirtieth Father McKeown sent Mary Callan's brother to Dundalk Garda Station. This call produced some slight response, for two Gardaí called to the house, and questioned the priest, Toal and Peggy Gallagher, a close friend of Mary Callan's acting as housekeeper in her place. The two policemen then departed, saying that the Superintendent would call the next day, and Father McKeown instructed Toal to be available for the Superintendent's visit. That night Toal burned some objects in his room, making quite a large fire, and alarming Father McKeown, and in the open on the following day he burned some more things, which he said were papers. There was nothing secretive about this, for he borrowed matches from Miss Gallagher. The Superintendent did not call, however, and police activity seemed to have faded again.

About a week later Father McKeown spoke to Toal about Mary Callan, and Toal said he had forgotten to mention that at about 5 o'clock in the afternoon of the seventeenth, when he was working in the garage, a car had come into the yard, turned and gone out again. Toal could not say what was the number of this car, as he had taken no notice of it. The priest thought the car might have come for Mary's clothes, as she couldn't have carried them on a bicycle, but this was surmise and Toal said nothing to it. On Toal's statement, the reasonable conclusion was that the car had used the yard for turning as the road was narrow.

The strange disappearance remained unexplained. No letter or message of any kind was received from Mary Callan; wages were due to her but she did not apply for them; nobody had seen or met her since 17 May, and the police were doing nothing. Of course, there was much local talk and speculation as to where she had gone, or what might have happened to her, but nobody could answer the disturbing questions. Father McKeown was as mystified as everyone else, but powerless, and uneasy as time went by and

Mary Callan's silence continued. In the summer he went away for two months, an unhappy man, and returned to find the cause of his unhappiness still there, as potent as ever.

He had never been inside Toal's room, kept locked by the boy since the disappearance. But one day in November 1927, the priest saw that the room was unlocked and went in. He looked around without actually making a search, and saw a blanket in the loft over the bed, not the proper place for that article. He showed the blanket to Peggy Gallagher and asked for an explanation, and she said the blanket was from Mary Callan's bed, and had been missing along with another of her blankets since she left. Toal now had to explain what Mary Callan's blanket was doing in the loft, but he insisted that the blanket was his and not hers. It was in the loft, he said, because the weather was not cold enough to need it. Father McKeown was satisfied with this explanation, although the weather was now noticeably cold.

But Peggy Gallagher was not satisfied, and as well as being distressed over her friend, was now suspicious. She conducted a few investigations on her own account, and finally on 28 March 1928 succeeded in arousing Father McKeown's suspicions, and persuaded him to look into Toal's room again. This time he searched, and found concealed a wheel, front fork, mudguard, saddle, and dress cords for a ladies' bicycle, in almost new condition. On a window sill was a small box containing the parts of three dismantled watches, one a lady's watch, which Peggy Gallagher felt nearly sure was Mary Callan's. When Toal came in that evening from work, Father McKeown asked him what the bicycle parts were doing in his room, but said nothing about the watch parts as he knew Toal was interested in mending old watches and assumed they were innocently in Toal's possession. Toal said the fork and wheel were from an old machine bought from a man named Carvill, but did not say where the other parts came from. By now, Father McKeown was thoroughly alert, 'I don't believe you,' he said. 'Those are not old parts, they are nearly new. They are from Mary's bicycle. I am suspicious of you and believe you were responsible for Mary's disappearance.' 'I know nothing about Mary Callan,' Toal replied, and walked away. The priest said no more then, but next day questioned Toal about the other parts. Toal said that the saddle and dress cords belonged to a Miss Lennon whose bicycle he was repairing, and that he had these parts in his room for examination. Father McKeown did not believe this either and said so, but Toal persisted in his story. The mudguard, he added, was bought from a youth named Halpenny who lived in Blackrock, about ten miles away. So the priest told Toal to get into his car and they drove to Halpenny's house. Father McKeown went inside, and learnt from Halpenny's mother that her son had gone to America thirteen months before.

Father McKeown returned to the car, grim and gravely distressed. 'You have told me another lie,' he said and repeated what Mrs Halpenny had told him. 'I will have to bring you to the Guards.' Toal said nothing and they drove off, but after about ten minutes he spoke. 'Father, I will tell you what happened. I broke into Williamson's (a bicycle shop in Dundalk) and stole those things.' He then told what the priest thought was a fantastic story, about bringing old parts — spanners, mudguards and the like — to Williamson's, stealing new parts and substituting the old so that the stolen ones would not be missed. Father McKeown remarked that if Toal had done that the burglary would have been discovered and reported.

The priest was now convinced that Toal had murdered the missing woman, and drove him to the Garda Station in Dundalk. There he accused Toal of the murder, and warned the Garda to watch the boy in case he might try to escape. He made a statement to the Sergeant in charge, and to Inspector Donovan, and departed, having done as much as could reasonably be expected of him in a disturbing situation. Toal was still in the station but not arrested, and was brought in to the sergeant and the inspector. He made a statement, not about Mary Callan's disappearance, but about the bicycle parts. He was not asked anything about the former topic, but this omission was due to Inspector Donovan's wish to report to his superiors and get instructions. He is not to be blamed for wanting guidance, for he had a suspected murder on his hands but no body, a situation which would puzzle most provincial police inspectors. Toal changed his story about the Williamson theft, and told the police that the thief — whose name he had promised not to disclose — had given him the wheel, fork and two or three cranks and only told him some two weeks later that they were stolen. The saddle, he said, was Mrs Lennon's, being repaired for her, and both mudguards were his own, one having been given to him by a man named Owen Cumiskey.

At about 8.30 p.m. that evening Toal was brought to the priest's house by the two Gardaí, and all went to his room which was in darkness and without artificial lighting. Toal stood by the window for a moment or two, then lit a match and the Gardaí searched the room. More bicycle parts were found, but the box with the watch parts was missing, although Father McKeown had seen it there four hours before. Inspector Donovan went over to the house, spoke to Father McKeown and came back. He asked Toal if he had the missing box, whereupon Toal produced it, obviously having pocketed it as he stood by the window. He explained that he got one of the watches for 6d. from a man he did not know, one night at a nearby place called Dowdall's Hill. The fireplace was full of hot ashes which contained a piece of burned fabric like sacking, and the remains of clothing. Toal said he had burned newspapers and his old clothes there. The Gardaí finished their investigations in about an hour and then went away. But to Father McKeown's astonishment they left Toal behind, and he slept in his room that night and for the next few nights as usual.

Father McKeown's astonishment was natural, for after five attempts to interest the Gardaí, he was left with a suspected murderer in his house and no prospect of getting any advice from anyone as to what his next step should be. Toal had for some time been considering emigrating to Canada, and he made no secret of his intention, even telling Inspector Donovan and the Gardaí about it! So, after a few days Father McKeown felt he had had enough of the boy and gave him two weeks notice, and on 7 April Toal, suspected murderer, departed for Belfast, without hindrance, on his way to Canada. Father McKeown drove him to the station and saw him on the train, almost eleven months after the day his housekeeper had disappeared.

As he drove homewards Father McKeown was a worried and unhappy man, for now he was afraid he had perhaps done Toal an injustice in accusing him. He had vacillated in those eleven months between thoughts of the boy's innocence and his guilt, and now decided that perhaps he had been wrong after all. But with Toal gone, he felt he might look forward to some peace of mind, or at least to less worry. He had done all he could. And the Gardaí thought they too had done what they could for, after all, the evidence of murder or even of death was at best flimsy. True, Mary Callan had not been heard of for almost a year, but if she were dead, where was the body? There were no blood stains, no clues. And now, there was no Toal.

But he came back ten days later, under arrest, but not for the murder. He had been staying with a relative waiting for a boat to Canada, but was suspected of having broken into a clothier's in Dundalk before he went away, and when arrested he had some of the stolen clothes in his possession. When brought back to Dundalk he was questioned about Mary Callan, as well as the housebreaking, and repeated substantially what he had told Father McKeown about 17 May 1927, but told the Gardaí that he had said all this to the priest on the seventeenth instead of the next day. He mentioned a quarrel with Mary Callan, due to her having reported to Father McKeown that he stole eggs and gave them to neighbours. 'After that,' said Toal, 'we never spoke a civil word to each other.'

This was the only new fact which came out of the questioning and its significance was slight. The stalemate continued.

But a month later things changed. Superintendent Hunt, from Garda Headquarters in Dublin, came to Dundalk and revived the investigations. Toal was again interviewed, for the fourth time, and asked about the bicycle parts which were nagging at everyone's mind. He repeated substantially what he had said to Father McKeown about breaking in to Williamson's, thus contradicting what he had already told the Gardaí. He added that the priest had promised not to tell the Gardaí if he told him the truth — a statement no one could believe. He described the supposed theft in detail.

'I stole these from Williamson's about eight months ago. Two or three nights before I stole them I arranged with another man whose name I will not give that we would go to Williamson's and break into the shop. . . . The man who was with me had a key and I opened the back door with this key. I entered the shop but he remained outside . . . I looked around for the bicycles and I selected one from which I removed the front wheel and fork . . . I then put the fork and wheel I brought from Father McKeown's on the bicycle, and left it in the same position in the shop. I then selected three other bicycles from which I removed the cranks and replaced them with the cranks I brought with me.'

Superintendent Hunt was certain Toal was lying, so on 22 May he and a party of Gardaí went to Father McKeown's house and searched the grounds. In an ash-pit and refuse heap they found:

Part of the bottom brackèt of a ladies' bicycle
Part of the frame of a ladies' handbag
Some men's clothing, which included a trousers from which
    the left leg and lower part of the right leg were missing
A penknife in the trousers pocket

Then they dug, and unearthed, near a boundary fence, the following:

3 parts of three ladies' coats
Part of a blanket
A piece of a ladies' coat buckle
Part of a ladies' jumper
Scraps of ladies' clothing

all of which had pieces of lime adhering. Toal was shown these things, told where they were found, and asked whose they were. Without looking he answered, 'I don't know.' 'Examine them carefully and see did you ever see them before,' said the Superintendent. 'No,' was the answer. He was shown the handlebars on a bicycle he had sold to Father McKeown when leaving for Belfast, and asked where they came from. 'I bought a bicycle frame and these handlebars in Higginson's of Dundalk last August.'

Superintendent Hunt felt certain now that this was a murder case and Toal was the murderer, but the discoveries in the garden did not advance the proof, and the frustrating stalemate remained. The body was not buried in the garden, though one freshly dug patch suggested this, but it yielded nothing on being dug again. Hunt now studied the environs of the priest's house. It was near a road junction, and he walked to it one evening, crossed a little bridge and found himself at a small wood. He went in and followed a steeply rising path for a short way, and at the summit he came out from the trees and saw a fence ahead. He looked down and there, forty feet below, were the waters of Falmore Quarry. It was about 500 yards from the priest's house.

The quarry was 390 feet long, and 100 feet wide at its widest point, narrowing to 65 feet. It was 45 feet deep in parts, and the banks were sheer save at the place where Hunt was standing. Trees surrounded the quarry on nearly all sides, so that the waters were dark. Even on a sunny day the place might be gloomy. The quarry stone had been used for building bridges and churches locally, and for years the quarry itself had been the subject of public agitation. It was considered dangerous, and several people were thought to have been drowned there. But the demand to have the quarry filled was never met, and so there it lay, forty feet below Hunt's gaze. Looking down, if you had not a good head for heights, you could easily imagine the fence giving way and falling into the sinister waters. You would have little chance of survival unless you were a very good swimmer.

Hunt had no such imaginings, for his mind was on other things. After a good look down, he walked quickly back to Father McKeown's and telephoned to Dublin. In response to his call a

37

section of the Dublin Fire Brigade arrived in a few hours, and began pumping the quarry. After four days and and nights more than four million gallons had been pumped out, and the depth of the water was down to twelve feet. On the fourth day Fireman O'Connor saw something about six inches below the surface, some distance out in the quarry, and as the water level fell a little more he could see that it was a sack. He retrieved the sack with a shovel, cut it open, and saw inside the remains of a woman's body extensively decomposed in places. It was what Hunt had expected.

The news spread, attracting large crowds to the place, among them Joseph McArdle, the missing woman's fiancée, who broke down and had to be led away. But it was too soon to say for certain whether the body was Mary Callan's, though everybody was quite certain it was. After pathological examinations had been made of the remains, Superintendent Hunt felt he had enough proof, and on 4 June charged Toal with the murder. When cautioned and invited to make a statement, Toal said nothing.

The Trial

The trial began in Dublin on 23 July 1928, before Mr Justice Hanna, K.C. and a jury, and took four days. Mr William Carrigan, K.C. and Mr Dudley White K.C. prosecuted; Mr Patrick J. Roe, Barrister-at-Law, defended.

Mr Carrigan opened with a vigorous speech, and an attack on Father McKeown, whom he called an innocent and very credulous man, who had searched everywhere except the one place where there was a mine of information — Toal's bedroom. 'You would think', he said, 'that the powers of darkness had darkened Father McKeown's understanding.' As the priest had shown much more energy that the local Gardaí before Superintendent Hunt arrived, this was unfair, and when it came out in evidence that Father McKeown had been five times altogether to the Gardaí with no appreciable result, Mr Carrigan was as much surprised as everyone else. Clearly, *that* detail was not in his brief.

Mr Carrigan told the jury that the remains in the sack could not be identified owing to decomposition, but there were valuable clues, such as patched shoes on the feet, a piece of lace owned by the dead girl lying across the face, and clothes of hers in the sack, which was fastened by articles belonging to Toal — a shirt sleeve among them. Mr Carrigan spoke as if confident that he would prove the case, and his first two witnesses, a dentist and dental mechanic, easily identified false teeth in the mouth as Mary Callan's. A shoemaker proved that the shoes were hers, repaired by him with a distinctive patch.

Uncertainty crept in when the cause of death came to be proved. Dr Dungan, a pathologist, said that there was no evidence of heart of other disease, or pregnancy, and that the cause of death was unknown. He advanced a theory, however, concerning the hyoid bone, part of which had been present in the body. This bone, situated above the Adam's apple, starts in the human body as a piece of gristle, usually hardens with growth, and ossifies at about age 30. It is shaped like a horseshoe, the tips facing the back of the body. In the body found in the sack, one tip was missing and the question was: What had happened to it? — assuming of course that the tip had been present before death, and as bone instead of gristle. The pathologist's theory was that the tip could have been lost by fracture from external pressure, and that this pressure *might* produce strangulation. Another pathologist, Dr O'Kelly, thought the pressure required would be very slight, but both doctors agreed that the absence of the tongue in the body, missing from decomposition, made it impossible to say whether strangulation had occurred. There were no marks on the body to suggest it.

The legs had been severed from the body, and the prosecution wanted to show that such dismemberment required skill or practice. Dr Dungan said it would be decidedly easier for someone with such experience to do the severance, which called for knowledge of the function of the thigh bone with the pelvis, and a skill somewhat similar to that required by a butcher when disjointing a carcass. Dr O'Kelly was less sure when asked the same question. 'Well, yes,' was his answer, seized upon by Mr Roe, who then got both doctors to agree that dismemberment would be difficult in good light and almost impossible without some light — and there was no artificial light in Toal's living quarters in the yard. With further questions, Mr Roe showed that dismemberment would cause a moderate flow of blood for some days until decomposition began and that even then a little more blood might escape from the veins. Mr Roe was leading to the point that no trace of blood, nor any blood stained garments, had ever been found in the priest's house or in Toal's quarters.

Joseph Quinn, the next witness, introduced one of the central points of controversy in the case. He had been at Artane Industrial School in Dublin with Toal, and said Toal had worked for six months in the butcher's shop there, helping the butcher twice a week, and he had watched Toal removing hides from carcasses, and separating heads from bodies. He said he had seen this from outside, through the slaughter-house windows. Mr Roe tackled Quinn strongly and put it to him that he was lying, but Quinn persisted, even when told that the butcher from Artane would swear that Toal had never worked with him. As Toal was only 13 and a half at the time, it seemed unlikely that such skill as he might have acquired working as butcher's helper for six months — if he *had* so worked — would enable him six years later to dismember a human body.

An acquaintance of Toal named Brodigan and Joseph McArdle were the next witnesses. Brodigan told of meeting Toal on the road in July 1927, when Toal offered to show him a trick — how to choke a man — which he promised would not hurt. But it did hurt, for Toal, though shorter and smaller than the other, put his arm around Brodigan's neck and, with his other arm around the head, cracked Brodigan's sinews by sharply shooting the latter's head forward. His sinews pained him for a fortnight, Brodigan said, but he was not disabled. 'A hard shot like that,' said Toal, 'would kill a man.'

McArdle told a fuller story. In January 1927 Toal offered to show McArdle some tricks, and showed three in all. The first was 'how to break a man's neck', and McArdle said that as the pressure came on from Toal's hands he felt as if something was going to break, and cried out to Toal to stop. Toal then showed 'how to break a man's back', and tackled the willing McArdle by putting his legs behind McArdle's and straining his back. The third was designed 'to floor a man no matter how strong he was', and Toal, catching McArdle's wrist, nearly tumbled him, although McArdle was a much bigger and stronger man. Toal told McArdle he had learnt these tricks from a book on ju-jitsu.

Mr Roe objected to this evidence, on the grounds that as the cause of death had not been proved, a skill possessed by the accused which *could* have caused death was irrelevant. The objection seems valid but it was overruled, and so the jury heard what the doctors could not provide, namely, a cause of death, founded upon a theory or guess about the missing tip of the hyoid bone, which could never be proved. When the two men had left the witness box, the jury must have thought that if Mary Callan had been in a struggle with Toal, she would not have had a chance. The gallows had come a little nearer to Toal.

Peggy Gallagher brought it another bit nearer. She said Toal and Mary Callan were unfriendly, though not bitter, and had been cool with each other after Toal was reported for stealing eggs. They ate at different tables in the kitchen, rarely spoke to each other, and once, a few months before the disappearance when Mary had asked Toal to do a small task he said, 'Don't be annoying me, for I hate the sight of you.' Miss Gallagher identified the shirt sleeve around the sack as part of a shirt she had once ironed for Toal, and the woman's clothes in the sack as Mary's. Amongst these were two deadly articles, namely, part of the checked overall Mary Callan had worn when Father McKeown saw her last, and the waist-band of the brown skirt Toal said she was wearing on the same day. All the clothes were missing from Mary Callan's bedroom, but Miss Gallagher produced two articles which, significantly, were not missing — Mary's only suitcase, empty, and her handbag with her references inside. The missing woman would never have left these behind if departing permanently, nor her savings of £120 which lay unclaimed in the bank.

Unknown to Toal, Miss Gallagher had searched his room twice, and there found Mary Callan's comb, watch, scapula from her overcoat, prayer book (with Toal's name written in and Mary's torn out) and scissors. She had asked Toal about the scissors a few weeks before the find, and he said he knew nothing of it, and that Mary must have taken it when she left. She had been puzzled as to how Mary could have transported her clothes on a bicycle, and said so to Toal, who made no comment; she then asked if a car had come for Mary that day, and he said no. A week later, however, he told her about the car turning in the yard and going out, which in fact was true as the driver had been traced and verified. The prosecution alleged that Toal had used the car incident, learned of by him after his talk with Peggy Gallagher, to suggest that Mary's clothes had gone in the car.

Toal had done great damage to his case by blowing hot and cold about whether Mary Callan had or had not disappeared, saying several times that she was at home with her mother, or that others knew where she was. He had told Miss Gallagher that Mrs Callan barely raised her head to him on the morning he called. 'She did not let me inside the house. I supposed Mary was inside and she did not want me to see her,' and he said of McArdle, who had cycled past the priest's house a day or two after the disappearance, 'I suppose Joe only went to meet Mary to bluff people, he knowing all about her leaving.'

41

To a man named McEntee he had more than once said there was no news of Mary Callan, and yet had remarked on other occasions that her people knew where she was. Nevertheless on the evening of 17 May, when he called to a neighbour, Mrs Livingstone, for milk, she had asked him to give some senna pods to Mary. He took the pods, but did not tell her Mary had gone away.

Toal may have thought his clumsy suggestions about Mary Callan's whereabouts would divert suspicion from him, but they had had the opposite effect with Gallagher and, one may surmise, with the jury. She had found the wash-tub on 18 May with some unwashed clothes in it, and this was a highly suspicious circumstance for it suggested a time for the murder, if murder it was. Mary Callan had been about to start the washing when Father McKeown was leaving the house, Toal was back at the house within half an hour, and the orderly careful housekeeper would never have willingly left a tub of washing unfinished.

Peggy Gallagher had made two other discoveries. In Toal's room there was a comb, on which there was hair 'like' some hair combings on Mary Callan's dressing-table. This was the only proof of the identity of the hair, but the other discovery was dramatic. At a gap in the hedge between Father McKeown's garden and an adjoining field, Peggy Gallagher had found a piece of sacking which fitted a hole in the sack fished out of the quarry. This was an achievement for Miss Gallagher, for the police had not seen it, and the inference was that the sack with the body inside was brought through the gap, and unknown to the carrier, torn by the brambles.

Mr Roe did his best with this obviously truthful witness, but it was almost impossible to shake her, as is usual with truthful witnesses. He got her to agree that Mary Callan had found Toal's unpleasantness a disagreeable feature of her work, though she was otherwise content with it. That was, of course, a possible reason why she might want to leave her job. Furthermore, she had told Miss Gallagher she might have to go home and help her mother because her sister had married. So there were two reasons for Mary Callan to leave Father McKeown, though not so abruptly. But this was mere shadow boxing, because if she had gone home she should have been in Court to say so, or her mother should have been.

Her mother's absence was one of the strange features of the trial, for neither side had her in Court. But when you have no case, or a very bad one, you have to shadow box, and so Mr Roe proved through Peggy Gallagher that Mary Goss, the missing girl's predecessor, had left Father McKeown's service without notice, and suggested that Mary had threatened the same thing. Miss Gallagher said it had not happened in her hearing, but McArdle had said he heard Mary threaten to leave. So the defence gained a crumb of comfort.

The prosecution called on two more witnesses. One was James McLaren, a boy who had met Toal on 17 May at about 3 p.m., in a field near the priest's house, and said that Toal told him Mary had gone away. If he had murdered her, the body must then have been hidden somewhere in the house or outbuildings for Toal, said McLaren, was then wearing the shirt, a sleeve of which had been around the sack. A few days later the two met again and Toal, in answer to a question, told McLaren Mary Callan must have gone home, for he had seen what looked like her bicycle track on the road to her home. This was an obvious lie, although people in the district were saying that she must have gone home, but that proved nothing. What could these people *know*? But the prosecution proved that if the missing woman had cycled away from her employer's house, she had not used her own bicycle, for the handlebars on Toal's bicycle, and other parts found in the fire were, according to the manufacturer, from a bicycle he had made specially to her order though there was some doubt whether the fork was from a ladies' or man's bicycle.

The prosecution's last witness, from Williamson's of Dundalk, exploded Toal's absurd story about the burglary there by saying that nothing had been missing from stock, and nothing was substituted for stock, nor could have been without detection.

The Defence

So now it was Mr Roe's turn to call witnesses, but he first made a short speech strongly attacking the prosecution for failing to discover that Quinn's evidence about Toal and the butcher's shop could be discredited and forcing the defence to call witnesses who would show that Quinn was wrong. The State, said Mr Roe, were inviting the jury to hang Toal on the word of a youth who worked nowhere save occasionally at the Guards' barracks in Dundalk. Disgraceful, was his comment. Mr Carrigan objected, and some sharp words followed between the two Counsel, until the Judge intervened, whereupon Mr Roe resumed unabashed, and accused the police of partiality in their attempt to find the murderer.

There was another row when the defence's first witness, Mr Connolly, a teacher from Artane School, was proving the date of Toal's admission there, and a question arose as to the whereabouts of the written record of the admission. Mr Carrigan complained that this record had been withheld by the school authorities from Superintendent Hunt, and Mr Roe heatedly defended the authorities. When the record finally was produced it showed that Quinn and Toal had been only eight months together in the school — from November 1920 to July 1921. The records did not show what trade any particular boy was learning, but the witness said it would be very unusual for a boy to learn a trade before the age of 13 and a half, or to help the butcher when he was under 14. Toal, he said, had gone to the fitter's shop to learn engineering, at the age of 13 and a half, for he had a strong aptitude for that work. The boys might do odd jobs about the school premises but not in the butcher's shop, which was strictly forbidden, but Mr Connolly agreed that this rule might be broken.

The two butchers, Martin Joyce and Christopher Joyce, then gave evidence, and neither could even recognise Toal in Court. Each said that if Toal had ever worked in the shop he would have remembered him. The steward from Artane then proved that the only boys ever employed in the slaughterhouse were those who worked on the farm, and Toal was not one of these. The superintendent of the fitter's shop put the matter beyond all doubt when he said Toal was under his charge from January 1921 to July 1924, learning to be a fitter, working an eight hour day, with only 45 minutes for lunch. So Quinn's evidence should have been wholly discredited. But was it?

Toal was the last witness. He had taken very little interest in the trial, sitting with his head bowed and staring at his hands most of the time. It was not his first time in a criminal court, for he had been sent to Artane School in consequence of convictions for theft when a child.

The first question he was asked was: Did you kill Mary Callan? 'No,' he said. 'I know nothing at all about her murder.' Then he told about his time in Artane. He said that at first he was in the kitchen there, and later learnt to be a fitter. He had never been in or near the slaughterhouse nor helped there. 'There is no truth in that at all,' was his comment on Quinn's evidence.

His narrative of the events of 17 May tallied with what he had already told Father McKeown and the Gardaí. After dinner he had worked in the garden, and came up to the house after 3 p.m. for a barrow with which he collected weeds. At about 4 p.m. he was up again at the house and 'noticed' that Mary was not there. The next day's interview with her mother was very brief. He simply asked her had Mary come home the day before, as she had left Father McKeown's and not returned. Mrs Callan said no, Mary had not come home, showing a very strange lack of interest in her daughter's safety.

Toal then proceeded to explain the possession of various incriminating articles. The bicycle handlebars belonged to a frame he had bought second-hand; the watch, identified as Mary Callan's, he had bought for 6d. from an unknown man one night, as he thought the parts might be useful; he knew nothing of Mary Callan's comb found in his room, which was obviously untrue. He might have been wise to admit stealing it, as he did the prayer book. The scissors he said he had found inside a newspaper parcel along with cut flower stems, and he took it and kept it — in other words stole it — but it was before Mary left, and she had missed the article which, if Toal was telling the truth, he said she had mistakenly thrown into the parcel with the flower stems. This might have been true, though Peggy Gallagher had said Mary Callan used the scissors for fine embroidery work, and not for cutting flower stems. The scapula was 'like' one he had when he first came to Father McKeown's, but he never removed one from Mary Callan's coat, or even saw one there. He had no idea where the bicycle dress cords in his room came from except, perhaps, that as he used to repair bicycles for people they might have come from someone's machine, but not Mary Callan's. The bicycle saddle in his room was Miss Grant's, one of his customers.

The burning of papers in his room was a tidying up process, as Peggy Gallagher told him to do this because the Garda Superintendent was coming next day. It sounded implausible, as did his denial of burning things in the garden. Peggy Gallagher had seen him near the smoke in the garden, but Toal said he had been boiling pitch for house repairs in a wooden bucket which got burnt. He admitted, however, that a brown trousers found in the garden was his, and explained that the torn leg was used to patch another trousers; and he insisted that the blanket in the loft above his bed was his, and not Mary Callan's. He had to admit lying to the police about the bicycle fork, and other things supposedly from Williamson's, found in his room, which he now said were stolen by him only and not with another man. Mr Roe ended his questioning there and sat down.

45

Toal now had to face an ordeal. He was but 19 years old, and was about to be cross-examined by one of the most experienced prosecutors at the Irish Bar. Whatever chance he might have had of surviving the questioning if he were truthful, he had none with lies, and as soon as Mr Carrigan began, Toal had to admit to more lies — first, the story to Father McKeown about getting the bicycle wheel from Halpenny. Then he repeated the lie he had told to the police, about Father McKeown's promise to conceal from them Toal's theft of the bicycle parts, and that the priest had even lied to the police for him by saying that Toal had got the stolen parts elsewhere. When the Judge intervened to ask how he had got into Williamson's, Toal produced a grotesque lie. He said he had used a key in Father McKeown's house which had happened to fit the door, and that he had gone to commit the crime on the chance that it would fit. By now the jury must have found it impossible to believe anything Toal said, but all these lies about stolen parts from Williamson's were pointless, unless they were believed as explaining his possession of the bicycle parts which were in fact from Mary Callan's bicycle. And if they were not believed, then he was several steps nearer to the gallows.

Mr Carrigan's questioning about the events of the seventeenth gave Toal surprisingly little trouble, for he stuck to his previously told story, memorised by now probably, unlike the Williamson story. Mr Carrigan asked Toal had he seen anyone about the house that afternoon, and he said no, but agreed that if Mary Callan had been murdered in the kitchen someone must have got in, and was unable to explain how this could happen without his knowledge. Mr Carrigan did not pursue this line by asking how the stranger could have got rid of the body without Toal's knowledge, but got Toal to agree that Mary Callan could not have carried her clothes on the bicycle — if she left on it — and that the clothes did not go in the car which turned in the yard. Yet, said Mr Carrigan, these clothes were found in the garden? But Toal could not suggest how they got there. Nor, of course, could he explain why he stole Mary Callan's scissors.

When Mr Carrigan came to the alleged killing, he first suggested that Toal was wearing the torn trousers found in the ash-pit, and that some blood had got on to the trousers and the floor, thus necessitating the removal of the trousers leg and washing of the floor. Toal said no to all this, which was an alternative to the prosecution's hyoid bone theory, since strangulation does not cause bleeding. But then Mr Carrigan came back to the strangulation theory, and suggested that the woman, if she had had her back to him at the wash tub, could have offered no resistance to an attack such as he had demonstrated with McArdle and Brodigan. But Toal would not admit having effectively attacked either man. He said he could not remember the Brodigan incident, while McArdle, he said, was not really thrown but 'let himself come with me' in the trick. Perhaps the jury believed this, though it is unlikely.

One of the most incriminating articles was the shirt sleeve with which the sack had been tied, recognised by young McLaren as the shirt Toal was wearing when he met him on the fatal afternoon — though one wonders how the boy could have remembered this, or indeed, would even have noticed the shirt. However, that was his evidence, and Miss Gallagher said she had ironed the shirt for Toal. There was another shirt, found in the ash-pit, damaged and torn but intact, which Toal insisted was the one she had ironed, and McLaren had seen on him. He denied emphatically owning the shirt which was used to tie the sack. Each shirt was of a common design and somewhat alike, so possibly he was telling the truth, or was believed. But if this denial was false, it was absolutely necessary, for the admission that his shirt sleeve tied the sack would have been fatal.

Toal's remark to McLaren that afternoon that Mary had gone away was a serious embarrassment to him, and when Mr Carrigan asked him about it Toal said he could not remember saying it. The Judge asked Toal if, as McLaren had said, he had had a water can on wheels with him when he met McLaren. This was used for supplying water to the priest's house, and Toal said he could not recall going for water that afternoon, but if he had it was because he had taken the priest to the station in the morning and had not had time to do it then.

Judge. Do you recollect it now?

Toal. It could have happened all right.

Judge. Every incident of this day would be burned into your memory even if you are innocent.

Toal. I don't remember it now. I have only a kind of idea and I don't really remember it.

Judge. How long would it take up to fill the water can on wheels and carry it up to the bridge?

Toal. I would leave the big can at the bridge and I would only take four or five ordinary cans of water to it.

Judge. How long would it take you? — twenty minutes?

Toal. Yes, about twenty minutes.

Judge. Did you ever tell anybody — Father McKeown, Peggy Gallagher, or any of the Guards to whom you made a statement, that you were away from the house for twenty minutes for water?

Toal. (No reply).

Judge. Why didn't you?

Toal. I don't remember it.

Judge. You mean you had forgotten it?

Toal. I don't really remember it yet.

Judge. In one of your statements you said that at a certain period you got tired working?

Toal. Yes, that would be about four o'clock or afterwards.

Judge. Can you recollect was it with the water can you got tired?

Toal. I was in the garden at that time and I don't remember the water at all.

After that passage, the jury must have felt certain that the Judge thought Toal guilty. 'Even if you are innocent' could have one meaning only, and the Judge should never have said that. Indeed if Toal *was* innocent, there was no reason why, in a day which was perfectly ordinary — save for the departure of Mary Callan — everything should have been burned into his mind.

Toal's ordeal ended there, and he returned to the dock, after two and a half hours of questions which, strangely, did not include the topic of his total indifference to Mary Callan's safety. He had never once expressed to anyone either concern, or sympathy, about her fate.

———

Mr Roe's closing speech was delivered with an assurance he cannot have felt, but he confidently asked for an acquittal. He stressed that Toal had had no motive save unfriendly feeling, and asked the jury did they really think Toal had had the courage, or the skill, to dismember the body? He attacked Quinn again, and the jury should, on a fair view of the case, have refused to believe Quinn. Mr Roe made it sound as if there was a defence to the charge of murder. But there wasn't, really, and Mr Carrigan had an easy task when he made his closing speech. He defended Quinn against Mr Roe, and said that the defence was in effect saying that only a skilled butcher could have murdered Mary Callan, whereas Toal, with his knowledge of ju-jitsu could have done it. And then, of course, there were all Toal's lies, the buried clothes, the shirt sleeve around the sack, the bicycle parts and all the other things in Toal's possession. Mr Carrigan made a half-hearted apology to Father McKeown for having attacked him in his opening speech.

It was 6.40 p.m. Everybody was tired on this the fourth day of the trial, but the Judge thought the case should go on that night and he began his charge. The first question was: Had Mary Callan been murdered, and the Judge, having dealt with the dismembering of the body, which by now everyone seemed to accept was Mary Callan's, asked was it likely that if she had left the house voluntarily she would have left behind her suitcase, her rosary, references and so on. And he said the jury must consider whether they could accept Toal's evidence that when he last saw Mary Callan she was wearing her best clothes and shoes, since the body had working shoes on the feet, and there was in the sack a piece of the check overall she wore when Father McKeown saw her last. And did they think a careful girl like her would prepare a meal wearing her best clothes? As to where the murder took place, the jury were invited to conclude from the unmade state of her bed, the clothes, and the unfinished washing, that it was in or about the house, and that the killer knew the ways of the house and where the woman's clothes were kept. This, of course, was another way of saying Toal was the murderer, unless, said the Judge, someone came in unknown to Toal, murdered the woman, moved the wash tub, disarranged the bed and at some other time unknown, and still without Toal's knowledge, disposed of the body, placed incriminating articles in and on the sack, and threw the sack into the quarry. This was all utterly improbable, as of course the jury well knew.

The Judge's comments as he proceeded showed clearly what he thought of the case. It was 'an extraordinary incident' that Toal had not told Miss Livingstone, when collecting the milk, that Mary had gone away. So it was, looked at in one way, yet Toal's taciturnity could explain it. The Judge thought highly of Miss Gallagher and told the jury so, though he said it was for them to agree or disagree with that. This was an invitation to the jury to believe everything she said, including of course the damning bit about the shirt. The Judge said little about Mrs Callan's absence from the trial, which was crying out for severe comment, but he did say that as she was absent the jury should assume that Toal's account of the interview with her was true.

When the Judge was discussing Toal's supposed skill in dismemberment, he told the jury about a murder trial two years before at which he had presided, where a brother and sister had murdered their brother and cut the body into twenty-six parts, and the two accused were simple, ignorant, country people. This judicial reminiscence did not help Toal.

The charge finished at 9 p.m. and the jury retired. They came back at 9.37 p.m. and asked this question:

'We have, of course, no evidence to show whether Toal deliberately killed Mary Callan or whether, being angry or intending to hurt her, he did more damage than he intended. If the latter, would it be murder or manslaughter?'

Judge: 'There is nothing in the case which would justify you bringing in a verdict of manslaughter.'

The jury went in again and fifteen minutes later brought in a verdict of guilty. When the Judge asked Toal if he had anything to say why sentence of death should not be passed upon him he answered, calmly and quietly, 'I am not guilty'; he tried to say something else but failed, the unformed words trembling on his lips. When he was sentenced he was calm.

He appealed, but without success, and his petition to the Government for a reprieve failed too. When he was told he must die, he seemed unconcerned. 'I knew neither would succeed' he said. Such fortitude at age 19 is moving, until one remembers his crime. He was executed on 29 August 1928.

———————

Did Toal murder Mary Callan? He very probably, almost certainly, killed her, but the murder is less certain. Was the jury's question near the truth? Suppose, for instance, that the hostility between Toal and the housekeeper had flared into a quarrel when he came back that day from Dundalk station, and that she had aroused his temper either with a blow, or even with words; if he had struck her and she fell hitting her head and sustaining concussion, which can occur without a fracture of the skull, Toal might have panicked and thought she was dead. Or suppose he had attacked her from behind, not intending to kill but merely to hurt, and unwittingly used too much force, killing her? What could he do in such a position? Call a doctor, or the police? Would anyone believe him if he gave an innocent account of what happened — he, the known ju-jitsu student? One can imagine how the police, who never

50

believe protestations of innocence, would receive such a story. A jury might well believe it, for juries often find manslaughter on thin grounds, but how could Toal know that?

So, if the killing had been accidental Toal might naturally have tried to cover it up — and he nearly succeeded, guilty or innocent. A little while longer and he would have been on the way to Canada, where he might have disappeared, anonymous, safe from extradition. But his arrest for the smaller crime of housebreaking was his undoing.

The Gardaí thought Toal had not been alone in the murder, and asked him who he was screening. Toal did not answer directly but said ambiguously to Superintendent Hunt, 'I have no one belonging to me, but with others it is different.' The Gardaí had to be content with that answer to their suspicions, and police suspicions are frequently themselves suspect. But there were other graver suspicions. Two prior murders in the district had never been cleared up. An elderly woman had been found dead in a barrel, and in February 1927, the body of a young girl had been discovered in the quarry. She had disappeared on a stormy day, and when found, the bundle of sticks she had gathered was in her arms. She might have been blown into the quarry, but tongues had wagged and said she had seen something which incriminated Toal in the murder of the woman in the barrel. So his youth was of no avail to save him from the hangman.

3.

The Anatomists

(Attorney-General v. Cornelius and Hannah O'Leary, 1925)

IMAGINE this scene: In a field in County Cork, on a dark cold night in March, two policemen are questioning a man. On the ground is a human head crudely dismembered from the body, and beside it the sack in which it was found concealed in the bushes. The police want to know if the head is that of the man's brother. The man looks calmly at the head in the light from a bicycle lamp and a torch, and after a moment says, 'Yes. That is Pat.'

Incredible? Almost, but it happened on 7 March 1924. What was a dismembered human head in a sack doing in a field?

Patrick O'Leary, whose head it was, had lived at his farm at Kilkerrin, County Cork, with his mother, Mrs Hannah O'Leary, a widow, his sisters Hannah and Mary Anne, and his brother Cornelius, known as Con. He was the man in the field with the Gardaí. Their father, Patrick O'Leary, had died three years before, leaving his small farm to his widow for life, and after her death to Patrick, but charged with the payment of £350 to Mary Anne, and a right of residence to Hannah and Con for life, a common arrangement amongst Irish farmers. The property was worth about £1,100, big money for a small farmer in rural Ireland at that time.

The dead man, who was in his forties, had not been seen in the neighbourhood since 26 February when a friend passing by saw him go into the hay loft behind the farmhouse at about 9.30 p.m., presumably on his way to bed, for he slept in the loft. When after about ten days he did not re-appear, tongues began to wag and one neighbour asked Con where his brother was, and did he not think the disappearance should be reported to the Gardaí? 'No,' said Con. 'There's no need. He'll be back soon.' The story given out by the O'Learys was that Patrick had gone to Bandon fair, a few miles away, on 27 February at 3 a.m. to sell a colt, and had often before stayed away for several days so his absence caused them no concern. But on 7 March Frank Walsh, a boy of ten, was crossing one of the O'Learys' fields and found a potato sack near a furze bush. He opened it, glanced inside, and ran home to tell his mother. Mrs Walsh immediately telephoned to the Gardaí.

The sack was the first of the horrors. In another sack, in an adjoining field, was a human arm, severed at the shoulder and still wearing a shirt sleeve. The horrors multiplied with each fresh discovery of dismembered human remains in various places of concealment, until the final horror when the O'Learys' dog trotted out of a wood with a human arm in its mouth. When all the dismembered parts had been collected, including the trunk, the body was still not complete, and the missing parts were never discovered.

The first thing the Gardaí did after going to the field was to call to the O'Leary house, where they saw Con. He was asked where his brother was, and told the story about his having gone to Bandon to sell the colt and not returning. 'Why didn't you report his disappearance?' asked the Garda.

'I didn't think it was necessary.'

'It's a long time for him to be missing, nearly ten days,' the Garda remarked.

'What need, wisha, was there for reporting it?' repeated Con calmly — perhaps too calmly.

He was asked to go to the field where the head had been found, and on the way Sergeant Devoy asked him whether he had made any inquiries concerning Patrick's whereabouts. Con said no, but 'he was in the habit of going away like that, and we expected him to turn up any day.' This was a lie, as the Sergeant found out a few days later. In fact, Patrick never stayed away in this fashion. When the two men arrived at the field Garda Reynolds, who was there already, pointed out the dismembered arm lying where it had been found in some bushes. 'That's awful,' said Con. But when the head was produced he was unmoved. Most people would have fainted on the spot, but Con O'Leary, when asked if it was his brother's head, simply looked at it and had the head turned around so that he could see the temples and their state of baldness. He then studied the head and said, 'Yes. That is Pat.'

Why did he take so long to identify the head? Had he a genuine doubt? The head and nose were gravely injured from violence and the face could, conceivably, have been less easy to identify in consequence, but Sergeant Devoy, who had known Patrick O'Leary, had had no difficulty in recognising the head. Later, at least three other people who knew Patrick identified his head. So, Con

O'Leary may have thought it safer to delay the identification. If he had genuinely believed his brother had gone to Bandon ten days before, he might have had a real difficulty in the identification; but, as events later showed, he knew perfectly well his brother had not gone away, and so he was privy to the murder either before, or after, or both. But that did not mean he was guilty of it.

Just then Superintendent Troy arrived and asked Con if the head was his brother's, but surprisingly, Con said, 'I do not know whose head it is.'

'But you have just identified it for me!' exclaimed the Sergeant.

'I did,' said Con, but gave no explanation of this turn about, and was not asked to. At the inquest, he said that when he was asked by Superintendent Troy he was in doubt, although he had not had any doubts when the Sergeant asked him. And, of course, the artificial light in the field was hardly ideal for the recognition. But he may have had second thoughts and decided to play it safe with the Superintendent.

Nothing more was done in the field, and the dismembered remains were taken into the nearby village, where Mary Anne and Hannah had been brought by a Garda. The sacks were placed on a table in a small room behind a public house, and Superintendent Troy interviewed Hannah. She told him the Bandon story and he asked:

'What time did he go?'

'Three o'clock in the morning,' she said.

'Did you make any inquiries about him, or speak to anyone about him being away?'

'No,' said Hannah. 'We were expecting him back.'

'Was your brother Con on speaking terms with Patrick?'

'No.'

'Had Patrick any enemies?' asked Troy.

'Our Patrick had no enemies.'

'Did he ever go away from home before?' asked Troy, and Hannah's answer contradicted Con's earlier answer to this question.

'No, he never did.'

'Would you be surprised or frightened if I told you he was dead?'

'No,' said the woman. 'I would not believe you. Why should he be dead? He was a fine stout man, and he could do as much work as two men.'

'I don't mean that,' explained Troy, 'I mean would you be surprised or frightened if I told you he was killed?'

'I would not believe you. Who would kill him?'

The rhetorical question, and the answers about Patrick's disappearance, may have sounded plausible, but they were all lies. Hannah knew perfectly well that her brother had been dead since 25 or the early morning of 26 February, and Superintendent Troy learnt it soon afterwards. But her laconic answers and lack of concern for her brother were in themselves highly suspicious. She should have been haggard with anxiety and grief if her story was true, and distraught at the news that her brother's head had been found.

Having finished his questions, the Superintendent took Hannah into the small room, leaving Mary Anne and Con outside. The light was somewhat better than in the field, for in addition to the torch and lamp there was a candle, and the constricted space prevented the diffusion of the light which had occurred in the field. When the two came in, Sergeant Devoy and Garda Reynolds were there already, with a Doctor Murphy.

The head was taken out of the sack and placed on the table, and Troy asked Hannah could she identify it. She said nothing, and did not even flinch, but looked at the head for a fraction of a second, and then looked away and glanced around the room. Troy pointed out the temples to her and their bald condition, and invited her to look again. She did so, and said no, she could not identify the head. Then the head was moved so that she could see it full face on, and she turned her eyes to it, but not her head. Nobody spoke, but the watchers looked at this unnatural sister with horror as she stood there, quite unmoved by the ghastly spectacle. Then she spoke, 'Paddy was not so thin in the poll.' Then Troy sent her out of the room and called in Mary Anne, who had no difficulty in recognising her brother's head. Troy then recalled Hannah.

When Hannah came in again Troy asked Mary whose head it was. 'It is Paddy's,' she said, without a moment's hesitation. Then Troy turned to Hannah and asked her again if she could identify the head. 'Have a good look,' said Troy, and she did. After a moment or two she spoke. 'It is not Paddy's head.' Troy asked her again, and she took a long look at the head, and as Troy said at the trial, 'She again began to display some interest in it,' and after a while she said, 'I am beginning to think it is him.' Then after another interval she agreed. 'Yes. It is Paddy, sure enough.'

It was a long drawn-out performance, which may or may not have been convincing. But one wonders what Hannah thought she was achieving. She was not very intelligent, but of course had the normal sense of self-preservation, and no doubt decided it was safer to pretend she did not recognise the head even though Mary Anne had done so. Troy, having secured two identifications, wanted the third and summoned Con. In his presence, the two women repeated that the head was their brother's but Con disagreed. Then he said he wasn't sure that it was like Paddy's. He looked at the head from different angles, had it turned around, hesitated and then, asked again by Troy, he said the head was Paddy's, and added the words, 'Oh, I am innocent. My hands are clean.'

'Nobody is suggesting anything against you,' said Troy. 'No one is saying you are guilty,' and inquired of Con how he identified the head. 'By his poll,' was the answer. 'He was getting a bit thin in the poll.' None of the three had mentioned their dead brother's face, the surest means of identification. The hair alone could mean very little. Was it guilty conscience which kept them away from the face, or some vestige of human feeling?

The dreadful scene was now at an end, the time was 9.30 p.m. and Garda Reynolds took the two women to their home.

The inquest was held next day, and the first witness, called by Superintendent Troy representing the Gardaí, was Con O'Leary. The Coroner asked him if he wanted to give evidence and he said he did. The Coroner then told him that he did not require him to give evidence, and that if he did it would be taken down in writing, and if he was later charged with any crime in connection with the death what he said could be given in evidence at his trial. Con still wanted to give evidence, and made a deposition, most of which simply could not have been true, but nevertheless did not directly implicate him in the murder though, if he were innocent, might have shown him to be an accessory after the fact if Hannah, or Mary Anne, or both were the murderers.

His deposition was:

I last saw my brother alive last fortnight. That was on a Monday night (25 February) about half past nine or ten o'clock. I was in the act of going into the house and he was coming out. I saw him open the door of the loft, go in, and close the door after him.

I heard my brother was at home in the dwelling house on the following Tuesday morning (26 February) but I did not see him. My sister Hannah told me this. The door to the dwelling house is bolted every night, but the bolt is a bad one and by shaking the door it would open. There would be some noise made if the door was opened by shaking.

Hannah said Patrick came in for breakfast, that he was going to Bandon fair, between three and four o'clock. Hannah said he had his breakfast, that she gave it to him (i.e. in the kitchen). She would have to light the fire to get breakfast. I am a heavy sleeper. I was in the next room to the kitchen that night and did not hear Patrick come in or go out.

I have no idea as to what was my brother's business at Bandon fair, but my sister Hannah said he was going to sell a colt. The colt was not sold and was not taken to Bandon. I saw the colt in the stable on Tuesday morning (26 February) and it was also there on Wednesday morning . . . I have been feeding the colt since last Friday but did not do so before then as I worked away from home. The chopped furze with which the horses are fed was stored in the loft where my brother slept. . . .

Some person used enter the loft every day to get food for the horses. There were potatoes stored in the loft . . . within a few yards of my brother's bed. Potatoes are kept nowhere else in the farm and are required in the house every day. I was in the loft at least once a day since my brother left. I am not sure whether my brother slept in the bed after that night of the Monday before he was going to Bandon fair. I did not look at the bed but I saw a red kind of quilt on it. I never noticed anything strange about the bed since last slept in by my brother. . . . His old clothes were left there. I saw them up beside the bed after my brother disappearing. They were thrown across the partition at the head of the bed. I must have made a mistake when I said I did not look at the bed [a bad slip]. What I meant was that I did not turn the clothes . . . I was not on speaking terms with my brother for the past four or five years. My father is dead about three years and it was before that that we commenced to disagree. The cause of the disagreement was that I would not stop home and work. My brother was mostly the cause of the disagreement, but he never made any objection to my sleeping inside the house. My brother did not disagree with any other member of the family . . . I made no search for my brother since 27 February, and never asked any person if they had seen him. I thought he would turn up every minute. I did not think he would go away and leave the place after him. I thought he was gone away to work somewhere, to Cork or England or somewhere else. My mother and sisters were also wondering why Patrick had not returned and they discussed it with me. . . .

When Con left the witness box Troy called Hannah, but when she was told by the Coroner that she did not have to give evidence she returned to her seat. Mary Anne and her mother both waived their rights and gave evidence.

When the inquest was over Con walked down the road with Garda McHugh.

'How do you think we got on today?' he asked the Garda. 'I think you got on very fine,' said McHugh. 'Why did Hannah refuse to give evidence?'

'She has ruined us by not giving evidence,' said Con.

'But why didn't she?'

'She is that kind of girl,' said Con cryptically. It is not clear why he thought she had ruined them, for it is unlikely that she would have told any significantly different story from the other three, or would have contradicted anything important. Perhaps Con thought the Coroner would be suspicious when she did not speak, for innocent people have nothing to hide, and so no reason for silence. But the Coroner's suspicions would have made no difference to Con's peril, for neither his suspicions nor his verdict could have been proved, or even mentioned, at the trial Con feared. But he couldn't know that bit of law. His remark to Garda McHugh about Hannah having 'ruined us' was proved at the trial.

How much damage had Con done by his deposition?

He had shown that he was lying and, that he, asleep in the room off the kitchen, would not hear his brother come in to the kitchen through the noisy door, eat his meal, talk to Hannah and go out again. But he may have been a heavy sleeper. However, he must have known next day that Patrick did not go to Bandon, for he saw the colt Patrick was supposed to have taken, still on the farm. Therefore he could not have thought Patrick 'would turn up every minute,' and, of course, could not have believed that Patrick would go away leaving behind him a farm worth £1,100. It must also have been untrue that the O'Leary family had discussed the disappearance since if they were puzzled or uneasy about Patrick's absence they would have asked the Gardaí to help. So Con knew next day Patrick had not gone to Bandon and therefore had disappeared. But his lies did not prove that he had struck the fatal blows.

The funeral took place from the O'Leary house on the day after the inquest. The remains had been removed to the house and were on view at the wake, in accordance with the custom in rural Ireland, this being an especially ghoulish instance of that custom. The neighbours had gathered, the open coffin was in the kitchen, and the four O'Learys were dispensing the customary hospitality, showing no great concern about what would have been a profoundly melancholy occasion. But one neighbour, William Whelton, spoke up, expressing the feelings of the neighbours present and absent, all of whom had been for days aghast and incredulous at the callousness of the O'Learys.

'I must certainly say, Con, it is a terrible state of affairs to see your brother cut up in pieces and you not a bit worried over it. I must also say, Con, that suspicions are strongly against you, and it is up to you to find the perpetrator and free yourself,' said Whelton boldly.

Con rubbed his hands together. 'I am innocent, anyway. My hands are clean.' The other three said nothing. Later in the evening another guest, Mrs McCarthy, had something to say. She addressed her remarks to Mrs O'Leary.

'It is a shame, Mrs O'Leary, to see your son in such a state, and it is easily known who done it.'

Mrs O'Leary did not answer her, nor did either of her daughters, but Con repeated his earlier words. 'I am innocent.' The silence of the O'Leary women shocked everyone.

It is a pity that there is no record of the suspicions of the neighbours, although, of course, suspicion is not proof, but who were they saying was the murderer? Con had perhaps the strongest motive for killing his brother. He had not been on speaking terms with him, and had only a right of residence on the farm under his father's will, whereas Patrick would be complete owner of the farm as soon as their mother died. And as Con's employer, Mr Travers, told the Court at the trial, Patrick was putting Con's job in danger. He objected to Con working for Travers instead of for him and had called three times to the Travers' farm to complain. Patrick was a loud-voiced, blustering, domineering man and Travers was finding him and his calls a nuisance. Travers told Con about the calls, and said he had better leave his employment as the annoyance was becoming too great. Con was very upset and explained that Patrick wanted to get him out of the district altogether to work at home for nothing. 'Paddy wouldn't pay me, and I won't work for him.' Patrick thought Con should work for him for nothing in return for his residence which however, was Con's legal right under the will.

What motive had Hannah? She had got the same as Con under the will, a right of residence, and may have been jealous that Mary

Anne had got the money and she hadn't, although the fact was that the residence right was worth much more than £350. After all, Mary Anne could have been put off the farm at any time, and, indeed, did not sleep in the place but in a neighbour's house. But whether Hannah's feelings were strong enough to drive her to murder is, perhaps, questionable. Had Mary Anne any motive? No specific motive as far as is known, but all three may have hated Patrick, who was noisy-voiced and quarrelsome, and made it clear that he was 'the boss' at Kilkerrin. And with Patrick out of the way, the trio would share the farm equally on their mother's death.

———————

The Gardaí investigations continued, and showed beyond doubt that the murder had been committed while Patrick was in bed asleep, and, of course, must have been committed by one of the family. But which one? Mary Anne, a big strong woman, would have been able to kill her brother single-handed while he slept. But so could Con or Hannah. Whoever struck the blows had either pre-arranged it with the others or sought their help afterwards. In the latter event the helpers would have been guilty only of being accessories after the fact, which carries the penalty of imprisonment only. But the most likely event was a conspiracy to murder. The Gardaí, however, did not try to solve these legal problems. They dealt with the matter by arresting all four, on 14 March, one week after the head had been found. All were charged with murder and conspiracy to murder. Con said nothing when charged. Hannah said, 'I had nothing to do with it,' and Mary Anne's answer was, 'I was not there at all that night. Ask the woman I slept with.' Mrs O'Leary said she was innocent, which was probably true. She was seventy-five years old.

While the trail was pending Mary Anne died in prison from cancer, and so, as the prosecution had no case against Mrs O'Leary, they entered a *nolle prosequi* for her, and the trial proceeded against Con and Hannah. They were not charged with conspiracy but with murder, and as Mr Carrigan K.C. told the jury in his opening speech, it was a case of concerted murder, meaning that the two together had acted equally as principals in the commission of the crime. Mary Anne being dead, nothing was said about her part in it, whatever it had been, nor did Mr Carrigan try to say which of the pair had struck the fatal blow. He couldn't nor could anyone else, except the two in the dock, and they did not give evidence.

60

The proof of the crime and its manner presented no problems for the prosecution. The head-board of Patrick O'Leary's bed showed evidence of having been wiped, but worm holes in the wood were still filled with dried droplets of blood. The bed frame, and the floor underneath, were blood stained, and the inside of the loft roof showed blood from arterial spouting. Potatoes on the floor near the bed and pieces of chaff were also blood stained. The bed-clothes and the remainder of the bed were free of stains, and indeed the bolster, pillow, and quilt and blankets on the bed when the Gardaí came to search looked fresh, as if the bed had not been used for some time, but of course the bed-clothes could have been substituted for those in use when Patrick O'Leary was murdered. Indeed, it is difficult to see how blood could be on a bed frame, and yet the bed-clothes escape. And the mattress was missing, but pieces of a blood-stained mattress were found in a field near the house, and these matched fragments of a mattress impefectly hidden in Patrick's loft bedroom.

When Superintendent Troy had finished searching he asked Con who owned some old clothes lying across the bed. Con said they were Patrick's, and Troy asked where were Patrick's best clothes.

'He had them on and he going away to the fair.'

Troy invited him to search for those clothes and Con agreed. So the two men went up to the back of the house, and in an overgrown garden, under a pile of weeds, found a pair of trousers, which Con said were his brother's best trousers, although he was supposed to have worn them going away. And Garda McHugh, who was searching in the next field, appeared with the jacket which matched the trousers. He had found it in a ditch, and Con obligingly confirmed that the jacket was Patrick's, thereby bringing himself several paces nearer the scaffold. Garda McHugh had been unwittingly assisted in his search by Hannah and Mary Anne O'Leary who, as he was combing the field, appeared at the back door of their house and watched him intently. He was on higher ground and was clearly visible to them. From their scrutiny he concluded there must be something important in his vicinity, and sure enough, he found Patrick's jacket, and a moment later, concealed in some furze, a dismembered human leg. When shown the leg Con said nothing.

The medical evidence was to the effect that the dismemberment was probably effected by a blunt non-surgical instrument, the jagged and rough edges of the cuts having been caused by a hatchet or slasher. The head of the unfortunate victim had been

61

severely injured, the right side being partly pulp from severe violence, and the base of the skull, left cheek bone and nose being extensively fractured. The head wounds were circular in shape and could have been inflicted with a hammer, or the blunt end of a hatchet. No hammer was ever found in the house or loft, though a hatchet was. In cross-examination by Mr Joseph A. McCarthy, Barrister-at-law, defending, the doctor agreed that a good sized stone could have caused the wounds, and that both the head injuries and the dismemberment could have been the work of one person. The cause of death was the skull fracture, the other head injuries not being sufficient to cause death. The first blow had probably been the one on the right side of the head which, if inflicted during sleep, would immediately produce stunning. It is very unlikely that the murderer or murderers tackled their victim while he was awake. A juror's question supported this view. 'Were there any marks on the arms, legs, or hands, that would indicate a struggle?' and the answer was no.

One of the striking things about the behaviour of the four O'Learys was their silence about Patrick's disappearance — the silence of death as Mr Justice Hanna, the trial Judge, called it. To no single person in the neighbourhood did any one of them volunteer the information that Patrick had gone away and never come back. Only when asked did any of the four give the story of his trip to Bandon fair. One neighbour who gave evidence, a Miss O'Regan who lived on the other side of the road from the O'Learys, said she only missed Patrick when she heard some gossip that he had gone away. On the day after the finding of the head she and her brother met Con O'Leary on the road. Her brother asked, 'Con, is it Paddy in the bag?'

'Yes.'

'It's a bad case then,' said O'Regan.

'It's awful,' replied Con, adding his oft made remark about his innocence, and clean hands and going to heaven. 'And everyone in Kilkerrin is innocent.' Then he said something new. 'The man that did the like of it, did it before.' Was this an attempt to introduce an imaginary outsider into the crime?

Con's anti-social behaviour after the day of the disappearance was spoken of by a Mrs Collins, whom he met while on a visit to the solicitor in Clonakilty who had his father's will. He had called on 7 March to ask that the will be read over, perhaps to refresh his memory about it or possibly, as the prosecution suggested, to see what the spoils would be for him with Patrick out of the way.

When he came out of the office Mrs Collins was passing by. She stopped and asked why he had given up coming to her house in the evenings, where he used to meet the other neighbours who were regular visitors too. He had been there only once in the twelve days since the disappearance. Con said he had had to deliver milk to a neighbour's house, Colman's, because they were laid low with influenza. The excuse was feeble, and not even true, for Colman proved that Con had last delivered milk to him on 27 February. Then Mrs Collins asked had Pat come back and Con said no. When she advised him to tell the Gardaí he made the same reply as to everyone else. 'There's no need. He'll be home soon.'

The Judge was curious about the disposition of the two O'Leary sisters, and at the end of the trial recalled Miss O'Regan.

Judge: What kind of a woman is Hannah in disposition — is she cross?

Miss O'Regan: She was not cross to us.

Judge: Had you any opportunity of observing her demeanour about her own place? Was she cross or good-tempered?

Miss O'Regan: When she would meet us, she would not want to talk. That is how she would treat us.

Judge: Was she different from Mary Anne?

Miss O'Regan: Yes.

Judge: Mary Anne was a good-tempered pleasant woman?

Miss O'Regan: Yes.

This evidence was dangerous for the defence, as the picture of this good-tempered pleasant woman was unlike that of a murderer. When Mr McCarthy was addressing the jury at the end of the evidence, he suggested to them that Mary Anne might have committed the murder, and that the two in the dock might have hidden the body for the sake of family pride.

The Judge intervened.

Judge: Mr McCarthy, you are not entitled to make the case to the jury that Mary Anne did it. . . .

Mr McCarthy: Does your lordship say I am not entitled to say to them that Mary Anne may have done it?

Judge: It is the same thing. What distinction do you make between suggesting she did it, and that she may have done it? You have given no evidence whatever as regards that.

63

Mr McCarthy: You seem to preclude me, my lord, from making any observations to show that neither of the prisoners participated in this crime.

Judge: When you are not producing either of the prisoners to give evidence you cannot make the case, or the suggestion that Mary Anne did it. If you can point out to the jury any portion of evidence which shows Mary Anne may have done it, you are entitled to.

Mr McCarthy: It is only a matter of comment on the evidence. It puts me in a very difficult position. It is hard enough to conduct a case such as this.

So it must have been, and one sympathises with Counsel in his difficulties, though not with his clients, who had either committed or concealed a revolting murder. The Judge's point was upheld on appeal, but seems unreal. The very absence of evidence as to which of the trio had done it — any one, or all, or two of them could have been guilty on the evidence — seems to validate Mr McCarthy's argument. And indeed, one item in the prosecution case seems to show that Mary Anne had been in it as much as Hannah. This was the incident when she and Hannah watched Garda McHugh searching. If that evidence implicated Hannah, did it not equally implicate Mary Anne?

The prosecution had not called Mrs Donovan to prove or disprove, whether Mary Anne had been in her house on the night of the murder, because on the trial of Con and Hannah the evidence was not relevant. 'I was not there at all that night. Ask the woman I slept with,' Mary Anne had said. If Mrs Donovan could have been called, and had confirmed Mary Anne's arrival in her house before 9.30 p.m. and that she had not gone out during the night, the jury might not have had to puzzle their heads over which of the trio was the murderer. But perhaps they did not do much puzzling. At a late stage in the trial one of the jury asked: 'Were there any bloodstains found on the clothing of the accused?'

The question refers to the two accused, but both juror and Judge were thinking only of Con O'Leary.

Judge: According to the evidence of Dr O'Kelly no bloodstains whatever were found on the clothes of the accused.

Dr O'Kelly, the pathologist, called by the prosecution, had examined the clothing only of Con O'Leary. He had not, nor had anybody else, Gardaí, prosecution, or Judge, considered whether

Hannah's clothing might have had bloodstains. It was an astonishing oversight. The juror then said -

'Well, if he had murdered his brother seven days before, he would have had plenty of time to get rid of them.'

This comment overlooked a vital piece of evidence in favour of Con O'Leary, namely, that on the morning of 26 February — i.e. presumably a few hours after the murder — he had come to work at Mr Travers' farm wearing his working clothes, which showed no bloodstains whatever. The Judge drew attention to this evidence in his summing up, and may have made that juror think again about the point, but one wonders what influence the juror may have had with the other eleven.

The jury heard from Mr Travers of an incident on 27 February, the second morning after the disappearance, when Con arrived wearing his best clothes at 5 a.m. It was still dark, and Con looked rather dazed and 'astray'. 'I met a man on the road,' he announced. 'He was not a tall man. He was a small man, and he had nothing in his hand. The man was facing towards the east.' O'Leary's words smacked of 'the little people' (leprechauns), and Travers said, jokingly, 'That was something from the other world.' When Con said it was, Travers realised he was deadly serious, and frightened. Asked to say exactly where he had met this man, Con said it was on the road going to the lake, a place where nobody would be likely to be at that early hour. After breakfast, while it was still dark, O'Leary and another employee harnessed two carts to go to the Rosscarbery fair. The usual route was by the Miltown road, which passed the O'Leary house, but Con chose a different road and avoided thereby his own dwelling. He had never before gone that way to Rosscarbery. The prosecution suggested that the small man was a hallucination, and that Con was afraid to pass his house in the dark, both incidents springing from a guilty conscience.

The jury retired for but half an hour, and found both accused guilty, but the foreman announced that the majority of the jury wished to recommend mercy for Hannah. Was that because of her sex, or did they think Con had struck the blows and that Hannah, though guilty in law as a participant, was less heinous? But what had the jury thought about Mary Anne's part in the murder? If they had been trying her as well, is it conceivable that she would have been acquitted?

Neither of the two had gone into the witness box, on their Counsel's advice. Nor did they exercise their right to make an unsworn statement of evidence from the dock (on which they could not be cross-examined). The prosecution in a criminal trial is by law prohibited from commenting on the failure of accused persons to give evidence, but the Judge is not, and Mr Justice Hanna spoke unfavourably on their refusal, and their failure to explain things which required explanation. Later, in his charge, however, he recalled Con O'Leary's deposition at the inquest, and remarked that it had been unnecessary for him to give evidence, as he couldn't very well say anything different from what was in his deposition. But, of course, if he had given evidence he might have contradicted some part of his deposition, or on cross-examination perhaps have been forced to admit it contained lies.

When the Judge asked Con O'Leary if he had anything to say as to why sentence of death should not be passed upon him, he said: 'I had not hand, act, or part in the murder.' He was then sentenced to death, the date being fixed as 28 July. Con repeated what he had said, and added: 'I am going to die an innocent man.' When the Judge asked Hannah the same question she answered in a strong clear voice: 'I did not kill my brother.'

Both accused appealed, but without success. (lReported at [1926] I.R. 445.)

The Court remarked upon the striking similarity of the behaviour of Con and Hannah O'Leary — the same false story told by these two persons, the almost identical conduct of the two when confronted with the head, and the strange callousness of the two when the remains were found, and on the night of the wake. One point argued for them at some length was the admissibility in law of the Judge's questions about the temperament and disposition of the O'Leary sisters.

Almost without exception, the only evidence allowed in a criminal trial concerning the personality of an accused person is that of character. The defence can always prove that an accused has a good character (if he has one). The prosecution cannot offer evidence of the accused's bad character, if he has one, save where he has by his defence sought to impute a bad character to one or more of the prosecution's witnesses or, himself being of bad character, has sought to prove that he is of good character. Evidence as to his temperament or manner is not admissible, usually because it is irrelevant, but in Hannah O'Leary's case the Court of Criminal Appeal held that the answers to the Judge's questions concerning her were relevant. Indeed, the Court said they were in her favour, proving that her sullen reticence on being shown her brother's head, and being spoken to by Gardaí, was her normal way of behaving and not the reflection of a guilty conscience.

The picture of Mary Anne as a good-tempered pleasant woman, in contrast to Hannah's temperament, had suggested that Mary Anne was not the kind of person who would have murdered her brother, and therefore, by a process of elimination, that the only murderers were the two in the dock. Counsel for the O'Learys argued forcibly that Mary Anne's temperament was irrelevant, and that it should not have been inquired into by the Judge, but the argument failed, the Court holding that the picture of her as a powerful and unpleasant looking woman likely to do murder (suggested by some of Mr McCarthy's questions at the trial) made it relevant to show that, on the contrary, her demeanour and manner were good tempered and pleasant.

Three days before the execution date Hannah O'Leary was reprieved, the Government commuting her sentence to life imprisonment. She was detained in Mountjoy Prison, Dublin until 18 September 1942, and then released on licence to enter a convent. Cornelius O'Leary was executed on 28 July 1925.

One last speculation is permissible. What would the result have been if the two had been tried separately? It is very unlikely that the defence could have achieved separate trials, for the prosecution would never have consented, and it is improbable that the Judge would have granted two trials. But, suppose that he had? It is usually easier to procure a conviction against two persons tried together than tried alone, which is why prosecutors resist such requests by defenders. But, if Hannah had been tried alone, would the jury have convicted her?

4.

Third Time Lucky

(Attorney - General v. Thomas J. Kelly, 1936)

IN 1935 Patrick Henry, a bachelor of about 67, lived by himself in a two-roomed cottage in Boyle, County Roscommon. He was seemingly alone in the world, for he never visited anyone nor had visitors, but he was well known by appearance to many of the townspeople. Henry was unemployed, and each week drew six shillings dole at the unemployment exchange. It was thought he had some money, though not known for certain, but a trader in the town to whom he had paid a small bill told of Henry carrying a wallet containing about £30 or £40 in notes, and some said that he owned a small farm outside Boyle, which he sold that year. In May 1935, he decided to take in a lodger, one Thomas Kelly, who paid half the rent of two shillings weekly, and during the summer worked with him saving turf for the winter's fires.

Kelly had had a nomadic life before going in with Henry. He was 56, born in County Roscommon near Boyle, and when eighteen had gone to Glasgow where he worked for about six years on the railway, and later on the tramways. Then he emigrated to Rochester, U.S.A. and lived there seven years doing the same kind of work, after which he moved to Cleveland, Ohio, where he worked for a year in a hospital. He and another man stole twenty-five dollars in the hospital, were caught, and convicted and sent to a reformatory institution for a year. When Kelly came out, in 1911, he changed his name to McHugh, took up other employment, and in 1917, when America entered the war, went to work in a munitions factory. After the war he resumed civil employment in Cleveland, until November 1931 when he returned to Ireland with £1,300 savings, a substantial sum then for a man in his position. He lived in Dublin for two years without working and then went to Longford where he married in 1933, but lived with his wife for a few weeks only, and left her to live in County Leitrim, where he used the name of Flynn and grew a moustache and beard. At his trial, he explained: 'I was after getting married, and I did not want to let people know, and point their fingers at me and say, "Where is his wife?"' Soon afterwards he went back to his wife, but they separated after a short time and did not live together again.

Kelly now went to Dublin for a short while, and thence to Belfast, where he lived in a Corporation lodging-house under the name of Mooney for about nine months. It was now 1934, he had not worked for nearly four years and his funds were running low. From Belfast he went to Sligo, twenty-one miles from Boyle, and after a month came to Boyle where he stayed in various lodging houses, sometimes under the name Mooney, until May 1935 when he went to live in Henry's house. His rent was a mere one shilling weekly, and his food only six shillings, but he was going to live in squalor. The cottage had no water or sanitation, was uncarpeted, and without artificial light. Heat was no problem as there was a fireplace for burning turf, but the floors were of clay or stone, and there was the barest minimum of miserable furniture; two broken-down beds with makeshift bedding, a poor deal table, some battered cooking utensils and a couple of uncomfortable kitchen chairs.

And the place was grimy and dirty as might be expected of a poor man living alone. Kelly had always managed to live in reasonable comfort, but had now come down in the world.

The front door of Henry's dwelling had neither handle nor lock, but was secured on the outside by a hasp and padlock when the two men were out, and by bolts on the inside when they were in. As the two were constantly out and about in the town during the day, the locked padlock was a common sight to any passer-by.

Henry had always paid his rent punctually, but on Saturday 7 September 1935 he failed to pay and never paid afterwards. Miss O'Callaghan, his landlady, at first ignored the default, but after a few weeks she called to the cottage and found it locked on the outside. She assumed the two occupants were out, came back several times in the following weeks, but the house was always locked. Then she realised she had not seen Henry for a long time, since Monday 9 September in fact, whereas she used to see him several times a week as he passed her house. Finally, on 31 December she told the Gardaí, two of whom came with her to the cottage, forced the padlock and opened the door. Miss O'Callaghan followed them in, but when she saw the body of a man in the room she ran outside.

The dead man was her tenant, Patrick Henry, and he lay partly in the fireplace and partly on the floor, and had been savagely murdered. His skull was fractured from a severe blow with an instrument of some kind, his jaw was dislocated and broken, other facial bones were broken, and both body and clothing were horribly burned in places, some of the burns preceding death and perhaps accelerating it. The State pathologist thought Henry had been dead two or three months.

The state of the room was horrifying, with bloodstains everywhere on the floor, under the bed, on the walls, on a bucket, a hammer, and even on some sods of turf. But how had the assailant got in to commit this crime? The interior of the cottage was as secure as it could be. The back door was closed, and securely held by a stout timber beam; no windows were open, or broken, and none of the small articles on the window sills, such as bottles, had been disturbed for months. Obviously the last person to enter and leave the house, and therefore the murderer, had used the front door. Henry's bed seemed not to have been slept in, a daily newspaper lay on it — the *Irish Press* of 10 September — and on the floor was an unaddressed donation envelope, obviously pushed under the front door from outside. There was no money in the house, nor any valuables; the linings of Henry's jacket and waistcoat had been cut open as though in a search for concealed paper money, and his gold watch was missing.

Kelly too was missing, although Miss O'Callaghan did not know this, as she had never seen him, but she knew Henry had taken in a lodger. But others now realised Kelly was missing, and of course his absence was suspicious. Where was he? And when had he seen Henry or been with him? The padlocking of the front door required explanation, although a stranger might conceivably have killed Henry and locked the place after him, if he knew where to find the key, but this could only have happened if Kelly was then away from Boyle. If he had still been in the town and found himself locked out he would, of course, have summoned help. But Kelly had disappeared without trace, and police enquiries in the few places where he was known were unproductive.

The date of Henry's death was, of course, uncertain on the meagre information available but the newspaper which Henry read every day was for 10 September, and Miss O'Callaghan had last seen Henry on Monday 9 September. Others had last seen him on the tenth, but Henry's unemployment money, due to be collected regularly, was still waiting for him at the unemployment office. Kelly, too, had failed to draw his unemployment money, so it looked as though he had decamped on the eleventh and that Henry might have been murdered on that day or the night before.

But without Kelly it was all guesswork, and despite exhaustive enquiries and liaison with English police, newspaper announcements and the like, there was no news of Kelly, and the Gardaí could only wait.

They waited for five months and then something happened. On 21 May 1936 the Hibernian Bank in Sligo, where Kelly had had a small deposit account, received the deposit receipt from a bank in Coatbridge, Scotland, for collection. The Sligo bank claimed the right to ten days notice of withdrawal, and sent back the receipt to Scotland to be presented again after ten days, i.e. 31 May, and told the Gardaí.

On the 22 May a party of four Gardaí left Dublin for Glasgow, a few miles from Coatbridge. Two of the party knew Kelly by sight, and they, assisted by Scottish police, began their surveillance of the Coatbridge branch of the Bank of the North of Scotland, from a premises opposite. It was a tedious yet exciting business, watching day after day the many people go in and come out of the bank, but after thirteen days the reward came. On 5 June at 2.30 p.m. Kelly appeared in the street, wearing a moustache and glasses, which he had never worn in Boyle, and went into the bank. Garda Hawkshaw from Boyle and Constable Young of the Scottish police, both in plain clothes, crossed the street, and when Kelly came out followed him for a short distance. Then Young caught up with Kelly and asked him his name.

'John Hill,' was the reply.

'Where do you live?'

'Coatbridge.'

Hawkshaw then stepped forward and asked him to come to the police barracks for an interview. Kelly said nothing. Hawkshaw asked him his name and Kelly said, 'Tom Kelly.' 'Do you know me?' asked the Garda, and Kelly half admitted that he did. The three then walked to the police station, and at the door Young went in first, and Kelly next. When Young was ahead Kelly quickly pulled his hand out of his trousers pocket, and holding a razor blade slashed the left side of his neck. The two men grabbed him, but despite his years Kelly was nearly too strong for them, and they had to get the help of several other police before they could subdue him. First aid was applied to the wound, but Kelly resisted even that, and his fierce struggle had to be very forcibly overcome before a doctor could stitch the wound.

Kelly was then brought to a Glasgow hospital, and when well enough was taken back to Ireland to stand his trial for murder. He was charged with having murdered Henry on 13 September, a date which the Gardaí presumably thought was safe, and said nothing in reply. That choice of date was to give rise to difficulties later, for John McKee, the booking clerk employed by the Belfast Corporation at one of their lodging-houses, came to Boyle on 14 July and identified Kelly as a man who, under the name Thomas Mooney, had arrived at the house on 12 September 1935, and stayed there for a week. So, if Henry was alive on the 13 September Kelly could not have been his murderer.

This information about the date Kelly reached Belfast upset the Gardaí theory about the date of the crime, for up to then they did not know when Kelly had left Boyle. The bank official in Sligo had said that Kelly drew £10 on the twelfth, immediately the bank opened, but didn't know where he had gone after leaving the bank. The booking clerk at Sligo Railway Station had issued one ticket to Belfast on the twelfth, for the 10.30 a.m. train, but did not know to whom. But when Mr McKee identified Kelly the Gardaí changed the murder date to the eleventh, and this was the date for which Kelly was indicted.

The Trial

Kelly's trial began on Tuesday 10 November 1936, presided over by Justice John O'Byrne, K.C., and ended on Saturday 14 November. Prosecuting were Mr Martin Maguire, S.C. and Mr Kevin Haugh; for the defence were Mr Ralph Brereton-Barry, K.C., and Mr Robert Hogan. The date alleged for the crime being 11 September 1935, a vital question was: when had Henry last been seen alive? Indeed, the really controversial part of the trial and the major part of the evidence centred round this issue.

Miss O'Callaghan repeated in the witness box what she had told the Gardaí, that she had last seen Henry on Monday 9 September. Thomas Mayne, a cattle dealer who lived two doors from Henry, saw him on the tenth, which was a fair day in Boyle. But when cross-examined by Mr Barry he said that on 11 September Henry could have been outside the cottage, though he was quite sure he had no recollection of seeing him there. Yet at the preliminary enquiry in the District Court he had sworn: 'I last saw Henry on the evening of the 10th or 11th September. I cannot recollect which date. I saw him outside his house between 6 and 7 p.m.' Asked to say was he now quite sure that he did not remem-

72

ber which was the date, he said it was very hard to remember, but 'I firmly believe it was on Tuesday.' The first seeds of doubt had been cast.

Mrs Brennan, who lived in the adjoining cottage and shared the one roof with Henry, and whose cottage was separated by a wall from his, spoke of his regular habit of going out every morning for the newspaper, and was quite definite that she had seen him on the tenth entering his cottage between 7 and 8 p.m., and never saw him again. She last saw Kelly on Wednesday the eleventh, going into the cottage between 1 and 2 p.m. and coming out ten or fifteen minutes later wearing an overcoat over a brown suit, and carrying no suitcase. When he came to live there he had brought two cases. The dividing wall did not prevent her hearing some sounds from Henry's, such as voices, and the setting and lighting of the fire every morning between 8 and 9 a.m. when the two men usually got up, but on the eleventh she heard these latter sounds between 7 and 8 a.m., earlier than ever before. She remembered the eleventh because the Court had sat in the town that day. There had been silence, she said, from Henry's between Tuesday evening and Wednesday morning, a small point in favour of the defence, who contended though not convincingly that the murder must have been a noisy, violent affair. Why should it have been, if Henry had been felled by the first blow?

When had the front door been padlocked? Clearly, if Kelly had padlocked it on leaving, he was the murderer, for if Henry had been alive inside when Kelly locked him in, he only had to open the back door to get out. Mrs Brennan said she had not looked at Henry's front door when she went out of her house on the Wednesday after seeing Kelly leave, but on Thursday at about 10.30 a.m. she saw that the door was padlocked. But in the District Court she had sworn: 'After he (Kelly) had gone I looked at Henry's door, and it had no padlock on it,' though she did not remember having said this even when shown her deposition. But she was now confused, and became more so as Mr Hogan cross-examined her.

Q. Some time between 3 and 4 o'clock that day (Wednesday) did you look at the door of Henry's house?
A. Yes.
Q. And when you looked at Henry's house was there any padlock on the door?
A. I didn't look.
Q. When did you first see the padlock on Henry's house?
A. On the Thursday morning between 10 and 10.30.

However, a witness named Muldoon said that on the twelfth he had seen a man come out of Henry's in the afternoon and padlock the door, but could not say who it was, nor the time. The milkman, who used to deliver a pint to Henry every evening, said that on a day during Show Week, but he couldn't say which day, when he came with the bottle the door was padlocked, so he left it with Mr McLacklen who lived next door, in a big house on the other side of Henry's. Next day Henry's was still locked, so the milkman took back the bottle from McLacklen and never delivered milk again to Henry's. He had often before left the milk next door and Henry had collected it. McLacklen confirmed this evidence but he too could not give the date save to say that it was in the early part of Show Week.

The prosecution were able to show that all had not been well between Henry and Kelly. In August 1935, as Kelly and an acquaintance named John O'Connor were chatting in the street Henry passed by, and he and Kelly looked away from each other. 'Are you not talking to him?' asked O'Connor. 'No one could talk to that contrary old bastard,' said Kelly angrily. A week later O'Connor saw the two men again cut each other in the street, and on 10 September, as Kelly was talking to James Lynch, Henry came out of the Labour Exchange and crossed the street to keep away from the two, upon which Lynch drew Kelly's attention to him. 'I will do in the old f——,' said Kelly viciously. But neither Mrs Brennan nor McLacklen, the immediate neighbours of Henry and Kelly, had ever heard them quarrelling. Lynch used to see Henry regularly at the Labour Exchange, but had seen neither him nor Kelly since 10 September, a date he remembered because a circus had been in the town that day.

Charles McCormack gave the same date for seeing Kelly last, though with less certainty — 'in or about 10th September, about two nights previous to the Boyle Show,' which had been held on the twelfth. He had seen Kelly at The Diamond, a workmen's club in Boyle, where he often met Kelly who used to play a game of nap, and generally was in the club from about 7 p.m. to about 11 p.m. On the tenth, Kelly was playing cards and asked McCormack to stand in for him as he was going out with Reynolds, another club member. McCormack agreed, and played with the small coins Kelly had left on the table. When Kelly came back, an hour later, he showed signs of having had drink, and refused the money McCormack had won in his absence, an odd thing for a man living on relief money. At midnight Kelly, contrary to his custom, was still in the club and as the place was closing he seemed unwilling to go. 'What's your hurry?' he asked, but finally left at 12.15 a.m. Reynolds gave evidence too, and placed the date with certainty as the tenth. Kelly had asked him out for a drink — an unprecedented event — and had bought two drinks for each of them, surprising for a man drawing the dole. As the two chatted over their drinks, Kelly said he had met friends from Longford and had had a lot of drink with them. 'He is a contrary old son of a gun,' said Kelly out of the blue, without saying who he meant, but presumably it was Henry. Next day Reynolds went as usual to the Labour Exchange to sign on, but neither Kelly nor Henry turned up that day or ever again although, as the manager of the Labour Exchange confirmed and the two knew, there was six shillings waiting to be collected by each. Both, he said, had been at the Exchange on the tenth to sign on.

A publican gave evidence of serving Kelly one morning at 9 a.m. 'about the second week in September.' This was too vague to be of much use, but Kelly's evidence made it clear that this was 10 September. Kelly was wearing a blue suit which looked as if it had been slept in, according to the publican, seemed to have a hangover, and bought a glass of whiskey and a pint of stout, expensive drinking for a man in his position. A townsman named Patrick Casey gave evidence that he had last seen Kelly on either the day of the Show, or the day before. They had met in the street, and Kelly was showing signs of drink, though he was not drunk. 'Is the bus to Dublin gone?' asked Kelly. Casey told him it was and asked in what direction Kelly wanted to go. 'I don't mind which direction so long as I get away from this place,' said Kelly.

The prosecution had now finished their case, and Mr Maguire asked for leave to amend the murder date from that charged, 11 September, to 10 September, the second change of date. Mr Brereton-Barry did not object, the amendment was allowed, and Kelly came to the witness box. He said he had been at the fair in Boyle on 10 September, met friends from Longford with whom he had drinks, and went to the Diamond Club that evening as McCormack and Reynolds had said, Henry then being at home in the cottage. When the Club closed, he went straight home. Henry was in bed, and he (Kelly) went to bed as usual in the other room. Next morning at 8.30 when he got up, he was feeling the after-effects of the night's drinking; Henry was making the fire in the kitchen, and he went out to a public house for drinks. When he returned Henry was at breakfast, and they ate together, talking about the forthcoming show, cattle fairs and the like.

Q. Had you made up your mind to go away at that time?
A. Yes, sir.
Q. How long before?
A. I was speaking about it two or three weeks before that.
Judge: Q. Speaking about it to whom?
A. Myself and Henry used to talk about it.
Judge: Q. Had you made up your mind where you were going when you left Boyle?
A. Yes, sir going to Glasgow.
Judge: Q. Did you ever tell Henry that?
A. I told him at 1.30 that day.
Judge: Q. Did he make much comment about it?
A. No, he did not, we just talked about it that week.

After breakfast Henry went out, and Kelly followed at about 10.30 to get bread, and en route met Henry returning and spoke to him. He stayed about the town till about 1 p.m. when he came back to the cottage, and Henry was there reading the paper. Kelly did not again mention the bread errand, nor was he asked about it. The Judge interposed at this point with two questions, and Kelly almost certainly lied when answering the first one.

Judge: Q. But can you say of what date? (the newspaper).
A. He got it that morning or the morning before. I think it was the tenth.
Judge: Q. Did you look at the paper at all?
A. No, my lord, I did not.

Kelly knew, as well as everyone else, the importance of the dates 10 and 11 September, and that the newspaper found on the bed bore the former date. It was very unlikely that Henry, who used to go out every morning for the paper, would be reading the issue of the tenth on the eleventh, even if he could have bought it on the eleventh. So when Kelly answered the Judge's first question he was trying to do two things: to dodge the awkward question; and at the same time by saying 'I think it was the tenth,' to provide an explanation, weak though it was, for the improbability that Henry would be reading a day-old newspaper. But he did not look at the paper, he said, thus seeking, very weakly again, to pretend that his after-acquired knowledge of the date of the newspaper had been acquired in fact on the eleventh.

Kelly said he had left Boyle on the eleventh by the afternoon bus for Sligo, where he arrived to find the bank closed. He stayed in Sligo, for the night, and next day drew £10 from his deposit moneys, and as he had had £53 in cash leaving Boyle that gave him a total of £63. He took an early train to Belfast, very probably being the unidentified purchaser of the only ticket sold that day at Sligo for Belfast. He spent a week in Belfast, went to Glasgow, and on later to Coatbridge, where he got occasional work, looking after cattle at five shillings a day. Kelly denied emphatically that he had had any suitcase with him on leaving Boyle, a seemingly pointless lie, as it would be more natural for him to travel with luggage than not, and he was asked to explain the absence of luggage. 'I intended to go back sometime,' he said, which explained nothing.

He also had to explain his attempted suicide, and told the Court he had read about Henry's murder in Coatbridge in the *Irish Independent* some months before his arrest, and that the Gardaí wanted to see him to find out if he could help them in their enquiries. 'I had been intending to go back to Boyle before I read this,' he said, 'but then I did not know what to do because I might be blamed for the murder.' This could have been true, for if he was innocent, he would be in a most dangerous position as the last known person to have seen Henry alive. 'So I did nothing, although I was worried.' On the morning of his arrest, he said, he went blank and he did not know what he was doing, and did not remember cutting his throat. Mr Hogan's last question to Kelly was: 'Is there any truth in the suggestion that you killed Patrick Henry?' and Kelly answered, 'I never had anything to do with it.'

Kelly had to do some more explaining when Mr Maguire cross-examined him. He had been down to £100 in the bank in May 1935, and Mr Maguire suggested it was all he had in the world, but Kelly said he had also £60 or £70 on his person. Then he was asked why he had drawn £10 from the bank in May 1935, if he had that amount of cash and could live on his six shillings weekly dole, as he had said he could. 'I don't know what I did it for. I had money in my pocket. I didn't need it at all.' And the £10 withdrawal on 12 September had also to be explained but again could not be, unless, of course, he was penniless save for the £90 left in the bank. But, as Mr Barry pointed out to the jury, the trip to Sligo was very unlike the action of a fugitive to whom time was vital.

77

Mr Maguire wanted to know why Kelly had gone away in September 1935, and his answer was unconvincing: 'I was going to look for work in the summer time,' but when reminded that he had departed at the end of the summer, he said, 'In the following spring.' His stay in Glasgow 'would be according to how things would be'. 'What things?' asked Mr Maguire. 'Work,' said Kelly, but to further questions he agreed he had not done a tap of work in Ireland for four years, and he idled in Belfast without looking for work. He had chosen Glasgow, he said, because he knew it in his youth. In the nine months he was in Scotland before arrest, he had worked casually for about three or four months.

When he went back to Coatbridge the first time to negotiate the deposit receipt, he gave a false address, and also told the bank official that he was working in Ayrshire, twenty miles away, and so could not come back again for a few days. He could give no explanation for these falsehoods, nor for wearing glasses, nor for using the name Hill to Constable Young. He was again asked why he had left his suitcase in Henry's cottage, and said he had no clothes to put in it, as his blue suit was worn out, and there was no sense in taking an empty case, though it had been with him in his travels all over America and Ireland, and was of some value.

The trousers of Kelly's blue suit were missing and he could not say why, though the jacket had been left hanging in the cottage, and the suggestion was that they had been either been burnt or otherwise disposed of because of bloodstains. Mr Maguire handed Kelly two pairs of trousers which had been found in the cottage and asked was either his. Kelly hesitated and was silent. 'If you have any doubt about it I will ask you to put them on.' Then Kelly answered, 'I have a pair like them.'

Kelly had to admit that he had not said goodbye to anyone except Henry before leaving Boyle, but asserted he had told several acquaintances he was going. 'When did you tell them?' asked Mr Maguire, but Kelly could not remember, and denied telling Casey he did not care where he went so long as he got out of Boyle. He could not deny that he had not collected his six shillings unemployment money that morning. Asked why, he said, 'I was going away and I did not think of it.' It was lame, but even lamer answers followed.

> Q. So that is the reason you did not turn up (at the Labour Exchange)?
> A. Yes.

78

Q. Will you suggest why poor Henry did not turn up?
A. I don't know. I could give you no explanation.
A. You left him alive and well, according to your story, about 1.30 on the Wednesday?
A. When I left the house at 1.30 he was in the house.
Q. Alive and well?
A. Yes.
Judge: Q. You say he was well and alive that morning?
A. Yes, my lord, at 10.30.
Judge: Q. Is that not the time he usually went to the unemployment office?
A. Yes.

The picture was not only of a sudden departure, but of a senseless one which meant, as Kelly admitted, ending the cheapest living he had had for years — one shilling a week, which he could not get while in Scotland. In 1935 one could survive on that money.

The prosecution had no evidence about Henry's money affairs except what Redigan had said about the roll of notes, so Mr Maguire set about trying to get some information from Kelly. Kelly said he did not know if Henry had had any money, but Henry had told him he sometimes received £5 from a sister in America, where Henry himself had lived for twenty-seven years. Kelly denied knowing anything of Henry's business life there, but Mr Maguire elicited that Henry had told him he had some money when he came back from abroad, but did not say how much, and, 'I don't know where he kept it,' Kelly added. Neither did the prosecution, if the money still existed, which was pure speculation. Kelly denied cutting open Henry's garments to look for money, but said he had heard in the town that Henry had sold a farm in Boyle, and Henry had told him also, but not the price, nor had he asked Henry what the price was.

He had to make more denials as the cross-examination went on, and of course was contradicting disinterested and apparently honest witnesses. He denied that Henry and he had ever fallen out, that he had even called him an old bastard, or 'the old f——,' or threatened to kill him. The two of us, he said, were on normal friendly terms.

Kelly could not explain why he had changed his name after leaving, but said he had done that in Ireland, which was true, for he had used false names with landladies, and even with a laundry in Boyle where he was a customer. The fact was that Kelly was something of a wanderer, and had sudden impulses to leave and move on from place to place, as two of his Boyle landladies told the Court. He had more than once left them without notice and had come back in a few days, but of course he had not come back to Henry. And he had left his wife in the same abrupt way and come back to her, but a wife is not a landlady.

When Kelly's cross-examination ended, the defence dealt with an answer McCormack had given him when asked had he seen Henry on the twelfth at Boyle Show. 'No, I did not. I'm sure I did not,' he said emphatically, but others had seen Henry there, and the first one called was Kathleen McPherson of Boyle, aged 23, who knew Henry to see and said that she saw him on 12 September at the Show. She was an exhibitor of crochet-work, and on her way to the exhibits building saw him, at about 3 p.m., a few inches away. She had no doubt about it, until she was cross-examined, and was asked could it have been at the 1934 Show she had seen Henry. 'No sir, — well it could have been, but I don't think so.' Then Mr Maguire enquired if she had been interviewed in December 1935, by Superintendent Twomey of the Gardaí, and she said yes, but was not sure when, and not even sure she recognised Twomey when he was asked to stand up, which sounded as if she might be a poor judge of faces. Worse, she could not remember what she had told Twomey, but might have said she did not know when she last saw Henry. Miss McPherson lived less than a mile from the Garda Station, but had never called in there to tell any Garda that Henry was alive on the twelfth, nor had she disclosed this vital information when being interviewed. 'I was never asked,' was her explanation and this was true, for the Gardaí when interviewing witnesses were assuming that Henry had been murdered on the thirteenth and everyone in Boyle naturally thought the same. It was some time after the District Court proceedings that she realised the date 12 September might be important to Kelly.

Her brother Paul was the next witness, and he was certain he too had seen Henry at the Show. He had no doubt it was Henry, and Mary McPherson, another sister, corroborated him saying that Henry in fact 'was in our way' as they went towards the exhibits. Paul McPherson gave a convincing explanation for not telling this to the Garda who interviewed him. 'He asked me whether Henry owned a gold watch, and I told him he did because I had seen it, but he never asked me when I had last seen Henry alive.' Further questioning elicited the information that when McPherson read in the newspaper that the murder date had been changed from

80

the thirteenth to the tenth, he knew the tenth was wrong because Henry was alive on the twelfth. And the last few answers in the cross-examination ring true.

> Q. And to whom outside your family did you first divulge this information?
> A. Well, I told it to several. Plenty here too know he was alive then.

Judge: Q. For instance, who are these?
> A. Well, two witnesses who gave evidence (in the District Court), one is Johnston, and my own two sisters.
> Q. But who outside your own two sisters knows he was alive?
> A. There are plenty.
> Q. Do you know their names?
> A. Yes.
> Q. What are their names?
> A. John Harrington, Luke Dempsey and James Pettit.
> Q. Any others?
> A. That is all.

The defence then put up George Johnston whom McPherson had named, and who said he saw Henry on the twelfth at about 9 a.m., standing beside the Labour Exchange, but if this were true it was odd that Henry had not gone inside and collected his six shillings. But when asked the routine question why he had not told the Gardaí this, his answer created a surprise: 'I did. When the three detectives were at my house making enquiries about Kelly (*not* about Henry) I mentioned that the last time I saw Henry was on the day of the Show.' So the detectives had either forgotten this, or else rejected it as being unimportant because at that time they thought the murder had been committed on the thirteenth.

The next defence witness, Edward Doherty, an old age pensioner, not only corroborated Johnston as to where Henry was on the twelfth, but had actually spoken to Henry. Between 10 a.m. and 11 a.m. Doherty asked him if he was going to the Show, and Henry answered that he did not know yet. 'Do you remember seeing Thomas Kelly that morning? asked Mr Maguire. 'I thought I did, but I wouldn't swear to it. A man was standing at the corner. He had a brown suit on him, and he was about the same size as Kelly, but I didn't see his face.' This was somewhat different from what he had told the Gardaí, which was, 'I saw Henry, and Kelly standing about five yards from where Henry was standing,' and he was invited to explain the difference, the question being intended to discredit him. But Doherty's reply demolished the question, and ought to have impressed the jury with his regard for both accuracy and the truth. 'Yes,' he said, 'but a short time afterwards I made up my mind that it would be wrong to swear it when he had his back to me, because I did not see Kelly's face.'

There were other differences, however. His written statement to the Garda said he saw Henry between noon and 1 p.m., and that he had spoken to Henry after lunch as he was going back to the Show. 'I never said that,' Doherty asserted, but added that he was not now sure of the time in the morning when he had seen Henry. If this was true, the Garda had taken down wrongly what Doherty told him, but the statement contained the usual words: 'This statement has been read over to me before signature and is correct,' above Doherty's signature. How much damage had this contradiction done to his testimony? The important thing was that, unlike all the others who had seen Henry on the twelfth, Doherty had spoken to the man, and he should have been believed, especially as he had spoken about the Show, a realistic corroboration that the day was the twelfth.

The evidence for the defence closed then, and after Counsel's speeches were over it was 7.30 p.m. so the jury were locked up for another night. Next morning the Judge began his charge to the jury, and his contribution to Kelly's destiny. The Judge's charge in a criminal trial, both in Ireland and England, is supposed to be impartial but rarely is. The form of the charge is a combined statement of the law, which the jury must accept and act upon, and a summary of the facts, with any comments thereon which the Judge thinks he should make, but which the jury need not accept.

But the authority of the Judge's position, and of his personality if he is a strong Judge, together ensure that the jury will either totally accept the Judge's view of the case, or be seriously influenced by it. And as the Judge is the last speaker whom the jury hear, the speech of defending Counsel will probably be obscured, if not indeed obliterated, by the Judge's words, especially if the defender spoke the night before. It would indeed be a strong jury which would reject or totally ignore the Judge's opinions, even though the Judge will warn them that they are not bound to accept his opinions, so that one wonders why the Judge bothers to express opinions to the jury at all, since they are not obliged to listen to them. Anyone who thinks that a trial by jury in Ireland and England is really a trial by twelve people is being deceived; it is in fact a trial by the twelve, with a strong gloss put on it by the Judge. Much, therefore, depends on the man who is going to charge the jury.

Mr Justice O'Byrne was a judge of distinction, conscientious, principled, a sound and experienced lawyer, and a man of balanced and level mind. But he had a fatal defect for a judge. He was too strong minded, and once he had made up his mind found it difficult to entertain anything which might change it. The ideal judge is one possessing the admirable qualities stated above, and a flexible intellect which keeps open the question for decision until the last possible moment of the trial, so that all the facts and arguments are fully and properly considered and weighed.

As Judge O'Byrne's charge proceeded it became clear what he thought of Kelly's guilt. His statement of the law to the jury, and of the onus on the prosecution to prove the case beyond a reasonable doubt, was unexceptionable. 'The evidence must . . . be such as to be reasonably inconsistent with any hypothesis, save that the accused committed the crime; it must . . . point irresistibly to the conclusion that the accused committed it'. Faultless words, but followed by words which showed that the Judge thought the evidence *did* point to that conclusion. Kelly really had very little chance by the time the charge was over.

The motive for the crime, according to prosecution theory, was gain. This was inconsistent with the prosecution's evidence that the two men were on bad terms, and that the murder could have followed from an angry quarrel; and as the defence pointed out, if gain was the motive then Kelly's withdrawal of £10 from the bank was not only pointless but, indeed, dangerous if he was a fugitive and therefore pressed for time. And of course if Kelly was in flight it was incomprehensible that he should leave £80 in the bank. The Judge dealt adequately with these points, but when he came to the defence argument, that anybody had the same opportunity of committing the crime as Kelly had had, he said, 'You have only to consider for a moment to see that it is not so . . . '. He mentioned the very lonely life of the two men, whose threshold no visitor ever crossed, and asked, 'Who had such an opportunity for committing the crime as this man had? — the man who was living in the house; the man who could go into the house without arousing any suspicion; the man who could get into position to deliver such a blow without arousing any suspicion on the part of Patrick Henry.'

Of Johnston's evidence that he had said, in the presence of three detectives, he had seen Henry on the twelfth, the Judge was frankly incredulous, and he invited the jury to be of the same frame of mind. 'Gentlemen, do you believe that for a moment?' and asked did they believe that the Gardaí hearing Johnston would fail to take a statement from him? But the Judge overlooked the fact that none of the three detectives had been called to contradict Johnston, and one of them was actually sitting in Court. Of Bernard Doherty the Judge's comment was: 'Now Doherty is a man on whom I don't intend to spend much time, because I don't believe you will pay much attention to his evidence . . . I am not suggesting that he is telling you what he believes to be untrue . . . but he is obviously a man whose accuracy is not to be relied on.' He then referred unfavourably to the differences between Doherty's signed statement to the Gardaí and his testimony in Court, without suggesting that perhaps the Garda wrote down incorrectly what he was told, which does happen. The Judge even criticised Doherty for not identifying Kelly from behind: 'For a man living side by side with him (Kelly) in Boyle, a man who knew him to see day after day, I think the back of the man would be as well known as his face.' As to the date of Henry's death, the Judge correctly pointed out that if he had been alive on the twelfth, one would expect he should be seen by Mrs Brennan of next door, though she used not to see him every day, and that he would have collected his unemployment money, and taken in the milk.

The jury retired at 1.25 p.m. and took two hours to find Kelly guilty. When the Judge asked Kelly had he anything to say why sentence should not be pronounced according to law, he answered, 'Nothing.' Judge O'Byrne then sentenced him to be executed on 3 December 1936, saying that he entirely agreed with the jury's verdict, and appealing to Kelly to use the short time at his disposal in this life to make his peace 'with your Creator — the Great Judge — before whom we shall all have to appear'.

The trial ended on 14 November, and death was only nineteen days away for Kelly. He appealed on various grounds but within four days after the trial his solicitor, Mr Christopher Callan of Boyle, was told by three townspeople — Edward Farrell, John Tuite, and Thomas Johnston — that each had read about the trial and could prove that Henry was alive on 12 September 1936. Others came forward later with the same information, and by 27 November the total was seven, none of whom had been known to Mr Callan before the trial. So the Court of Criminal Appeal was asked, for the first time since its formation, to allow the appeal on the additional ground that these witnesses could prove that Henry was alive on the twelfth, and a new trial should be directed so that

84

another jury could hear them. The Court directed the attendance of the seven before them, and when they had been heard, quashed the conviction and ordered a new trial, but only on that ground, rejecting the other grounds of appeal. So, Kelly's time on this earth was extended considerably past 3 December, and he was tried again on 15 April 1937, before Mr Justice Hanna and a jury. The former evidence was repeated by the prosecution and they offered some new evidence about Henry's money affairs. It appeared that he was an undischarged bankrupt, and had withdrawn the last of his bank savings, about £73, in June 1933, so that unless he had put away money in some unexpected place he was penniless apart from the cash he carried on his person. The prosecution also called a man named Grady, who had seen Henry going into his house on the tenth at 4.30 p.m. followed by Kelly.

The new defence witnesses were remarkably consistent, and gave realistic and convincing details. John Tuite saw Henry between 9.30 a.m. and 10 a.m. on Show Day, the twelfth, standing with his back to the workhouse, and John Ryan saw him soon after that at the workhouse gate. Edward Farrell actually spoke to Henry at about five minutes to eleven on the road leading to the Show, and remarked to him that he was up early. 'I'm going down to see the bulls,' said Henry. Robert Irwin saw Henry twice on the twelfth, in the morning when Henry was with some others, and in the afternoon when Henry was alone. Martin Forde met Henry when on his (Forde's) way to the Show in the evening, and exchanged greetings with him. A Mrs Kenny met him as she stood on a bridge. 'Not much of a crowd at the Show,' he said, after they had exchanged 'good evening'.

Mary McPherson gave her evidence again, and a new bit came out when she was asked who she was with when she saw Henry at the Show. 'Sonny Gannon,' she replied, and then had to explain why she had not mentioned him before. 'He told me not to say his name.' No doubt she was an unreliable witness, as perhaps Farrell was, for both had told Superintendent Twomey that they did not know when they had last seen Henry. And Broder too, a Show steward, may have been unreliable when he said that at 4.30 a.m. on the way home from the Show dance he had seen a light in Henry's home, and in Mrs Brennan's next door, for his companion, Edward Dempsey, had seen no such lights. But the other seven, (Johnston, Tuite, Regan, Forde, Doherty, Paul McPherson and his sister Kathleen) were unshaken by the prosecution's reiterated question, why had they withheld the information when interviewed, in some cases, or not gone to the Gardaí, in other cases. 'I was not asked,' or 'they were asking about Kelly and not about Henry', or 'I didn't want to get involved' were the answers. When the Judge asked one of them why he didn't go to the Gardaí the answer was refreshingly different. 'I thought I'd just as soon tell Mr Callan.'

These people could not *all* have made the same mistake as to the day they had seen Henry, and as several of them did not even know Kelly, the prosecution's suggestion of a conspiracy amongst them to commit perjury sounded far-fetched. And, as the Judge told the jury, the various times and occasions spoken of by the seven fitted hour by hour right through the day, like a jig-saw puzzle, and if believed 'provided the best possible alibi for the accused'. And the defence case was strengthened when Dr Leyland, another new defence witness, said that in his opinion Henry had not been dead as long as three months when his body was discovered, and Dr McGrath the State pathologist agreed Henry had been dead for about two months. So, when the jury retired Kelly seemed to have quite a good chance of an acquittal.

Two hours later the jury returned, and when the foreman rose to speak a death-like silence fell, but all he said was that the jury wanted to hear the evidence of a man named Mulvanny, who had not been called by the prosecution, and might be able to give important evidence. The jury also wanted to know why this witness had not been called, and as he would have been a prosecution witness it was for Mr Maguire to say why, but he said nothing, and the Judge, who should have insisted on an explanation, let the matter go.

Mulvanny was called to the box by the Judge and said he had seen Henry on 12 September in Boyle. Mr Maguire rose to cross-examine whereupon Mr Brereton-Barry objected strongly, pointing out that if Mr Maguire had called Mulvanny as part of the prosecution's case he could not have cross-examined him, and should not now be in a better position by not having called the witness. The objection seems faultless, but Judge Hanna overruled it, and Mr Maguire elicited from Mulvanny that he had told the Gardaí he had not seen Henry, whom he knew well, on the day of the Show, and a month later had called again to the barracks and repeated this statement to the Superintendent. So, with some more confusion added to 12 September, the jury retired again, and Kelly had to wait for two more hours. Then the twelve reappeared, and once again there was that terrible silence, as the registrar stood to ask had they reached their verdict. 'No, my lord,' said the foreman. 'We cannot agree.' So Kelly was put back to await his third trial, which was delayed until 15 November 1937 and took six days. This third Judge was Mr Justice Gavan Duffy.

When the Court sat, Mr Brereton-Barry raised a legal point, and applied to the Judge to quash the indictment on the ground that the retrial directed by the Court of Criminal Appeal had already been held, resulting in disagreement, and that therefore Kelly could not be tried again. But the application was rejected, for it had been decided a hundred years earlier that a trial which ends in disagreement is a partial trial only, and therefore a complete trial must still be held. So Kelly heard himself being charged, for the fifth time, with Henry's murder — three times in the Central Criminal Court, once in the District Court, and once in the barracks at Boyle — and all the evidence was put forward again. The defence had two new witnesses, Edward Flanagan, who had said 'good evening' to Henry as they met on the road from the Show on the twelfth, and Edward Johnston who had seen Henry that day standing on the corner of the Northern Bank building in Boyle. But Johnston had told his solicitor he was 'almost sure' it was Henry, and was asked in cross-examination if he was still of that mind. 'I'm sure of it, because I never saw Henry since that day.'

The third jury now had heard eleven people, all of whom had seen Henry alive on the twelfth. Surely this must have helped Kelly? The Judge reminded the jury that most of these witnesses did not even know Kelly's appearance, and any who did not know him was not a friend of his, a point, he said, which was in his favour. Mr Brereton-Barry emphasised that most of the new witnesses had come from Boyle, 130 miles away, at very great inconvenience, but with a desire to prevent a 'hideous miscarriage of justice'. One cannot feel that *none* of these eleven should have been believed; if only *one* were to be believed then that was the end of the case, and Kelly must be acquitted. But even another disagreement would give Kelly a good chance that the prosecution would drop the case.

But there was no disagreement, and Kelly was found guilty. For the second time he heard himself being sentenced to death, and for the second time he said 'Nothing' when asked if he had anything to say. The Judge created a precedent by not donning the black cap, as he said the fatal words of the death sentence. Kelly's appeal failed, but on 21 December the Cabinet spared him, and commuted the death sentence to penal servitude for life, which rarely means life and for Kelly was ten years, for he was released from prison on 17 December 1947. He was fortunate, but the Cabinet may have felt it was dangerous to pass over the evidence of those eleven witnesses and so Kelly who had been close to death three times, once by his own act, survived its perils.

One may wonder why the third jury did not have the doubts which some of the second jury must have had. Could one really feel *certain* that every one of the eleven witnesses was wrong?

5.

The Strongest Motive of All

(Attorney-General v. John Fleming, 1933)

THE police say that when a wife is murdered, the husband is the first suspect, and it may have been in reliance on this cynical theory that the Gardaí, on 26 July 1933, within a quarter of an hour of seeing the body of Ellen Fleming, set off for the house where her husband was spending the evening. And there when they spoke to Fleming they got their best clue. Detective-Sergeant Mark Byrne, after some preliminaries, said to him: 'I am arresting you on a charge of murder,' but did not say who had been murdered, whereupon Fleming answered, 'Oh! My God! I will go with you,' without asking *who* had been murdered. An innocent man would, of course, enquire who was the victim — even a guilty man would do that as a precaution — but no innocent man would meekly assent to an arrest for a murder he knew nothing about. In fact, Ellen Fleming had been found murdered in her home about an hour or so before.

She had married John Fleming in 1921, and in 1933 they were living in Drumcondra, a north-side suburb of Dublin. She was several years older than her husband, who was thirty-four and worked as a shoe salesman in a city outfitter's. Mrs Fleming also worked in the city, in her uncle's shop. She had usually enjoyed reasonably good health, though occasionally getting dizzy spells of short duration and nervous attacks, but on 31 March 1932, she had a violent attack at about midnight. Fleming asked his wife's nephew, a youth who was living in the house, to summon Mrs O'Rourke from next door as Mrs Fleming had had a stroke, and Mrs O'Rourke came in immediately. She was told by Fleming of the stroke, ran up to the bedroom and found Mrs Fleming in bed in obvious agony, with glaring eyes, in the grip of severe spasm, opening and clenching her hands and rubbing her jaws. She was barely able to speak but managed to ask Mrs O'Rourke to pull her legs up and down and rub her hands and jaws. Whatever was wrong it was no stroke.

Mrs O'Rourke did her best to help, and in a few minutes her brother-in-law Patrick O'Rourke arrived. He was a qualified compounder and dispenser of medicines, and knew from looking at Mrs Fleming, whose spasms and contractions were now getting acute, that she was not having a stroke. He helped Mrs Fleming with muscle massage, but then her face dropped which he knew, if his suspicions were correct, was a bad sign. He called Fleming, who was downstairs, and advised him to get a doctor, advice which one would have thought unnecessary to a husband whose wife was in such distress. Fleming came into the room carrying a hot glass of milk, which he offered to his wife. She refused it, with a question: 'Why do you insist on my taking it, Jack?' and he did not press her but left, taking the milk with him, and presumably going to get a doctor.

In a few minutes Fleming returned bearing a wine-glass containing some coloured liquid, which he told his wife, in answer to her question, was port and whiskey. She was able to speak more easily now.

'It is not,' she said, 'because there is none in the house.'

'There was a little in the bottom of the bottles,' said Fleming offering her the glass. She tried it and spat out immediately.

'It tastes like the chocolates you gave me,' she complained. 'Bitter and taste of aspirin.'

'Did you put aspirin in it?' asked Mrs O'Rourke.

'I might have,' was Fleming's peculiar answer, but if he intended to convey that he *had* put in aspirin it was a lie, for, unknown to him, Mrs O'Rourke had a few minutes before gone to another room, to the medicine chest, and taken from it the only aspirin in the house.

'How could you have put in aspirin when I have it in my pocket?' she asked, and Fleming said nothing.

Mrs Fleming had put the wine-glass on the bedside table, and Fleming took it and left the room saying he was going for the doctor as his wife and O'Rourke had asked. It was now about 1.45 a.m. and Mrs Fleming was still in serious distress, but Fleming went down to the kitchen instead of going out. O'Rourke, however, was suspicious, followed him, and found he was holding the glass under the running tap, the coloured liquid having disappeared.

O'Rourke spoke plainly. 'I will hold you responsible if anything happens to Mrs Fleming. I can get a doctor in the wilds of Connemara in half an hour, and it's queer that you can't get one in the city of Dublin in an hour and a half.'

Fleming said, 'I will get a doctor,' and went out, but he came back without having made contact with Dr Cotter, Mrs Fleming's physician for years, or Dr Sheil, who will be mentioned later in this narrative and who lived only a few minutes walk from the house. Fleming went out a second time, and came back still without Dr Cotter, saying that the doctor's maid had answered him from a bedroom window, and from the way she spoke he knew the doctor was drunk.

This was a falsehood, as he had not even knocked at the doctor's door, and was a grave slander on a professional man of high reputation. Mrs Fleming, who nearly wept on hearing this, said the doctor must be very drunk when he would not come to her. Fleming went out a third time, again supposedly for the doctor, but came back without him.

Finally, Mr O'Rourke said that at least a nurse should be called, and the young nephew went out and got Miss McDonagh, a midwife and mental nurse, who came in at 2.45 a.m. When she asked Fleming what was wrong with his wife he said, 'She has taken a bad turn, that is all,' — an astonishing statement when in fact she had presented an alarming appearance for over two hours, and O'Rourke, who knew from experience, thought it was a case of strychnine poisoning, though he did not say so to Fleming. Miss McDonagh found Mrs Fleming apparently all right, but applied hot fomentations to her leg and jaw to ease the stiffness and contractions. Mrs Fleming slept then and Miss McDonagh stayed till 8 a.m. Fleming came in to the bedroom once or twice to enquire could he do anything, but not once did he discuss or ask the nurse what was wrong with his wife. At midday Miss McDonagh sent for Dr Cotter, and when Fleming came home for lunch the doctor was there.

'I have seen your wife,' he told Fleming. 'She is suffering from nerves and needs tonics and building up. I will take her in hand now.' From this diagnosis it is clear that Dr Cotter was not told of the symptoms of strychnine poisoning of the night before, and was treating Mrs Fleming for her former nervous condition. In fact, she was approaching the menopause.

Fleming's reply to the doctor was either brilliant, or exceptionally stupid, depending on how one looks at it. 'Yes. I knew it was nerves she was suffering from. I pretended last night to go for you.' It was as well Fleming did not mention that the night before he had told his wife he believed the doctor to have been drunk, or Dr Cotter would have had something to say. At the trial Dr Cotter made it clear that there had been no call for his services from Fleming on that night, and that if there had been he would have responded.

Earlier in the morning Fleming had called in to the O'Rourkes. 'About this poisoning,' he said, 'I was down in the country recently and got Joe (Mrs Fleming's brother) to get strychnine poison from the chemist to poison the dog next door. Some of it might have got loose in my pocket and got on to the chocolate. I buried the rest of it in the back lane. For the life of you don't tell Nellie (Mrs Fleming) or Miss O'Brien (a next door neighbour and friend of Mrs Fleming).

The two listened in silence to this remarkable recital, as well they might, for Fleming was now admitting that he knew his wife had been poisoned, and had not had any stroke, and that despite the grave illness he had not procured a doctor. He had not even gone for the nurse. Fleming's treatment of his wife that night was called 'disgraceful' by prosecuting counsel at his trial, and indeed it was an understatement. Mrs O'Rourke said nothing, but her husband commented. 'It is dangerous to carry things like that in your pocket.' Next day Mrs O'Rourke was at Fleming's place of employment and he asked her: 'If Nellie had eaten the chocolate would she have died in an hour?' Mrs O'Rourke was taken back, but answered 'It might take three hours.' Mr O'Rourke's suspicion that Mrs Fleming's symptoms were of strychnine poisoning were verified by medical evidence at the trial. He was asked by the defence did he not think it was his duty to report to the police, if he suspected Fleming of having tried to poison his wife. His answer was that once nursing and medical attention were provided the responsibility was off his shoulders, which was reasonable enough.

A few days later Mrs Fleming left her house and lived for some months with her sister in the Midlands. One may surmise that she was afraid of what Fleming might do to her, for there had been trouble between them once before. She had reproached him during Easter for neglecting to go to Mass — they were Catholics — and he became very angry and assaulted her severely.

The 26 July 1933 was a Wednesday, the weekly half-holiday for both the Flemings. Mrs Fleming was living again at Drumcondra, and reached home at 1.30 p.m. Fleming came in soon afterwards, and after lunch both of them were in the tiny back garden of their house. Fleming was cutting the grass and Mrs Fleming was chatting with Mrs O'Rourke across the garden wall. 'I intended going to Cahill's for dinner today, but Jack insisted on coming home to cut the grass, so I brought home some steak for the dinner, and we had tea and steak for dinner. When I tidy up the house I'm going to meet my sister on the 7 o'clock train. If she doesn't come I'll go on to Cahill's.' Fleming was nearby and could hear what his wife said. After some more talk the women separated, met again later, and the last time Mrs O'Rourke saw Mrs Fleming alive was at about 4.30 p.m., at her own front door, still wearing the working overalls she had worn earlier. Fleming was then in the back garden working with a pair of shears and wearing a blue suit, and Mrs O'Rourke was about to go into the city.

At 5 p.m. Mrs Fleming, still wearing overalls, crossed the road to speak to a neighbour, and left her ten minutes later, to return to No. 48. That was the last time she was seen alive. About 6.30 Mrs O'Rourke returned from the city, and saw that the back door of the Fleming house was closed, and nobody was about, and the windows which had been open were also closed. Fleming was last seen, at the house, at about 4.30 and next seen at about 6.30 by a man who lived on his road, walking at a place called the Bull Wall, in Dollymount, which is on the sea, and about three miles from Drumcondra. Fleming's next known appearance was at about 7.30 or 7.35 p.m. when he arrived at the house in Clontarf where he was later arrested. He came in through the back door, looking his normal self, and greeted the maid who was in the kitchen. 'I'm after being in Dollymount. I had a great swim and was sun bathing.' He had no towel or bathing costume with him either in Dollymount or Clontarf. He went through the kitchen into the dining room and met his hostess. 'I've been to Dollymount. I am sorry I'm late,' and repeated what he had said to the maid about his swim.

Meanwhile, Mrs Fleming's sister and nephew arrived in Dublin by train at 7.20, and as Mrs Fleming was not at the station to meet them, took a taxi to her house, fifteen minutes away. There was no reply to their knock on the door, so the boy got the key from O'Rourke's, leaving his aunt there, and let himself in to the house. He walked down to the kitchen door at the end of the hall but could only open it a few inches, as there was something on the floor behind the door holding it. He squeezed his head through and saw the obstruction. It was Mrs Fleming's dead body, and he immediately ran for help. Garda Wilson and Dr Sheil arrived, and forced the door sufficiently to get in to the kitchen, where the doctor was able to examine the body. Mrs Fleming was no longer wearing overalls, but was dressed to go out, wearing hat, jumper, and skirt, all of which were soaked in blood, and she lay in a large pool of blood. Her upper denture was on the floor, her spectacles were partly on her face, and a necklace, with the clasp broken, lay on her chest. The one window in the room was secured by a bolt on the inside, and the room was in an orderly and undisturbed condition, milk and water in vessels being unspilt. Mrs Fleming's handbag lay on a table and contained £4, so, clearly, robbery was not the motive for the murder.

Off the kitchen there was a scullery, the door from which to the back garden was unbolted, as was the door from the garden to a back lane which ran the length of the road. Clearly the assailant could have left, and at Fleming's trial the prosecution urged that he did leave, by the lane. There were no blood stains in the bathroom, which was next to the scullery, nor in the waste pipes, and no sign that bath, washbasin or sink had been recently used. Fleming owned four hammers which he kept in a tool shed in the garden, and one of these was missing. It had a blunt round edge on one side and a sharp edge on the other.

Mrs Fleming had been dead, according to Dr Sheil's opinion, between two and three hours, but *could* have been dead for only an hour and a half, though he thought not. His opinion was based upon the body temperature which, however, he estimated by touch and not with a thermometer. As she had been alive at 5.10 p.m. and had been found dead at 7.40, Dr Shiel's estimate of three hours was wrong, and two and a half hours was the maximum time she had been dead. So she had died not later than about 5.40 p.m.

Mrs Fleming's injuries were horrifying. She had been struck twenty times which suggested a frenzied attack, but the first blow probably felled her, and it and others had been given by a blunt instrument, whilst others had been administered by a fist. There were several severe skull fractures, injuries and fractures over the right eye and ear and heavy bruises on her forearms, indicating that she might have tried to protect her head and face, but there was no sign of any sexual assault.

Back in Clontarf, Fleming was working in the garden with his friend's young son. It was a lovely warm evening and they were finishing a task they had been doing the night before, during which Fleming had cut his right index finger. He had asked Mrs Ryan, his host's wife, to help him to bandage the cut, which was bleeding freely. At the time he was wearing a blue trousers and waistcoat, the jacket of which was hanging on a hook, and a brown striped shirt. Later in the evening the finger bled again, and Fleming washed but did not re-bandage it. He called attention to the second bleeding, and the next day at work pointed out the cut to two fellow workers. When he came in this evening to the Ryans' house he was asked if his finger was better, and told them it had bled that morning at work. Before starting in the garden and joking with his hosts, and was 'in great form' as they said.

When Detective Sergeant Byrne and the other two detectives arrived at 9 p.m. two of them drew Fleming on one side, and when Mr Ryan came forward to see what this was about, the third detective intercepted him and whispered that Mrs Fleming was dead. Fleming was wearing the same blue suit as the night before, but a white shirt, and Byrne drew attention to some spots on the front and left sleeve and cuff, and said they looked like blood. Byrne had not mentioned murder yet, and one might expect Fleming to have asked him what business it was of his whether it was blood or not, and what exactly Byrne wanted. But Fleming said nothing like that; instead he told Byrne he had cut his finger the evening before and showed him the cut. After arresting him, Byrne asked Fleming for his shirt, collar and tie, which he gave, borrowing replacements from Mr Ryan. Then he was brought to the Garda Station where his suit, shoes and socks were taken and replaced with ones fetched from his home. To all that had happened since 9 o'clock Fleming had responded with docility, and never once asked, nor was he told, who had been murdered, until 1.20 a.m., when he was charged with the murder of his wife. It was singular behaviour.

He made a brief statement. 'I know nothing about it because I was not at home at that time. It was between 4.30 and 4.45 when I left home. At the time I left home my wife was waiting for Mr Cunningham, insurance agent, 7 Dargle Road, to call. He usually calls on Tuesday evening.'

That was all he said. At no time did he show concern over his dead wife who had been so cruelly murdered; nor ask how it had happened. He seemed not to be interested.

The Trial

Fleming's trial lasted from 14 November 1933 to 21 November. He was defended by Mr Sean Hooper, then a young junior, whose able performance in the case brought him to the forefront of the Irish Criminal Bar. For the prosecution Mr Martin Maguire, S.C.

and Mr Kevin Haugh appeared, and the Judge was Mr Justice James Creed Meredith K.C., a chancery lawyer with little or no criminal experience, and a kindly genial man. As Mr Maguire was opening the case to the jury he was about to mention the poisoning incident of March 1932 and the incident of Fleming's assault on his wife when Mr Hooper objected. The jury were sent to their room and the legal argument proceeded, Mr Hooper urging that the prosecution could not give evidence of these matters, because to do so would violate the fundamental rule that, in a criminal trial, evidence of an offence by the accused other than the one being tried may not be given. But there are exceptions to that rule, one of which is that where the relations between accused and victim are explicable by reference to other evidence to be offered by the prosecution, and that other evidence is connected with another attempt by the accused on the life of the victim, it is open to the prosecution to adduce evidence of the other offence of attempted murder.

The Judge held that in the present case the exception applied, and the attempted murder by poisoning could be proved, but ruled that the assault could not.

The other evidence which the prosecution were going to offer to show Fleming's feeling towards his wife was that he had been conducting an affair with a young girl for about four years, unknown to his wife. Fleming was twenty-nine when he met this girl, then only sixteen, who was a waitress in the restaurant where he lunched daily. After about a year he invited her out, and a friendship began, but intercourse between them did not take place until the third year of the association. Fleming grossly deceived this girl, who had become deeply attached to him, by telling her he was unmarried and lived with his aunt, and by promising to marry her. As long as his wife lived Fleming could never keep this promise, for in Ireland there is no divorce but only judicial separation. The girl believed what Fleming told her and came to his house when Mrs Fleming was living away, and he told her everything in the house would be hers when they married. One Sunday morning in 1932 Mrs Fleming's nephew found Fleming was using his bed and asked why. Fleming said there was a cousin of his in the front bedroom. The 'cousin' was the girl, with whose father he had arranged for her late return home on the pretext that they were going to an all night dance. She appeared later on for breakfast but Fleming did not introduce the boy to her. On a second occasion two 'cousins' were in the house, according to Fleming, the second one presumably being a friend of the girl, but the boy saw neither.

If Fleming wanted to keep this affair secret from his wife he had gone the wrong way about it. His house was in a narrow road of small houses of a lower middle class type, literally on top of each other, in two long terraces in which privacy was scarce. The people next door, on each side, and opposite, must have seen the girl go in and out on Sunday morning and, of course, were perfectly well aware that Mrs Fleming was away. The houses have no front gardens, the hall doors opening directly on to the footpath, and almost touching each other in pairs, so nobody could go in or out of the house without the knowledge of the occupant of the second one of the pair. And, of course, the road must have buzzed with the story of Fleming's attempt to poison his wife. Fleming had also brought the girl to a local hall and sat with her in full view of many of his neighbours, and this had provided the gossips with plenty of material. Yet this seems not to have reached Mrs Fleming, though it seems unlikely some of the many women she knew on the road did not drop her a hint. But there was other gossip, and this reached the girl's family in July 1933.

The girl had to give evidence, of course, but she had been in the box only a few minutes when, asked if she had believed Fleming's promise of marriage, she broke down and wept. She recovered but in a moment collapsed again and sobbed bitterly, and finally had to be led from the witness chair. While she was outside her mother gave evidence of a talk she had had with Fleming in July, about the rumour which had reached her husband and herself that Fleming was a married man. At this time Fleming was 'engaged' to the girl.

'A desperate state of affairs is going on about me being a married man,' Fleming said to her, ' and it is all lies. I'm very upset about it.'

'It has upset me and the family too,' said the girl's mother.

'As far as I am concerned, I can marry your daughter in August,' said Fleming recklessly, and she believed what he said. At this time, unknown to her parents, the girl was pregnant, and as the baby was due in September obviously the fact could not be concealed much longer. That evening Fleming met the girl's father, who recounted in the witness box what had passed between them. Fleming assured him, said the father, that he was single and lived with his aunt, and thought the rumour about him being married was due to jealousy.

'I have an aunt who keeps house for me, and cleans the brasses and so on. I take her out sometimes for walks. When I am out walking people actually stand on the street and look at me as much as to say — "Surely he is not married to her".' The last bit should have made the father suspicious but seemingly didn't. 'I know the anxiety of a father's mind about things,' continued Fleming, with disgusting hypocrisy. 'We have never been bad friends, have we?' 'No,' said the father, a simple man, who though not suspicious was nevertheless uneasy. 'And we won't be if you can prove to me that you are a single man.'

'I have suspicions of the people who live on my road, but I am not quite sure,' said Fleming, embellishing to gain credence. 'You know, it's terrible to accuse a person of anything except you can prove it against him. I hope to find out who has been accusing me in a few days.'

The Judge was curious about the father's attitude:

Q. I don't understand why there should be all this talk about a rumour when you could have gone to the house and found out. Didn't that occur to you?

A. No, because I thought my daughter was all right. I was taking my time about it. I gave orders to my daughter, but I did not go to the house.

Q. That would have set the matter at rest at once — if you had gone to the house and inquired and asked for Mr Fleming.

A. Well, I did not like to go as far as that, my lord.

The next witness was a jeweller who told of Fleming and the girl coming to his shop in February, where Fleming chose with her a wedding ring and an engagement ring but did not pay for them then, but asked to have the articles put aside until he called back in a few days. He never came back, nor paid for the rings, and after a week the jeweller put them back into his window. When the jeweller left the witness box, Mr Maguire informed the Judge that the girl had been seen by a doctor, and was now ready to resume her evidence. Mr Maguire proposed, reasonably enough, that instead of putting her back into the witness chair she be allowed to sit in a seat behind counsel. Mr Hooper objected, equally reasonably, and some acrimony followed.

Judge: Yes. To put the witness up in the chair on the table would be trying to her.

98

Mr Hooper: I respectfully submit that the witness must take the chair in the ordinary way.

Mr Maguire: This is perfect nonsense.

Mr Hooper: I don't think it is a proper position for the witness to be examined in — away from the witness chair, with two people beside her.

Mr Maguire: It is very hard to understand why such observations should be made.

Mr Hooper: I don't see why this observation should be made.

Judge: Can you point out to any definite rule on this matter, saying that a witness may not give evidence from any part of the Court but the witness box or the chair?

Mr Hooper: I don't know of any rule, but I have never yet seen a witness examined except in a witness chair.

Mr Maguire: I submit, my lord, that this is obstruction and nothing else.

Mr Hooper: I think that I am entitled to make the submission without interruption. It is an established practice in the Courts that the witness should be examined and cross-examined from a witness chair. I have never heard or seen a witness in a case where the witness was being examined in a position between two persons.

Judge: It has been done. They have been questioned in different parts of the Court.

Mr Hooper: My attitude is perfectly proper.

Judge: It is very trying to the witness and it is being complained that people have been staring at her, and it is most trying for her.

Mr Hooper: It will be equally trying for me if I have to cross-examine. I might make a similar application with regard to the accused and with regard to my witnesses.

Mr Hooper's last observation was unreasonable, as, of course, there could be no comparison between the plight of this young girl, and the slight inconvenience to counsel of cross-examining a witness seated in an unusual place. But Mr Hooper was nettled by Mr Maguire's unreasonable comments, and he was under the strain of having to conduct a most difficult defence alone, against two opponents, one being perhaps the most experienced criminal lawyer of the day. The Judge was anxious to mitigate the girl's ordeal, and of course, ensure that her evidence would be given so that the trial would not suffer, and he was conscious that in the packed court which the case had attracted, hundreds were staring at the girl as if she were a freak.

In the end the Judge ruled that she should sit where Mr Maguire had suggested, but that there must be no communication of any kind with the person seated on either side of her. She was then brought in, but sobbing, as she had broken down again at the thought of giving evidence. But gradually the girl calmed down and was able to answer, and as she did Fleming's perfidy was fully exposed. She told how as she slept in Fleming's house, in his aunt's bed as she believed, Fleming came into the room, got into bed with her and seduced her. That was soon after the poisoning incident and was the beginning of their intimacy. When in January 1933 she told him she was pregnant he seemed delighted. 'It was always my ambition to have children,' he said, which probably was true, for there had been only one child of his marriage, stillborn, and it was very unlikely now that his wife would again conceive. Fleming's apparent delight gave no hint to the girl of her predicament.

'Of course, we'll be married?' she asked.

'Yes. Before Lent.'

Some weeks after the visit to the jeweller, as the rings had not materialised, the girl asked Fleming when she would get them, for she had of course told her parents and friends that the rings had been chosen. He said he was getting some money from the bank, but first had to obtain a signature for it, and this was the cause of the delay. She never received the rings, but he frequently reassured her about their marriage, and in March 1933, said it would take place as soon as his aunt left the house to go back to the country, in about a month. Later, he said he had bought a house in Galway, where they would live when married, but he would not get possession for about two months. He even told the girl his aunt had had a stroke, and that another one would kill her. But she was becoming uneasy as her confinement came nearer but her wedding did not. On 20 July, sick with anxiety about her condition and fearful that her parents would discover it, she taxed him with the rumour that he was married.

Fleming laughed at the absurdity, as he called it, of the story, but she was not satisfied. 'If you can prove you are not married, you should prove it to my mammy and daddy,' she said. Fleming still would not admit the truth and made up another lie.

'There are two Flemings living on my road, and the other one is married, and they've mixed him up with me.'

100

The girl thought this was true, and Fleming arranged to see her father next day and reassure him, and did so as already narrated, after which he met the girl and told her of the interview. On the 24th, two days before the murder, they met again briefly and made an appointment for that night, but he failed to turn up, and failed to appear again on the 26th, for which date another appointment had been arranged. She never met Fleming again after 24 July, and her child was born on 22 September.

The girl had borne up fairly well during the questioning by Mr Maguire, and had told her story coherently. When Mr Hooper started to cross-examine she showed signs of distress, broke down again and then fainted and had to be carried out of Court. A doctor examined her and said she was unfit to go on again that day. This was, of course, most difficult for Mr Hooper, and might have been disastrous for his client, but fortunately there was no real point of controversy in her evidence, and the only matter Mr Hooper wanted to establish was that the original suggestion of marriage had come from her and not Fleming. She got into the box next day and was sufficiently composed to answer questions about this, her answers substantially agreeing with what was being suggested to her. Then she was allowed to leave Court and go home.

The nature of the injuries inflicted on Mrs Fleming were such that the attacker should have been covered with blood, as the unfortunate woman had bled profusely, and the murder weapon should have been in the same condition. Yet there was no blood on Fleming's shoes, socks, tie or collar, but there were nine small human blood spots — splashes — on his waistcoat, seven on the trousers below the knee, and thirty on the front of the left sleeve of the jacket, between elbow and wrist. His white shirt, not the brown one he wore at Ryan's the evening before the murder, had four spots about four inches from the collar band, seven on the left cuff, and one on the left sleeve below the shoulder. All seemed to have got there by sprinkling or splashing. Dr McGrath, the State pathologist, who had examined all the garments, thought some splashes could be due to a bleeding finger which had been shaken, but if so he would have expected blood over other parts of the garments. He considered it unlikely that blood would have come on the jacket sleeve from the taking of cigarettes out of the jacket pocket. Some attempt, he said, had been made to wipe or remove the stains or spots below the knee, and a jacket button had been wiped lightly but there was a remnant of blood on the thread of the button. Dr McGrath agreed, when Mr Hooper cross-examined, that if the murder weapon had been taken out of the house unwashed then there must have been blood on the clothes of the assailant in large quantity, Mr Hooper's point being that the sink, washbasin, and bath wastes showed no sign of blood and, therefore, that Fleming was not the murderer. Of major importance, as Mr Hooper emphasised, was whose blood had fallen on Fleming's clothes, and the pathologist could not say, as he had not been furnished with a specimen of either Fleming's or Mrs Fleming's blood, which may have been hard luck on Fleming.

In his statement Fleming had said he left the house between 4.30 and 4.45 p.m., and that his wife was then waiting for Mr Cunningham, the insurance agent, to call. This witness said he had called on Mrs Fleming at 4 p.m. and collected some premiums, and his superior, a Mr McPartland who was working with him that day, corroborated as to the time. But a woman living opposite had seen the agent call at 4.50 p.m., and if she was right then Fleming could have been telling the truth in saying that his wife was waiting for Cunningham when he left. But nothing really turned on this, as the real question was: when did Fleming leave the house?

The prosecution had now proved all the facts narrated, and Mr Hooper applied to the Judge to withdraw the case from the jury and direct them to find a verdict of not guilty. Mr Hooper urged that there was no evidence of any kind to implicate Fleming in the crime, pointing out that the poisoning was evidence of a motive, as was Fleming's desire to marry the girl, but there was no proof that Fleming was in the house at the time Mrs Fleming was last seen alive. Albeit, said Mr Hooper, the case was one of suspicion. The Judge refused the application, however, and the trial proceeded.

Of course, in one sense Mr Hooper was right. There was no evidence, except a few spots of blood, a missing hammer and Fleming's failure to ask the Detective-Sergeant who had been murdered, all highly important circumstantial evidence, yet it was inconceivable that anyone else could have murdered Mrs Fleming. Can one imagine a stranger, in daylight, entering the house stealthily by some means or other, risking being seen, murdering Mrs Fleming, leaving undetected, without stealing anything or even attempting a sexual assault on the unfortunate woman? At dead of night, perhaps, but on a bright summer's afternoon in a house cheek by jowl with the others, it was inconceivable. So Fleming took the oath and started his evidence.

He freely admitted his association with the girl, that she had become pregnant and that he was the father of her child, and said that when she told him in January 1933, and asked him to marry her he agreed, and they visited the jewellers. At one stage, the questioning took on an unreal air.

Q. Had you any actual intention of marrying her or had you
    not?
A. No.

The strychnine incident took some explaining. Fleming stuck to the story that he wanted the poison to kill the dog next door, and said emphatically 'No, never,' to the question had he had any intention of poisoning his wife. The next question produced a strange answer.

Q. Had you any desire to poison your wife?
A. Never. She was a bread winner the same as I was.

But nobody asked him what his wife's capacity to earn could possibly have to do with any desire to kill her. He denied having put poison into the drinks in the bedroom, or into the chocolates, and repeated the unlikely story he had told the O'Rourkes about the poison getting on to the chocolates, adding some new detail. 'I had the poison in my pocket. I had made up my mind to bring to town two sandwiches for the poison, and had the chocolates afterwards in my pocket.'

He gave his wife some chocolates, 'but I cannot definitely say that she ate them,' but he ate some chocolates 'out of the same pocket anyway'. This was verging on the absurd. His wife who as far as he knew did not eat the chocolates (and if he was even slightly interested in her he should have found out whether she did or not) got an attack of strychnine poisoning. He *did* eat the chocolates and got no attack. His wife, he said, was delicate and had had several attacks like the poisoning one, the second last in January 1932, and 'several attacks on previous occasions that no one knew anything about only myself. I would waken in the night to get at her knees'— knee bending being a symptom of strychnine poisoning.

Also to be explained was what he had said about Dr Cotter's absence on 31 March, but he did not explain this. He simply denied what the other witnesses said. 'I did not say anything about drunkenness. I did not see the maid at all.'

103

The blood stains or spots on his jacket were, perhaps, accounted for by his describing how at Clontarf, on the day before the murder, when his finger was bleeding, he had gone to the jacket to get cigarettes, the implication being that blood had fallen on the garment. It had bled again next day when he was at work and was wearing the same jacket.

The important thing was how he had passed the afternoon of the murder. He had arrived home, he said, at 1.30 p.m., lunched with his wife, and they had spoken about some new houses being built on another road in Drumcondra which she asked him to see, as they were thinking of changing house. She had also asked him to look in the shops for a new overcoat for himself, as his coat was getting shabby. The afternoon passed as already described, and after he spoke to the O'Rourkes before they left for the city, he went upstairs and took £4 in cash from a bag. On the way down he met his wife coming up and asked her was she ready to come out. She said not, as she wanted to see Cunningham the insurance collector, so Fleming went out without her at about 4.30 or 4.45 p.m. by the front door. Nobody saw him go out, and the prosecution contended that he had left by the back door to avoid being seen. Fleming then described in detail how he passed the time from then until he reached Clontarf. He had looked at the new house as his wife had asked, walking a considerable distance, then he had gone into the city and looked at overcoats in various shop windows. It was then about 6 p.m., and he took a bus to the sea, walked down the Bull Wall and had a swim, without a costume, sunbathed afterwards, and then went on to Clontarf. In the three hours he had met no person he knew (save on the Bull Wall), and so could not support his alibi.

The Judge spotted one of the weak points in this narrative, namely, Mrs Fleming's decision not to accompany Fleming when he left, and asked some questions.

Q. You went to see the new houses because she asked you?
A. Quite right.
Q. Before you said good-bye to her because she was not ready, was it your intention that she was to go with you?
A. That is right.
Q. To look at these houses together?
A. Yes.
Q. And although you had plenty of time to walk to the Bull Wall, you had no time to wait ten or fifteen minutes for your wife? How is that?

A. Well, she said she wanted to see Mr Cunningham, and she told me go on as she wanted to tidy upstairs.

Q. Then she was to follow you to the new houses?

A. No. No.

Q. Just because she was to keep you a few minutes you gave up?

A. I did on her saying she would be down later on.

Q. Did you go anywhere to meet her?

A. No. That would be when she would come to Mrs Ryan's.

Q. Well, this thing about the new houses was a serious business?

A. Yes. That is right.

Q. When you found out she was not ready why did you not say 'We will wait for another time?'

A. I had no particular reason.

It seems likely that Fleming had invented the house incident and had not fully considered all its implications. Why should he not wait, or be asked by his wife to wait, until she was ready to come with him for this important matter? It was his half-day, and he would not have another free afternoon for a week. And of course, if Mrs Fleming were to follow him to Ryan's house, she would not be able to meet her sister at the train as she had already announced to Mrs O'Rourke, though Fleming had denied she had said this. Asked by the Judge what Mrs Fleming's sister was to do if she was not met, and came on to the house to find the Flemings out, Fleming said she would follow on down to Ryan's after them, which sounded like another lie, or 'perhaps wait at the house'. When Fleming arrived at Ryan's he had said he had been delayed by his swim, but said nothing about looking at houses, a small point, perhaps, yet possibly significant. But, perhaps more significant, he did not say that his wife was coming along later, and that her sister too might be a visitor.

Mr Maguire began his cross-examination with questions about Fleming's behaviour to the girl.

Q. You brought her to your house in Drumcondra?

A. That is right.

Q. You showed her over the house, did you?

A. Yes, that is right.

Q. And did you tell her everything there would be hers when you got married?

A. Probably I did. More than likely I did.

Q. Did you mean that?

A. (*after hesitation*) Probably in the course of conversation I may have said it.

Q. What did you mean by saying that to a young girl of 17 or 18 — by showing her over the house and telling her that everything there would be hers when you were married? What did you mean?

A. More or less friendship had been growing between us. I had no particular meaning in telling her so.

Q. Did you tell her when you were saying that that you were a married man?

A. No. I did not.

Q. You kept it back from her?

A. I did.

Q. And from her parents?

A. I did.

Q. Am I right that you carried out that deception deliberately?

A. Yes. I did that.

Q. For what purpose were you deceiving the girl herself?

A. Well, friendship was growing between us, and I knew we were gone on each other, and I put it down to my not liking to tell her.

The last answer suggests that Fleming had a real fondness for the girl, but the next three answers contradicted this. But he may have deliberately tried to create a cynical attitude to her, so as to imply that his feelings for the girl were no motive for murdering his wife.

Q. Had you any genuine friendship for her?

A. I rather liked the girl, her manner and ways. I had no particular reason.

Q. For what?

A. I suppose it is a case of the weakness of human nature; the friendship grew between us.

Q. I am asking you if you have any genuine affection for the girl? — don't mind about the human nature.

A. No. I had not.

Q. Did you bring her to your house in August 1932?

A. I did.

Q. Did you seduce her there?

A. I did.

Judge:

Q. And do you say at that time you had no affection for her?

A. Well, I admit I liked the girl.

106

Mr Maguire:

Q. Did you bring her to your wife's bedroom and did the two of you occupy your wife's bed?

A. That is right.

Q. Did you realise, sir, that you were degrading this girl while you were doing that?

A. I never dreamt of such a thing at the time.

Mr Maguire next asked Fleming about his feelings towards his wife.

Q. Of course, when you developed this affection, such as it was, for this girl, you no longer had any time for your wife?

A. I had, certainly.

Q. Had you any affection for your wife?

A. I had always.

Q. How can you reconcile that with bringing this girl into your bedroom and occupying your wife's bed with her?

A. A friendship had grown with her and it was a matter of the weakness of human nature.

Judge:

Q. Do you still say that you had a real affection for your wife?

A. That is right.

Fleming's supposed wish to poison the dog next door looked very thin in cross-examination. He had never complained about the dog to the owner, with whom he was on cordial neighbourly terms, and the reason he swore to for wanting to kill the dog was that the dog's house was separated from his scullery only by a thin wall, and the odour from the dog came into his kitchenette. If true, this would have been objectionable, of course, but he was prepared to kill the dog and run the risk that the poisoning might be discovered, rather than ask his neighbour to keep the animal elsewhere.

He had kept the poison for four days before using it, and then, at his place of work, he had put it into some sandwiches which he carried all day in his jacket pocket, and laid in the garden next door after dark.

Q. Had you anything else in the pocket of the coat that day?

A. I don't remember anything else, except what I might have at business.

Q. Had you any chocolates in the pocket of the coat?

A. Not at the time I had the poison in it.

Q. So that no chocolates could have come into contact with the poison at that time?

107

A. It was afterwards I put the chocolates in my pocket.
Q. When?
A. That evening passing down to the garden I put the choco-
lates in my pocket.
Q. Where did you get the chocolates?
A. Down the road I was out for a walk and I went in for
cigarettes and I bought a few chocolates.
Q. After you had set the poison?
A. Yes.
Q. And were the chocolates in a paper parcel?
A. Just an ordinary little bag.

Could anybody believe that the chocolates could pick up some
strychnine from his pocket *after* the contents of the poison packet,
which he said was securely wrapped, had been used for the
sandwiches and the sandwiches had been laid? He described
again how he had given chocolates to his wife, and eaten one
himself, but he could not answer Mr Maguire's question as to what
had happened to the chocolates Mrs Fleming had partly eaten and
put into the bed chamber unconsumed. He emphatically denied
throwing out either the milk, or the whiskey and port wine, but
agreed with O'Rourke's testimony that Mrs Fleming had said the
drink tasted bitter like the chocolates.

Many of Mrs Fleming's injuries could have been caused with
the missing hammer, and Mr Maguire asked Fleming to explain its
absence. He had last seen the hammer, he said, about three weeks
before the murder, but had not 'the slightest idea where it was now'.

'Where was the hammer when you last saw it?' asked Mr Maguire,
and the answer was, 'In the coal shed.' But the coal shed was always
kept locked, and was locked when the body of Mrs Fleming was
discovered, and the keys of the shed were in their usual proper
place. The prosecution's case was that the hammer was the murder
weapon, and that Fleming had disposed of it in its bloody condition. But Fleming denied seeing or touching it on the day of the
murder, and the Gardaí had searched exhaustively for it, even at
the sea shore, without success.

The cross-examination ended soon afterwards, Fleming returned
to the dock, and his counsel stood up to make his final speech to
the jury. It was an unenviable task, but Mr Hooper made two good
points. He asked: How could a man who wanted to poison his wife
be so stupid as to ask her brother for the poison? And, indeed, the
very question makes it seem absurdly improbable that Fleming

could have intended murder, until one remembers his failure to get a doctor and his lies about trying to, and his three attempts to get his wife to consume the poison. The answer to Mr Hooper's question then is: Fleming *was* stupid and behaved very stupidly throughout his association with the girl.

Mr Hooper's second point stressed a fundamental legal principle, namely, that the jury could only convict Fleming of the murder if they were satisfied, beyond any reasonable doubt, that he was guilty. But it was clear that the jury were, in effect, also trying Fleming for the attempted murder by poisoning. And Mr Hooper urged that Fleming was entitled also to have the attempt proved beyond any reasonable doubt, and said that as they could not be satisfied of the attempt — that there *must* be a doubt about it — they should, before proceeding further with their deliberations, find the attempt not proved. Only then, with their minds freed from the overwhelming prejudice of the poisoning incident, could they hope to give Fleming what was his legal right — a fair trial on the murder charge. 'For all you know,' said counsel, 'it was mere misadventure that the strychnine got on to the chocolates, and that Fleming, when he realised this, decided to take advantage of it by not fetching the doctor. If that is what happened, it would have been manslaughter, and not murder if his wife had died in consequence of Fleming's neglect that night.'

The Judge's charge supported Mr Hooper on these two points, but otherwise his charge, as a whole, was unfavouable to Fleming. He pointed out that when considering if Fleming had told the truth in court, they were entitled to bear in mind all the lies he told the girl, and her parents. '. . . can you then place much reliance on his statements now as to the route he took, and just accept them because he said so and there is difficulty in disproving it?' And later on he said '. . . some people tell lies with great facility, and the strange thing is that they expect to be believed, and if they are questioned they reply: "I have said it. Can you disprove it?".' This was as good as telling the jury that Fleming was a habitual liar, whereas the fact was that he had made many unfavourable admissions against himself, corroborating several prosecution witnesses. A habitual liar would have denied *everything* which could tell against him.

The Judge implicitly supported the prosecution's theory that the murderer must have left the house by the back way, for otherwise he could not have got through the kitchen door past Mrs Fleming's body, which was proved not to have been moved

109

after falling. So the murderer, leaving by the back, locked the shed where the missing hammer was kept, and put the keys in the place where Fleming always kept them. And, said the prosecution, the murderer must have known Mrs Fleming's movements that afternoon, and therefore that she was at home; he had no sexual motive for the crime for she had not been sexually assaulted, and robbery was out of the case too. On this view of the facts, and any other was difficult to find, the jury could hardly have had any doubt. And in two hours they were back in Court with a verdict of guilty.

'I wish to make an appeal. I am not guilty,' said Fleming, when the Judge asked had he anything to say why sentence of death should not be passed upon him. After sentence, Mr Hooper asked for leave to appeal, and the Judge granted this on the legal ground as to whether the evidence of the poisoning should have been admitted, but it availed Fleming not, the Court of Criminal Appeal holding that the evidence had been properly admitted, and dismissing the appeal. Fleming was executed on 5 January 1934.

———————

He was guilty of vile murder, there can be no doubt of it, and one can only feel sorry for his victim, whose sole offence was that she had ceased to attract him, and so was forced to pay an appalling price. Hatred was not Fleming's only motive. The evidence to save face with the girl and her family were part of his motive, and it is possible that he also had in mind the sum of £250, the amount of a joint life policy on his and his wife's life, though it is unlikely that he murdered for it. If he had had the moral courage to tell the truth on the Saturday before the murder, Ellen Fleming might have lived. But when he parted from the girl's father on a mythical search for a mythical tale teller, he threw away his last chance of returning to the world of reality. He was then, or soon afterwards, in the grip of what Galsworthy called the strongest motive of all — the desire to save face. The Japanese commit suicide from that motive.

6.

The Identification Parade

(Attorney-General v. Edward Kelly and Edward Gorman, 1924)

IN the year 1923, in Lisalong, Co. Monaghan, the postmaster was one Samuel Atkinson. He was elderly and lived in the rooms behind and over the post office with his wife and children. On 8 March 1923 he closed the post office as usual, and after supper they were all seated in the kitchen behind the post office. Two young men, Owen McCabe and Patrick Connolly, called in for a chat around the fire, and Mr Atkinson took out his violin and provided a little music. Then he and the two visitors went out to the yard to attend to the cattle, and returned in a few minutes. At this period in Ireland the Civil War was raging, following upon the treaty with Britain which had created the Irish Free State. The serious disorder in the country was being taken advantage of by many common criminals who posed as Republicans as a cover for violent crime.

The three had just returned to the room and Mr Atkinson was about to seat himself when the door from the hall or porch to the kitchen was kicked open and two men appeared. The smaller one carried a revolver and he advanced just over the threshold, threatened McCabe and Connolly, and shouted 'Hands up'. They both stood and raised their hands over their heads. He then said the same thing to Mrs Atkinson but she did not comply, nor did Mr Atkinson. The man then demanded the keys of the post office and ordered Mr Atkinson to 'open the bloody offices'.

Sixteen months later, at the trial of Edward Kelly and Edward Gorman for the murder of Samuel Atkinson, Mrs Atkinson narrated the foregoing in the witness box, answering the questions of Mr Dudley White, K.C. who, with Mr William Carrigan, K.C., was prosecuting. Her evidence continued.

Q. What did your husband do?
A. He walked forward to the man. The man backed away out of the kitchen.

Q. Where was the bigger man this time?

A. Leaning against the kitchen door.

Q. The small one backed out?

A. Yes.

Q. Your husband following him?

A. Following him.

Q. Did you follow your husband.

A. Yes. I kept close to my husband.

Q. What light was there in the kitchen?

A. There was a lamp in the kitchen. I took it in my hand.

Q. Do you see in Court the man you describe as the small man who had the revolver?

A. Yes.

Q. Would you point him out?

A. That is the man now that had the revolver. He is looking at me.

Mrs Atkinson pointed to the dock, singling out Edward Kelly as the small man. Asked next where was the other man she, of course, picked out Gorman. 'Picked' is perhaps not the best word, for the only other person in the dock not in uniform was Gorman. The two warders in charge of the prisoners were naturally ignored. The dock, being isolated and raised above the level of the seats in Court, and containing only the accused and their custodians, makes satisfactory identification at a criminal trial almost impossible.

Most witnesses, when asked to point out the man they saw committing the crime, or running away, or whatever he was seen doing, assume that the man in the dock is the one they have been talking about, and in nine cases out of ten he is. The identification is then a formality. But when there is a controversy about the identity of the criminal, the accused, in his conspicuous and isolated position, is at a disadvantage, for witnesses will point him out just because he is in the dock. They not only assume he is the right man, but they also assume that the police know their business and since they have caught a man and got him into Court, then he must be the man they saw twelve months before waving a gun, or picking someone's pocket, or whatever it was he did. It rarely occurs to witnesses that the police may have the wrong man. There are only two ways of avoiding this kind of error by witnesses. One is to put seven or eight other men into the dock and place the accused amongst them. The other, which has been done very occasionally in the Republic of Ireland, is to remove the dock from court

rooms altogether, and allow the accused to sit in the ordinary public seating, near to his solicitor or counsel if he wishes, and with
members of the public seated beside him and in his vicinity.

Mrs Atkinson's evidence continued.

Q. When Kelly — that is, the small man — went back as far as
   Gorman, did they both back out together?
A. They both backed out together to the porch or hall.
Q. And your husband?
A. My husband followed after them pretty close.
Q. At this time where was Kelly's revolver?
A. Quite close to my husband's heart.
Q. Was anything said at this time?
A. We never said anything. We never spoke at all.
Q. Did Kelly and Gorman back out through the street door?
A. Yes. They just stood in this doorway leading out — in the
   outside door.
Q. Did you hear Gorman say anything then?
A. Yes. He said to 'pink him, pink him', and immediately
   after. . . .
Q. Wait now. Were you looking at Gorman when he said that?
A. Yes. I was looking at him.
Q. How near were you to him?
A. The hall is very small, and the four of us were standing in
   it — my husband, myself and the two strange men. I could
   have put my hand on him (i.e. Gorman). I was quite near
   him.
Q. Immediately after Gorman said, 'Pink him, pink him', did
   Kelly do anything?
A. Yes. He fired a shot. It did not hurt anyone. It did not touch.
Q. Did you see him firing the shot?
A. Yes. I was looking at him.
Q. Did you see the way he pointed his revolver?
A. He held it up. My husband was in the hall. I could not say
   whether he meant to hit him in the head, but it did not. It
   went through the partition and out through the back
   window through the kitchen. It did not hurt anybody.
Q. Did your husband say something then?
A. He asked them what they were doing, or what did they
   mean, and then closed the street door on them.
Q. Immediately after that door was closed did you hear
   anything?

113

A. The two shots were fired in quick succession — both entering
my husband's body.
Q. Fired from outside?
A. Yes — through the door.

Atkinson fell, gravely wounded, and died next evening. A doctor
was called, but when he arrived the stricken man was in a state of
partial paralysis, and before surgery could be attempted death had
caught him. The murder was brutal and senseless, for the two
men could gain nothing by killing Samuel Atkinson. There were
three other people there who could identify them, and they had
obtained no money from their crime. Their callousness contrasts
strikingly with the courage of their victim. Silent and unarmed,
the old man had faced a young man with a gun, and by sheer
moral force compelled him and the other scoundrel to withdraw.
But he was cruelly robbed of his victory.

Mrs Atkinson had never seen either of these men before that
night, and did not see them after they went out through the street
door. Next day, she described them to the Gardaí, and heard nothing more until 5 February 1924, when she was asked to attend
an identification parade at the internment camp in the military
barracks at the Curragh, in County Kildare. This camp was used to
intern opponents of the new State, and Kelly and Gorman had
been incarcerated there since August 1923. Mrs Atkinson was
brought to a room in the camp, into which six or seven men, she
wasn't sure which, were brought, two of whom were the accused.
The men were lined up in front of her, and present also were
Superintendent Murphy, in charge of the murder investigation,
and some Army officers.

Q. When you looked at this group of six or seven men did you
see anybody you recognised?
A. Yes. I saw the two prisoners.
Q. Which of them did you notice first?
A. The man that had the revolver.
Q. That is?
A. The man there.
Q. That is Kelly?
A. Yes — on the left.

After three minutes or more — a long time for the examination of
faces in an identification parade — the men were taken out and in
a short while brought back for a second inspection. This time

Kelly, who had not had a coat on, was wearing a trench coat and, though Mrs Atkinson did not remember it, a cap as well. The change of attire seems odd. Even more odd was his re-appearance for a second scrutiny. Was it hoped thus to jog Mrs Atkinson's memory? Her evidence on several points was going to be challenged, as was the use of the trench coat for Kelly's second appearance. That garment, and a cap or 'trilby' hat were in very common use amongst the 'Irregulars', the name given to the Republicans who were fighting against the new Free State. Indeed, these clothes had almost the status of a uniform.

Mrs Atkinson had said nothing about the clothes worn by the two men who came to her house, and had said that at the Curragh she did not notice anything about the clothes of the men on the first parade. But if the two criminals had worn the trench coat and cap when in Atkinson's, as many common criminals were doing at the time, Kelly's re-appearance wearing the coat might have deceived her into thinking that he was one of the men.

1. *Q.* Were they brought in on a second occasion?
   A. Yes. I seen both of them again.
2. *Q.* Did you do anything to Kelly?
   A. I put my hand on the man that had the revolver.
3. *A.* That is, on Kelly?
   A. Yes, on Kelly.
4. *Q.* On his shoulder?
   A. On his shoulder.
5. *Q.* What did you say?
   A. I said 'I seen that man once before, I am sorry to say.'
6. *Q.* Was he dressed differently on this second occasion to the first time?
   A. Yes. He had a trench coat on when I seen him again.
7. *Q.* What was it that you identified him by?
   A. His face.
8. *Q.* And on the first occasion when he had no trench coat on, what did you identify him by?
   A. I always said I would know his face.
9. *Q.* Well, now, did you see Gorman there on the second occasion too?
   A. Yes. I seen the two prisoners from the first.
10. *Q.* By what did you identify him?
    A. His face. I identified his face. I put my hand on his shoulder.

But these answers were misleading. She saw 'the two prisoners from the first', she said, but that was merely saying that the men on the parade were the men in the dock. Despite the leading questions, she was not saying that on first sight she *identified* the two men as those who were in her house. Question No. 9 seeks to put the words of identification into her mouth, but her answer, 'I always said I would know his face' not only did not help the prosecution, but showed that she *didn't* know Kelly's face — if he was the right man — after looking at him or having the opportunity of looking, for more than three minutes. Only when he came in the second time did she put out her hand to touch him. And she had to see Gorman *three* times before she put her hand on him. Answer No. 10 is incomplete, because she does not say that she put her hand on Gorman's shoulder only on the third time of seeing him.

Q. After the second parade were they removed?
A. Yes
Q. And did they come back?
A. Yes. They came back.
Q. All except Kelly?
A. Except Kelly.
Q. Was this owing to something you had said?
A. I asked Superintendent Murphy. . . .
Mr Lavery: (defending) I object.
Mr White: Very well.
Q. At any rate, you said something to Superintendent Murphy, and Kelly did not come in the third time?
A. Yes. He did not come.
Q. Did Gorman come in?
A. He did.
Q. What did you do to Gorman the third time?
A. I put my hand on his shoulder. I said 'I seen that man once before.'

Mr Cecil Lavery, then a junior counsel, began his cross-examination of Mrs Atkinson by asking about her state of mind and nerves on the night of the tragedy. She answered bravely, 'I have everything to meet since [the death]. I did not so much suffer from nervousness. I never felt myself so strong as I was that night — never. I attended to my husband and did everything I could for him. I never lost my head one bit — never was so strong.' One could not but admire her fortitude in the witness box as she had to recount her ordeal.

116

Q. After the death of your husband did you feel disturbed, or nervous, or feel any reaction from the events you had gone through?

A. Of course. I felt the loss of my husband. Why not? But I had everything to meet. But I say I never felt as strong.

Q. Of course the matter has been preying on your mind a great deal since March 1923?

A. No doubt it would.

Q. It is a subject more or less always near your mind?

A. I could never get away from those faces. They seemed to haunt me all the time. This is the memory that is with me — to see them coming up constantly, sleeping and awake.

She was identifying these men in conditions of bad light, for the lamp she carried, and such light as came from the range, were the only illumination. The hall or porch was in darkness, and that was where the second man had stood. And she was positive that she had the right men. Yet her memory for detail and her powers of observation were far from good, even for recent events, e.g. the identification parade. She could not say how many men were in the parade — five, or six, or seven, but knew there were more than four. She thought Kelly took up the position second on the left, and that all the men had open necks and wore mufflers.

Q. Had they caps on?

A. I do not think so.

Q. You do not know?

A. I am not sure what they had on.

Q. You are not sure whether they had caps on or not?

A. No.

Q. You remember this incident quite clearly?

A. Quite clear.

Q. You identified Kelly by his face?

A. Yes.

Q. Had he a cap on?

A. He had no cap then, when they came in parading in front of me. I think he had not. It was his face I had in mind.

Q. Had he a cap?

A. I say I could not tell whether he had anything on his head or not, but I knew the face.

Q. Had Gorman a cap?

A. I do not know whether they had anything on their heads or not.

117

Q. Had Gorman an overcoat on?

A. He had no overcoat when they came in first.

Q. None of them?

A. I do not think so.

Q. Why do you not think so? Which is it now?

Judge (Mr Justice O'Shaugnessy): Let her answer.

A. I could not know about the clothes. I could not take my eyes out of their faces. It was the faces I knew. I did not look for the clothes — what they had on. It was the faces I identified.

Mr Lavery tested Mrs Atkinson by asking her what the other men had worn. 'I did not look at them much,' and then she said 'No' to the question, 'You did not look at them?' She agreed she would be unable to recognise any of the other men if she saw them again. 'I do not suppose I could. I do not think so. I watched the man that had the revolver very close from when I first met him.'

Q. Had either of these men beards?

A. No. None of them.

Q. When they were on the parade?

A. No, none of them?

Q. Had they a growth of beard?

A. Well, they were not shaved or cleaned up, I am sure.

Q. Mrs Atkinson, I do not want to know what you think. They were in the room. You saw them?

A. Yes. I saw them.

Q. Had they beards or a growth of beard?

A. They had a growth of beard.

Q. Both Kelly and Gorman?

A. Yes.

Q. Had the other men in the parade — were they clean shaven or had they a growth of beard?

A. I think they were all much about the same — I did not mind very much about the other men.

Q. Had either of the men who came into your house on the 8 March 1923 a beard?

A. They might have had a growth of beard. They were not in the habit of wearing either beard or moustache.

Q. You know I am asking you about 8 March 1923?

A. Yes.

Q. Had either of the men who came in that night a growth of beard?

A. They had a growth of beard.

Q. Both of them?

A. Yes.

Q. A marked growth?

A. They were not in the habit of wearing beards but they might not have shaved for a day or two.

Q. But you did not know either of these two men? You could not say what they. . . .

Judge: They had not shaven for a day. Is that what you mean?

A. This is what I mean.

Mr Lavery: I want to know whether it was a day or three weeks. Had they a substantial growth?

A. No.

Q. They had a dirtying of hair on their faces?

A. Yes.

After the doctor had given evidence of Samuel Atkinson's injuries and the cause of death, the prosecution's case closed with Superintendent Murphy, who briefly narrated the arrest of the two accused, and the denial of each that he had had anything to do with the murder. Although Connolly and McCabe had been present in the Atkinsons' kitchen from the moment the two men burst in, the prosecution did not call either to give evidence. Mr Lavery described the omission as 'curious' and called them himself. He knew that they would raise considerable doubts about Mrs Atkinson's identification.

Connolly, who was eighteen, went into the box first. He said he and McCabe were in the kitchen, having come in from the yard with Mr Atkinson. Mrs Atkinson sat at a table near the door, her husband was opposite the range, and he and Mc Cabe were nearest the door. Florrie Atkinson, the young daughter of the Atkinsons, was at the farthest end of the room. When the gunman entered and shouted 'Hands up' Connolly and McCabe complied, and Mr Atkinson went forward to put out the man and his companion. But, according to Connolly, Mrs Atkinson did not follow her husband with the lamp.

Q. Where was Mrs Atkinson when the deceased went forward to the man at the door, as you have told? Did you observe what she did?

A. Yes. She was going for the keys to get the lamp.

Q. In what direction was she going?

A. On towards the window [i.e. away from the door].

Q. Where was she when the first shot was fired over Mr Atkinson's head?

119

A. She was looking for the keys of the office on the window.

Q. Where the lamp was?

A. Yes, sir.

Q. What did Mrs Atkinson do after her husband had been shot?

A. She came round with the keys and the lamp.

Q. She came across with the lamp in her hand?

A. Yes, right round into the hallway.

Q. The outer door was then shut?

A. Yes, sir.

Q. And Samuel Atkinson was lying on the floor?

A. Yes, sir.

If this evidence was correct, not only was Mrs Atkinson mistaken in her recollection, hardly surprising considering the shocking events which had just occurred, but her opportunity of seeing the murderers clearly enough to identify them eleven months later was very poor. This became clear as Connolly's testimony continued.

Q. You have told us that the first man came to the kitchen door?

A. He was standing on the door threshold.

Q. Could you see another man?

A. Yes.

Q. Where was he?

A. Further back, at the door leading into the street.

Q. At the outer door?

A. Yes, sir.

Q. Behind the front man?

A. Yes.

Q. Did either of the men come further into the room than that? One was at the threshold, and the other standing at the outer door?

A. Yes sir.

Q. Did they come in?

A. No, sir.

Q. Did you see the first man?

A. He was a tall man, about five feet eight inches, and he wore a beard about a week's growth and a white face.

Q. Could you see the other man?

A. I could not really see him right, from where I was standing.

Judge: You could not see the other man?

A. Not right.

Mr Lavery: Could you see him to recognise him?

120

A. Yes, sir.
Q. I thought you said you could not see him?
A. Yes, sir.
Q. What do you mean by you could not see him right?
A. I could not see him right, the description of him.

The foregoing explains the 'curious' failure of the prosecution to call Connolly, although their duty was to lay all the relevant facts before the jury, and not merely those facts which favoured their case and would probably bring about a conviction. If Connolly was right, then Mrs Atkinson could not have recognised the second man, for he never crossed the threshold, but stayed in the dark porch or hall. As for the description of the man with the revolver as 'short', Connolly said he was tall, if 5'8" can be so called, and the 'dirtying' or hair on that man's face was not one day's growth but a week's — quite a different thing. And that man was being seen by Mrs Atkinson in the light of an oil lamp on a table at the far end of the room from him, and perhaps throwing Connolly's or McCabe's shadow across his face as he stood on the threshold, and not inside the room as she had said. Was she wrong on that last point also? It does seem unlikely, at least, that the gunman would advance one inch more into the room that necessary for his purpose, because the farther in, the more danger of attack, and the longer his retreat route.

Connolly had been brought to the Curragh in February or March 1924, and seen a number of men paraded before him, but did not know or recognise any. It would have been interesting to learn whether either accused had been on that parade. Such a contradiction in the evidence of identity should not have been passed over. The prosecution, of course, knew exactly who had been on that parade, but did not tell the Court. At a later identification parade, this time in Monaghan Garda Station, Connolly had recognised nobody and could not say if the two men in the dock were amongst the paraders. Once again the prosecution was silent on the point. The Judge made no enquiry from either Mr Carrigan or Mr White on this vital point, and did not mention it when charging the jury.

Mr Carrigan cross-examined Connolly, which he could not have done if Connolly had been a prosecution witness. Connolly agreed with Mr Carrigan's suggestion that he had been frightened by the men coming in. Who wouldn't have been? But very little emerged from the questioning, save that the man with the

121

revolver had leaned into the room and kicked McCabe with the tip of his boot to make him stand up. This confirmed that he had taken up his position at the threshold and had not come into the room, and contradicted Mrs Atkinson on that point. Mr Carrigan suggested that Connolly had been distressed at having to look at the faces of the paraders in Monaghan, and averted his gaze from them, and had to be asked to look. Connolly denied this. He was not a bit distressed, he said, nor unwilling to attend the parade. When Mr Carrigan sat down, Connolly's evidence was unshaken, and despite vigorous questioning, he adhered to his statement that Mrs Atkinson did not reach the porch with the lamp until her husband had fallen, by which time the men had left.

Owen McCabe was next, and he corroborated Connolly with impressive certainty and detail, including the fact that when Samuel Atkinson was shot, Mrs Atkinson was just coming from the window at the other end of the kitchen, with the oil lamp and keys in her hand — 'rattling keys. I could not say what keys they were.' He, too, had attended an identification parade in Monaghan, though whether it was the same one that Connolly spoke about was not made clear. Probably it was not, for the two accused men *were* in that parade and, said McCabe, he could not identify either of the men, he saw in Atkinson's that night as being on the parade, and he could remember the faces of those two men. Indeed, when he was being cross-examined by Mr White he said that the two accused were *not* the men he saw that night. The cross-examination took a hostile turn, which was regrettable since McCabe, too, should have been a prosecution witness. He was picked up on one discrepancy, but it was not important.

Q. Was that the man who ordered you to put your hands up — had he a growth of beard?
A. I could not say.
Q. That is, the man who ordered you to put up your hands, had he a beard?
A. He had a beard but I could not say how long it might have been.
Q. Do you remember saying at the Coroner's inquest, 'I could not say whether the man who ordered us to put up our hands had a growth of beard?'
A. I do not remember.

He was then shown his deposition, and it was clear that he had said this at the inquest.

Judge: Can you say now?

A. I could not rightly remember.

Judge: You cannot remember?

A. Yes, sir.

Mr White: Yet, you undertake to say neither of these were the men there that night?

A. By the features of the men and stand [stance?] they could not.

Mr Lavery now called Eugene McQuaid, the internee along with the two accused at the Curragh, and one of the men on the parades there. The Court heard from him what went on behind the scenes at the parade, and how Mrs Atkinson's identification had proceeded. He was having dinner with Kelly and Gorman when an Army officer and a private came, took those two away to an office nearby, returned with them in a few minutes and told them to pack their belongings. When this was done they were taken away again to the office. It would be interesting to know why somebody in authority in the internment camp had decided that the two men should get ready to depart — not, of course, to freedom, but to civil custody — *before* they had been identified.

A short while later McQuaid, a man named Patrick Kelly and an unarmed man from Sligo were summoned to the office and there found Kelly and Gorman, along with Captain Fitzpatrick, the Commandant of the Camp, and some other officers. Fitzpatrick asked Kelly where was his coat, Kelly said he had none; Fitzpatrick said he had, but Kelly repeated his denial, so an officer was sent out and returned with two borrowed coats.

The five internees were then marched into the room or office where Mrs Atkinson was waiting, and paraded before her. If McQuaid's evidence about what happened then was even partly correct, any lingering doubt about acquitting which the jury may have had, should have been finally removed.

Q. When you came into the office where were you put?

A. We were lined up, the five of us opposite this woman.

Q. Can you say the order they were in?

A. Yes. Gorman was the second from the left. This other fellow from Sligo was in the centre, and Kelly was next to me on my left.

Q. How long did you remain in the office?

A. About three minutes.

Q. Was anything said while you were in the office?

A. No, there was nothing said. We were told to look in different directions.

Q. Then something must have been said. By whom?

A. By Captain Fitzpatrick.

Q. Did you all do that?

A. Yes.

Q. And after three minutes you were told to go out?

A. Yes, sir.

Q. You went out?

A. Yes, sir.

Mrs Atkinson said and did nothing to show she recognised anyone, although she had three minutes scrutiny time. Why? Either she was unsure, or had no idea at all, of the faces of the two murderers eleven months later. The questioning went on.

Q. When you got outside was anything done?

A. Those two trench coats were put on Kelly and Gorman.

Q. Who ordered or put them on?

A. Captain Fitzpatrick.

Q. Were there any caps?

A. He took the cap off me, and put it on Kelly.

Q. Had any of the other men caps?

A. None of the other men had caps.

Q. And in that way did you all go back to the office?

A. Yes.

Q. When you got in, what was done?

A. We were lined up in different positions, the second time. The woman looked for a while, got up, and tipped Kelly on the shoulder.

Q. Did she say anything?

A. No. This Captain, or Superintendent Murphy, I do not know which, asked did she see any man before her she knew and she said 'I think I do'.

Q. Did she go near anybody else or do anything to anybody else?

A. No, sir.

So on her second view of Gorman, Mrs Atkinson does not recognise him and can only say of Kelly, 'I think I do.' This was not, one would think, the kind of evidence on which to hang two men.

The five went outside a second time, said McQuaid, and Kelly was told to stand aside. After three minutes, the others were taken

124

in again, only four now, and stood looking in different directions as before. This time Mrs Atkinson, without looking at the others, got up and tipped Gorman on the shoulder. Why did she not do this the first time, or even the second time? Gorman's chances of being wrongly picked out increased enormously when the number of men fell to four. Even five was a dangerously small number, though Superintendent Murphy insisted there had been six, but the presentation of only four men to Mrs Atkinson on the third parade was a plain invitation to her to pick one of them. It was like telling her to try again and she would surely find the missing man. Perhaps she had been right in choosing Gorman, but she had missed him twice before. She could have thought he was *like* one of the two men she was looking for when she saw him the first time, and built up in her mind on the second and third times the conviction that he was the one.

But the Gardaí and the military should never have exposed the two accused men, nor McQuaid and the other two, who were volunteers, to the hazards involved in such a parade. Suppose that one of the volunteers had looked like one of the killers, and had been picked out by Mrs Atkinson, would anyone have believed her wrong? The usual number on an identification parade when one man is being sought is nine or ten, and even eleven or twelve, but rarely fewer than eight. But a parade of only five or six in a search for *two* men is unprecedented. As for the dressing up of Kelly in cap and trench coat, it is difficult to speak of this with moderation. As a prisoner, he had the right to be told he was not bound to go on the parade, and need not wear the coat or cap. These improprieties, however, went into evidence without any comment from the Judge. And nobody explained the intervention of the military into what was purely a civil matter. What business, one wonders, had Captain Fitzpatrick in dressing up Kelly?

Lest any reader thinks the foregoing is lawyer's talk, and that lawyers exaggerate the dangers of wrong identifications, he should think back on any person whom he has met only once, and for a moment or two, in the previous nine or twelve months and see whether he can recapture mentally that person's face. It can be a surprisingly difficult thing to do. Let him then imagine attending an identification parade knowing that a murderer is being sought, and being asked to pick that person out with certainty, and consider whether he would undertake such a task with even the slightest feeling of confidence.

We should also remember that in the year 1895 one Adolf Beck was wrongly identified as being a man who had defrauded women with whom he had lived. The identification was made by two or three women who had each lived with the real trickster for several months, yet they were utterly convinced that Beck, who had never seen the women before, was the man they had lived with, and in consequence he served several years in an English prison, before being pardoned, for a crime which he had never committed. And there have been many similar mistakes of identity in the history of the law.

McQuaid's cross-examination achieved nothing for the prosecution, and indeed helped the defence, for Mr Carrigan not only did not suggest that McQuaid was wrong about Mrs Atkinson's failure to identify Kelly and Gorman the first time, and Gorman the second time, but established that she had carefully looked along the line of men the first time. Thus, her scrutiny was real. She had said that was no scrutiny, as she had immediately recognised the two men. But that was now clearly incorrect, for it was proved up to the hilt that the first inspection took at least three minutes — McQuaid had said three or five minutes. What was happening after Mrs Atkinson's supposed immediate identification? Were they all standing in that room for three or four minutes, doing and saying nothing? Of course not. When Mr Carrigan was asking about the identification of Kelly and Gorman on the second parade, he put it this way.

> Q. And having done that on the first occasion you passed out and you came back and this time Kelly and Gorman were disguised?
> A. Yes.

Nobody questioned the word 'disguised', but could the garb, trench coat and cap, be properly called a disguise for a man suspected of violent crime in 1923 in Ireland? Disguise or no disguise, without looking at the man Mrs Atkinson picked out Kelly the second time. Each time, said McQuaid, when making her identification she touched the man without hesitation.

The last witness was Patrick Kelly. He corroborated McQuaid and added some interesting new information. There were four parades, he said, and not three, and when the parade went outside the first time, a 'conference' took place in the room between police and military, in which Mrs Atkinson may have actually taken part, but if not, of which she was within earshot. What can they have conferred about? What was there to discuss, unless it were some way of ensuring that there would be an identification by Mrs Atkinson? Was the 'disguise' the result of the conference? Asked if he agreed with McQuaid that Mrs Atkinson had touched Kelly without hesitation, Patrick Kelly said he thought she had hesitated. When Carrigan asked about the changes made in Kelly's garments, he got an unexpected answer.

> A. Yes. In changing, Captain Fitzpatrick pulled the cap down on Kelly's eyes, and pulled the collar of his trench coat and motioned him to come up to the head of the parade.

Mr Carrigan commented: 'That is what we were waiting for', a strange remark if the evidence was true, because, of course, if true it should have been brought out by the prosecution long before. If not true, Mr Carrigan could not have been waiting for it. Either way, the answer was very much against the prosecution and therefore not something they had been waiting for — unless with apprehension! Mr Lavery's comment was pithy: 'It was worth waiting for.'

McQuaid said that Fitzpatrick had done this in the presence of Murphy and Mrs Atkinson, which, if true, meant that she had *not* identified Kelly immediately upon his entering the room the second time. Later, Superintendent Murphy was recalled and asked about McQuaid's answer. It was 'an absolute falsehood, an utter falsehood', he said. One can almost feel his anger as one reads the transcript. The only question, if one's feeling is correct, is: Why was he angry? Perhaps Patrick Kelly had told a falsehood, but it was a plausible one, in keeping with the way Edward Kelly had been pushed around by Captain Fitzpatrick and Superintendent Murphy. It was equally likely to have been the truth.

Murphy was also asked what Mrs Atkinson had said when she put her hand on Kelly. He contradicted both McQuaid and Patrick Kelly. She said, according to him, 'I have seen this man before — he is the man who murdered my husband.' These, he said, were her exact words as far as he remembered, yet in his deposition made months earlier he had sworn she said nothing. This, when put to him, he said was a mistake.

At this stage the foreman of the jury spoke. 'My lord the jury request me to ask three questions. The first is, were any depositions taken from the late Mr Atkinson after he was shot?'

> 1. Judge: No. There was not, unfortunately. He was not in a condition to make a deposition, but there was none taken at all events.

2. Foreman: The second is: How long were the prisoners known to be living in the locality after the murder?

(This question was irrelevant and should have been disallowed. In fact the two accused lived only a few miles from the Atkinsons.)

3. Judge: I cannot answer that. Can you? (to Mr Carrigan).

4. Superintendent Murphy: Kelly was arrested in August 1923, and it was March 1923 the murder was committed — five months.

5. Mr Carrigan: Had he been living in the locality all that time?

6. Superintendent Murphy: He was being sought for. It is unknown really where he was, but he was being looked for.

7. Judge: I see. And ultimately interned, I suppose?

8. Superintendent Murphy: Interned. In fact he was fired at and shot while being. . . .

9. Mr Lavery: Of course, this is not evidence.

10. Judge: The jury has asked for it.

11. Mr Carrigan: The jury has asked the questions.

12. Mr Lavery: I know, but the Superintendent has no knowledge of it.

13. Superintendent Murphy: I have.

14. Mr Lavery: Yes, but no legal knowledge — no legal evidence.

15. Judge: Has he been in custody since August last?

16. Superintendent Murphy: Yes.

17. Judge: And you say he was sought for before August?

18. A Juror: Was he about the neighbourhood for any length of time after the murder was committed?

19. Superintendent Murphy: He may or may not have been, but he was being sought for the whole time.

20. A Juror: For what purpose?

21. Superintendent Murphy: For this murder, sir, and I will not say any more.

22. A Juror: That is all we want to know.

23. Foreman: (putting the third question). Was it on Mrs Atkinson's description that accused were identified by the authorities, and if so how soon after the arrest?

24. Superintendent Murphy: A month after the arrest.

25. Judge: Was it from the description of Mrs Atkinson?

26. Superintendent Murphy: Oh! Yes, my lord.

27. Foreman: That is all we want to know.

And it was too much! The Judge was in error in allowing the foreman to ask any questions, the proper procedure being for the questions to be stated to the Judge for his ruling on their admissibility and, if admissible, for him and no one else to have put them. Mr Lavery's objection at 12 dealt with the hearsay nature of the evidence, but there was a graver objection, namely that the police search, and the reasons for it (6,8,17,20 and 21) were wholly irrelevant, and were also inadmissible as being an attempt to prove the suspicions of the police. To say that a police officer is searching for a man 'for a murder' is another way of saying that the officer thinks he is guilty. But Question 23 was even worse, for the jury, convinced by now that the 'authorities' had 'identified' the two accused as the criminals, which they couldn't possibly do in or outside a court of law, wanted to know if what Mrs Atkinson had told them about the accused was what proved to the 'authorities' that the accused were the guilty ones. But *what* did she tell the authorities? Was it different from what she had now sworn? Whatever it was, it was inadmissible. The only admissible thing was what had been sworn by her in front of the jury. The twelve men, and not the authorities, were the ones to be satisfied, or otherwise, with the identification, or purported identification, by Mrs Atkinson in Court of the two accused as the murderers.

The Judge charged the jury after counsel had made their speeches, and the jury retired. They came back with a verdict of guilty and, very strangely, with a strong recommendation to mercy. What, one wonders, could they have found in the cruel and wanton murder of Samuel Atkinson to require the exercise of mercy? But the recommendation may have been the result of a compromise in the jury room. If a minority wanted to acquit, or were doubtful what to do, the majority may have prevailed on them to join in a verdict of guilty if accompanied by a recommendation of mercy. Juries sometimes do this to avoid a disagreement, which means, under Irish law, no verdict and a fresh trial later with a new jury.

The Judge promised to forward the recommendation to the Minister for Justice, and then asked each prisoner the usual question: Had he anything to say why sentence of death should not be passed upon him. Kelly did not answer. Nor did Gorman, but he thanked his solicitor, Mr Murphy, and Mr Lavery. The Judge then passed sentence of death on each for 5 August 1924. He refused Mr Lavery's request for a certificate of leave to appeal, saying there was no ground for one.

However, the Court of Criminal Appeal thought otherwise. They dealt with the irregularity arising from the jury's third question, and passed over the Judge's charge to the jury, to which no exception had been taken on appeal. But if the charge had been a ground of appeal, it was very likely that the appeal would have succeeded on that ground alone. Mr Justice O'Shaughnessy had failed to warn the jury of the need for a proper and sure identification of the accused, and of the grave risks known to the law of acting upon identification by one person only, especially considering what had gone on at the Curragh parades. He also failed to deal with the evidence of McQuaid and Kelly, and with the serious contradictions of Mrs Atkinson's evidence by McCabe and Connolly. Indeed, the most striking thing in the case was the prosecution's virtual acceptance of what McQuaid and Patrick Kelly said about Mrs Atkinson's hesitant identification at the Curragh. If those two witnesses were wrong in that evidence, there were at least four people who could have contradicted them: Superintendent Murphy, Captain Fitzpatrick, and two other Army officers, all present at the parades. Yet none of these was put into the box to say that the two witnesses were wrong. The Judge did not mention this to the jury either.

The Appeal Court considered that the third question had been put to test the description of the criminals given by Mrs Atkinson to the Gardaí on the morning after the murder (though that description was not given in evidence and could not have been, save by the defence); that the question, and Superintendent Murphy's answer to it, meant that some person or persons vaguely called 'the authorities' had compared the two accused with that description, and was or were of opinion that they were the two she had described. In this way, the Court said, the jury satisfied themselves that Mrs Atkinson's identification at the parade, and at the trial, agreed with her original description of the men, and more than probably the jury considered they should be so satisfied before finding a verdict. As this evidence was not admissible in law, being a mixture of hearsay and the opinion of someone unknown, and had been crucial in a verdict which depended entirely on identification, the Court quashed the conviction and acquitted the two accused. 'Possibly', said Chief Justice Kennedy, 'the result will be that the cowardly murder of a brave old man will go unpunished. Still, the greatest call is the strict, certain, and regular administration of justice, especially in criminal matters, and the duty of the Court is to answer that call, whatever the consequences.'

These were apt words in 1924, the year in which the appeal court was created. Prior to then, there was no right of appeal for convicted criminals, for British rule in Ireland had not thought the Irish needed such a right. After all, they had denied the same right to their own criminals for hundreds of years, only granting it in the year 1907.

But when Ireland became independent she removed this injustice by a statute of 1924. However, this statute contained a defect, namely that when a conviction was quashed on appeal, for whatever reason, the case was at an end no matter how strong had been the evidence of guilt. In 1938 the law was changed, and this anomaly, as many thought it, was removed by providing that where the Court of Criminal Appeal reverse a conviction they may direct a new trial, if the circumstances so require.

7.

The Body in the Street

(The People v. Mary Anne (Mamie) Cadden, 1956)

HUME STREET in Dublin is part of the well-known Georgian area of the city. It is off St Stephen's Green, one of Dublin's finest squares, which still retains much of its Georgian character despite the inroads of the developers. At the other end of Hume Street is Ely Place, a distinguished and beautiful street, where George Moore and, on the opposite side, Oliver St John Gogarty once lived. In April 1956, No. 17 Hume Street was let in flats and single residential rooms, and one of these rooms at the rear of the first floor was occupied by Mary Anne (Mamie) Cadden. She was a qualified midwife in her early sixties, formerly of Pennsylvania but living in Dublin for many years. She no longer practised midwifery, but treated patients for hair trouble, constipation and rheumatism. She was known as Nurse Cadden.

Early in the morning of 18 April 1956, a woman's body was found on the footpath outside No. 15 Hume Street, which is two doors from No. 17 and on the same side of the street — the left as one goes from St Stephen's Green to Ely Place. The first person believed to have seen anything strange that morning was a Mr Gleeson, a milk roundsman who was delivering milk at 5.04 a.m. to the hospital on the opposite side of the street. He noticed what he thought was a bundle of clothing partly on the footpath and partly in the gateway which gives access to the top step of the basement stairs. In fact, what Mr Gleeson saw was almost certainly a body so covered by clothes that, from where he was, no part of it was visible. He paid no further attention to what he saw and, finishing his deliveries in about fifteen minutes, departed in his van.

At about 5.40 a.m. Mr John Moran, who lived in No. 17 on the floor above Nurse Cadden, left the house for work and at the doorstep paused to light a cigarette. He looked up and down the street but noticed nothing strange, although the body was at that moment about twenty-five yards from him, to his left. He turned right and walked towards St Stephen's Green. About ten minutes later a nurse on night duty in the hospital looked out of a window towards No. 15 on the opposite side of the street but, like Mr Moran, noticed nothing. At about 6.25 a.m., however, Mr Patrick Rigney, another milk roundsman, drove his milk float into Hume Street from St Stephen's Green and saw what he too thought was a bundle of clothing on the path, but as he got nearer he saw two legs protruding from a black overcoat, and then realised it was a woman's body.

The head was covered by a skirt and partly pillowed upon it, and the remainder of the body was covered loosely with a black overcoat. It was clothed underneath the coat as far as the waist, but unclad below. There was a stocking tied loosely around the woman's neck, and her legs were held together above the knees by a stocking and by a torn pair of knickers. The legs were stretched out partly on the footpath, and partly on the first of the basement steps. On the fifth step there was a parcel containing, amongst other things, a pair of women's shoes, and beside the parcel was a woman's handbag. On the pavement there was a mark, about three feet long, as though something had been dragged along it sweeping the pavement clean. This mark led from the head towards No. 17.

The Gardaí were called immediately and a nursing sister came from the hospital to examine the body. She confirmed that the woman was dead — that was at 6.32 a.m. — and tried to raise one of the woman's arms which lay across the chest, but could not do so because it was stiff, though whether or not this was due to rigor mortis she could not say. She thought, however, that rigor mortis had not completely set in.

The State Pathologist, Dr Maurice Hickey, arrived at 8.20 a.m. He examined the body and later, in the city morgue, made a post mortem examination. The woman was aged about thirty, had been about five months pregnant, and had undergone an illegal operation i.e. an operation to bring about an abortion. In the operation the caul in which the foetus lay and part of the afterbirth had been forcibly separated from the womb wall, probably from the insertion into the neck of the womb of an instrument which pumped in either a liquid or gas. Death was caused, in the pathologist's opinion, by an air embolism which stopped the circulation of the blood, and was created by the entry of air through where the afterbirth had been forced away. Unconsciousness would have occurred about fifteen seconds from the insertion of the instrument, and death about two minutes thereafter. If the pathologist was right, it was almost certainly a case of murder.

Who was this woman who had died so, and whose body had suffered the indignity of being dumped in the public street? In her handbag were her bank book and some scraps of paper with names and addresses, and the Gardaí were soon able to establish not only her identity but her movements for two weeks before. She was Irish, married but living apart from her husband, and had come to Dublin from Preston in Lancashire on 4 April. She had stayed in a boarding-house until the thirteenth, on which day she was traced to an address in Ely Place. On the fourteenth and fifteenth she had spent her time in and out of public houses, lounge bars and restaurants in the city, staying at night in various premises with different men. She had worn a black overcoat during these two weeks, a fact which proved to be important, and she carried a new umbrella; the former lay around her body and the latter was found in the basement area of No. 15 Hume Street.

On 16 April this woman had passed most of the day until about 6.30 p.m. in the company of a woman friend. She had drawn £15 from her bank account and, as a bus ticket in her handbag showed, had travelled in a bus which passed along St Stephen's Green, but the ticket would have entitled her to go a long way past that point, and she might well have done this. After 6.30 p.m. her movements were unknown. Her handbag contained only £4 7s 2d, so she had spent at least £10 12s 0d of the money she drew from the bank.

Gardaí enquiries elicited that strange sounds had been heard in No. 17 Hume Street in the early hours of 18 April by a Mrs Farrelly who lived in two rooms on the same floor as Nurse Cadden. At 5 a.m. these noises awakened her; they were 'like dragging or pushing something, moving furniture', and came from the landing outside her door, or the stairs. These sounds went on until nearly 6.30, but stopped for about five minutes before Mr Moran passed down the stairs at about 5.45, his usual hour, and resumed when he had left. Nobody else in the house had heard these disturbances, nor had anybody moved furniture during the night. Two doors away, Mr James Kirwan, who lived in the first floor flat of No. 15 and slept in the front, had heard from outside a sound as if someone was pushing a brush up the street. This sound was continuous, not intermittent, and seemed to be coming towards him. It stopped twice, and lasted altogether about six or seven minutes. He could not say when he heard the sound, except that it was after 3.30 a.m. and that it was daylight then.

The Gardaí questioned everyone in No. 17 Hume Street, including Nurse Cadden, of course. Asked had she heard any unusual noises during the night or early morning, she replied: 'Sure, I could hear no noise. My room is away at the back, and as well as that I had the radio on all night' — to keep her company, she said, as she suffered from arthritis and it had kept her awake. But this differed from what she had told Mrs Farrelly, who had asked the same question. 'No, I was fast asleep in my bed.' When Mrs Farrelly insisted that there had been noise, Nurse Cadden said it was from next door. When the Gardaí told the women about the dead body outside, Mrs Farrelly exclaimed 'God bless us! Is it known who she is?' Nurse Cadden said 'Isn't it terrible,' and then, an odd remark, 'Sure it must have been a man who did that.' Her comment to Mr Moran was 'Ah! the poor bitch.'

The State Pathologist had found a distinctive smell of disinfectant from the womb of the dead woman, probably from the substance used to cause the abortion. As a bucket in Nurse Cadden's room gave off the same smell, and as she was contradicting herself on interrogation, the Gardaí were becoming suspicious. So, armed with a search warrant, they went to her room. 'Search away,' she said, with the utmost sang froid. 'You will not find anything here.' The search took time, and the Gardaí found — if that is the right word for articles that were in full view in a small room — two syringes, a forceps and, wrapped in a cloth in a hat box on top of a wardrobe, two duck billed specula, instruments which are used for examination of the womb. When the searcher lifted down the hat box, Nurse Cadden said, 'That box has not been taken down for years,' but finger marks in the dust on the lid contradicted her. On seeing the specula shown to her by the Garda, she said, 'I had these articles when I was in a nursing home in Rathmines.' The nursing home had closed down in 1939.

Beside one of the syringes were two pieces of rubber tubing which fitted on to the end of the syringe. 'I use that for enemas, it screws together,' she explained, and took up the pieces and joined them to the instrument. The Gardaí took all these things, and a book, *Manual of Practical Anatomy*, two very strong lamps commonly used in surgical examinations, and some rubber sheets — all articles which any working midwife might own, and Nurse Cadden's diary. She was then asked would she account for her movements on the seventeenth and eighteenth, and answered, 'Of course I will.'

135

She said that from 2 p.m. to 7 p.m. on the seventeenth she was in bed, and got up to make tea, talked with Mrs Farrelly in the latter's room for about twenty minutes, and then went back to bed till 10.30 p.m. At that time her bell rang and she went down to the hall door and discovered that the caller was a man patient who, she thought, came from Kilkenny — about 75 miles away. She had been treating him for hair trouble, and did not know his name, nor indeed the name of any of her patients. Most of this narrative was contradicted by Mrs Farrelly, who had told the Gardaí that Nurse Cadden had been in her own room talking with two women during the afternoon, and was up and down the stairs in the evening washing and drawing water at a sink on one of the landings where she had spilt water, and answering the hall door.

Nurse Cadden said she spoke with this man for about an hour — this was amply corroborated by several visitors to the house — and then went to bed, sleeping soundly till 8 a.m. on the eighteenth, and heard nothing during the night. As the talk with this man was at the hall door in full view and hearing of those coming in and out, it seems very unlikely that the pair were discussing a proposed abortion, or one that had taken place and had killed the woman.

The Gardaí went off then, and were back in a week to question Nurse Cadden about her diary, and about the instruments they had taken. Superintendent Lawlor had been studying some entries in the diary and cautioned her, before starting interrogation, that she was not obliged to answer his questions, but she answered willingly. He wanted an explanation of a diary entry on 17 April, the day before the body was found. The writing had been made almost illegible, by heavy writing and ink markings over the original writing of the entry, and the use of two inks, red and blue. Nurse Cadden said that the entry was '2 p.m. blue coats', and it meant that two patients wearing blue coats were to call at that hour for hair treatment, but in fact they had not turned up. She repeated what she had said at the earlier interview, that she never kept her patients' names, and several anonymous entries in the diary seemed to bear this out. Superintendent Lawlor suggested that the original entry had been 'black coat', and had been unnecessarily over-written and made unreadable. She said no, that her pen had run out of red ink and she had gone over the entry to make it clear. In fact she had made it hopelessly unclear, and the jury when they saw it could not have believed that explanation.

The Superintendent asked her then about an entry on 10 April, '6 p.m. black coats.' The 'coats' was illegible and could have been almost any other short word, but the word 'black' was clear. She said this entry referred to a woman patient whose treatment she could not remember. An entry for 30 March, £50, seemed to need explanation from a nurse whose fees varied from 3s to 12s 6d. She said it was £50 for 'professional services rendered on two or three of a family'. The most striking thing about the diary was that of the eighteen entries examined by the Gardaí, only the two mentioned had been written over to make them illegible.

At the end of this talk, Superintendent Lawlor said the dead woman had worn a black coat, and 'I have information that that woman was in your room on 17 April.' It is not clear if this statement was strictly accurate, for it was not proved at the trial, but of course may have been hearsay and therefore not admissible.

Nurse Cadden, who was a cool customer, responded to this by picking up the evening paper and showing Lawlor a photograph in it of the dead woman. 'I never saw her face before. I passed a remark, when I saw her photograph, to a man who was here, that she had the mouth of a prostitute.' This was dangerous talk, as it contained a hint that she knew the dead woman.

Lawlor wanted an explanation about the uses of the syringe and forceps. The former, Nurse Cadden said, was for enemas solely. 'It is not used for anything else.' The rubber extension was for her own convenience. 'It keeps me away from my patient.' She explained the function of the forceps: 'It is a clamp. It is used in maternity cases, to stop the bleeding after the umbilical cord is cut. I have had that instrument since I was in Rathmines' . . . and said that she now used it as a tongs for picking up things. 'I never used it since I was in Rathmines, for any surgical purpose . . . If there are any hairs or blood on it I cannot account for them.'

There were no hairs, in fact — was Lawlor bluffing? — but there was one drop of blood, on a limb of the forceps.

She made several mistakes when asked further about the late night caller on the seventeenth. 'I spoke to him about arthritis he was suffering from, also about cortisone. If I knew this dirt was going on I would have let him up to my room — to show him there was no corpse in my room. I did not know who he was until I went to the door. Then — I recognised him as one of my patients I had not seen for just two years. I was going to give him some stuff, but I was too fatigued and too tired and I told him to come again. He has not called back since — and came from nearly 200 miles away to see me.' She refused to name him as she did not want to drag his name 'into the dirt'. If she really did know this man's name, he was an exception to her other patients who, she had said, were all anonymous.

What brought this man to see Nurse Cadden that night, from 200 miles or 75 miles away, whichever it was? She said she had been too tired to treat him, yet she had stood with him for over an hour at the hall door, when ten minutes or so upstairs might have sufficed for his treatment. She told Superintendent Lawlor that she never saw patients except by appointment, but she saw this one without an appointment, yet to no purpose, if she only talked to him about his ailments — arthritis this time, and not hair trouble as she had first said.

The linoleum in the hall of No. 17, some carpet outside Nurse Cadden's door, and some matting in her room had been examined and all had minute traces of blood, and she was contradicting herself significantly. She denied that she had been washing anything or had spilt water on the evening of the seventeenth. And as the investigations proceeded, more suspicious evidence came into Gardaí hands. On 27 May they thought it was time to act, and she was arrested and charged with murder. 'I'll say nothing. I'll tell it to the Judge or Justice rather,' was her reply. In the District Court, when she was told she might say something if she wished, she said: 'I have nothing to say only that I deny the charge. As a matter of fact, I am unable to stand up. I will have a doctor to prove that at the trial, a specialist too, and I have never even heard of her. That statement is true.'

The Trial

Nurse Cadden's trial started on 22 October 1956 and took ten days, three of which were occupied by the evidence of pathologists. The murder charge lay because if she had performed an illegal operation, which is a felony, in consequence of which the woman died, it was murder even though she had not intended to kill, for the killing of a person during the commission of a felony is murder, regardless of intention. This somewhat strange law is the creation of the English Bench. The Judges of England from whom prior to 1922 came much of the present law of Ireland, decided a long time ago that the malice which is an ingredient in the felony of procuring an abortion should be equated with the malice which is the indispensable element in the crime of murder.

The crime popularly known as an illegal operation was created by Section 58 of the Offences Against the Person Act, 1861, which makes it a felony for any person, 'who . . . shall *unlawfully* use any instrument or other means whatsoever with intent to procure the miscarriage of a woman', and renders the offender liable to life imprisonment. Today this statement of the former English law may sound quaintly archaic, for the procuring of an abortion is no longer an offence in England, where the lawful procuring of abortions is big business. But it was the law of England and Ireland in 1956, and is still the law in Ireland. The question which Section 58 raises but does not answer is: What is meant by 'unlawfully'? One would think that such an important question in a statute, for breach of which life imprisonment — and even hanging — could follow, would have been answered in the statute itself or soon after 1861, but it was not answered until 1939, and even then not satisfactorily.

In that year, an English surgeon of high repute operated upon a girl under age 16, who was pregnant from a particularly vicious rape, and caused her to miscarry. The operation was done in the operating theatre in the surgeon's own hospital, in full view of his assistants and the theatre staff. He was charged with an offence under Section 58, and gave evidence that the girl's health, and possibly her life, would have been endangered if the child had been born, and that he had operated with the intent of saving her life. This was believed by the jury, but of course he had also had the intent of causing the miscarriage which was the means of saving her life. The question was whether what he had done was 'unlawful'. As his professional future and his personal liberty were at stake, one can only say that he was a brave man to have undertaken such grave risks.

The trial judge found nothing in the Statute of 1861 to help him to decide what was meant by 'unlawfully' but looked at another English statute, The Infant Life Preservation Act of 1929, which has nothing whatever to do with the 1861 Act or with abortion, but makes if a felony for any person by any wilful act to cause the death of a child which is capable of being born alive, before it has an existence independent of its mother. The felony is called child destruction. There is, however, a proviso to that statute which says it is no offence if the act which kills the child is done in good faith for preserving the life of the mother. So the judge decided that the operation Mr Bourne performed was lawful because it was done to preserve the expectant mother's life. Mr Bourne was indeed fortunate to find not only a jury which believed him, but a judge who found a defence for him. He was also lucky that he had not performed the operation in 1928, the year before the Infant Life Protection Act was passed. But no such defence was open to Nurse Cadden.

It seems strange that one can commit murder, the most serious of the non-political crimes, by accident. It also seems strange that the crime can be committed during the performance of an act to which the victim has consented, and which she has invited, for the abortionist does not usually seek out his customers. They come to him. If a professional abortionist should commit a common assault on somebody who falls from the blow, and dies as a result, the abortionist will not have committed murder, but manslaughter. The victim would not only not have invited the fatal blow, but would never have given permission for the assault, yet it would not be murder because common assault is a misdemeanour and not a felony. This does not mean that all felonies are more serious crimes that misdemeanours, but that they were when the English judges decided that a killing during a felony was murder. In those days felonies carried the most savage punishment.

So, for the crime of murder in the course of procuring an abortion Mary Anne Cadden stood her trial. The trial judge was Mr Justice Richard McLoughlin, S.C. Prosecuting were Mr Desmond Bell S.C. and Mr James Ryan, Barrister-at-Law. For the defence Mr Ernest Wood S.C. and Mr Noel Hartnett, Barrister-at-Law, appeared.

The prosecution were presenting a case founded wholly on circumstantial evidence, for there was no evidence that Nurse Cadden had ever even seen the murdered woman, so the State had to show that their case was consistent with guilt, and with no other rational conclusion. All the facts already narrated were fully proved by the various witnesses. Mr Rigney, the milk roundsman, in addition to what has already been stated, said that a few minutes before he entered Hume Street and found the body he had been going to St Stephen's Green, and when passing the end of Hume Street had looked to his left into the street. He saw a woman on the footpath, at the spot where later he found the body, in a crouched position and facing towards the hospital. She turned her head as his vehicle passed, and he noticed that she wore glasses, and saw the glint on the lenses. She was of stocky build and had something white on. 'I am not sure what it was. I was only passing by.'

When he was at the body, he said, he heard a sound from below, and leaned over the railings to look into the basement.

There was a woman in the area, standing with her back to the wall and looking at him.

Mr Bell was examining Mr Rigney and at this point the following questions were asked:

> Q. Can you give a description of the woman you saw looking up at you?
> A. I think she had fair hair.
> Q. Can you describe any more about it?
> A. It was raised up on her forehead — puffed, you know.
> Q. Anything more about her, do you remember?
> A. I don't.
> Q. Can you give any description or give us any help as to what she was wearing?
> A. No. You see, there is a downpipe and it would obscure my view owing to the position she was in.
> Q. Can you say whether or not the woman in the basement resembled the woman you had previously seen on the footpath?
> A. No, but I can tell you something I have learned since I came to this Court.
> Q. Don't.
> Judge:
> Q. Did the woman make any move during the time you were looking at her?
> A. Well, you see, I only glanced at her.
> Q. Only glanced?
> A. Yes. I wanted to get away as quickly as I could.
> Q. You say that at the time of your glance she was looking up?
> A. Yes.
> Q. Or was it when you glanced she looked up?
> A. She was looking up. Her head was turned in my direction and she wore glasses.

Some further questions followed, and at the conclusion of the examination of the witness, by Mr Bell, this occurred:

> Mr Bell: Now I propose to ask this witness, my lord, whether he has seen the woman he saw in Hume Street, or the woman he saw in the basement, at any time since. I don't know whether there is any objection to that, my lord.
> Mr Wood: I object, my lord. There is no notice of the question, my lord — of the evidence proposed to be tendered.

Judge: On the ground that you would be taken by surprise?

Mr Wood: Naturally, my lord.

Judge: I haven't read the depositions in this case. I suppose I had better read Mr Rigney's deposition from that point of view, otherwise I would allow the question.

Mr Wood: I am sure Mr Bell will agree that there is no such evidence in the deposition.

Mr Bell of course agreed, and the Judge intimated that he himself would have asked the question if Mr Bell had not. Mr Wood said that he wished to be taken as respectfully objecting. Mr Wood repeated his objection, but it was disallowed.

Judge:

Q. (to witness) What was there about the hair that would enable you to describe this person as a woman, you may answer that?

A. The way the hair was worn.

Q. What do you mean by the way it was worn?

A. It was puffed.

Q. What do you mean by puffed?

A. No man would wear his hair the same way.

Q. When you used the word woman, does that imply by you anything of the age of the person, young, old, or very old?

A. I couldn't say.

Q. Or as to build or stature?

A. I have a fair idea of the height of the person.

Q. What was your fair idea?

A. Judging from where I was standing.

Q. What is your fair idea, judging from where you were standing?

A. She would be over five feet.

Later the Judge asked four more questions of Mr Rigney:

Judge:

Q. You also said that you couldn't say what the person was wearing?

A. No.

Q. What clothes the person was wearing?

A. No.

Q. And you say you saw it first, the hair and spectacles?

A. Exactly.

Q. Was the person clothed or could you say that you saw sufficient of the person's clothing?

A. I didn't notice the clothes; I only noticed the face and hair;
I only glanced down.

The Judge did not ask Mr Rigney if he had seen the woman since
and the matter dropped. But the jury had only to look at Nurse
Cadden in the dock and they saw a woman who wore glasses and
had fair hair. It would have been surprising if they had not
thought she was the woman Mr Rigney saw.

Mr Wood cross-examined Mr Rigney on his opportunity of
seeing the woman crouched on the pavement. The speed at which
he had passed the end of Hume Street must, of course, have
affected the duration of his view. He did not agree he was going as
fast as 20 m.p.h. but said he was going slowly because a few
mornings before a car came tearing out of the street and he was
being careful. To the suggestion that he should have been looking
ahead and not to his left, he said: 'Something white attracted my
attention, and that is how I saw her.' However, it was clear that his
view of the woman was very brief — the time taken by his van to
pass the width of the pavement would be less than half a second.
And the shorter the view, of course the less reliable his description
of her.

Mr Rigney had been interviewed by a Dublin newspaper
reporter to whom he had said, after describing the finding of the
body, 'It was perfectly bright at the time; I didn't see anyone in the
vicinity.' Mr Wood asked him why he did not tell the reporter
about the woman in the basement, and he said he had wanted, at
the time, to say as little as was necessary. As he had not told the
Gardaí about the woman until he came to the District Court he
had to account for this too. 'I knew I had seen the woman in the
basement, and I knew that when I came to Court I would have to
tell that.' It seemed plausible enough.

Mr Wood questioned Mrs Farrelly about the voices of the two
women she had heard coming from Nurse Cadden's room when
the latter was supposed to be alone and resting. Mrs Farrelly had
gone out that afternoon and returned in about an hour, and the
voices of women were still audible. Mr Wood suggested the she
couldn't know that she had heard two women, and that if she had
she couldn't possibly know that they were the same two an hour
later. But Mrs Farrelly would not be shaken. Yet she had made an
extraordinary mistake when the Gardaí asked her, on the eighteenth, if she had heard any sounds in the night. At first she said
'no'. How did she forget about the pushing and dragging noises?

143

She was seventy-four years of age, which might have ex-plained the memory lapse.

When Nurse Cadden's diary was produced Detective-Guard Horgan, a photographer at the Garda Technical Bureau, gave evidence of photographing and enlarging the entries of 10 and 17 April. By using a filter he was able substantially to eliminate the red ink over-writing in the photograph of the former entry, so that only the black ink writing remained. It read clearly '2 p.m. blue coats', so Nurse Cadden had told the truth about that entry. In photographing the entry of 17 April the photographer eliminated the black over-writing, which called for a different technique, but he succeeded in producing a photograph which showed only the original red ink writing. The result was deadly. The entry clearly read '8 p.m. black coat'. So the jury now knew that Nurse Cadden had an appointment on the night before the body was found with someone wearing a black coat, and had tried to conceal the fact. It could only mean one thing.

Dr Hickey gave the lengthiest testimony, being in the box for more than two days. The syringe without the nozzle and rubber attached was, he said, in common medical use, and with the attachment could cause the injury suffered by the dead woman. He considered that the insertion and use of the adapted syringe could require some skill, to avoid injury to the vagina or the cervix, neither of which had been injured. He was asked about the age of the blood stain on the forceps, and said it was comparatively fresh, less than a month old. There was no way, however, of determining to what blood group the stain belonged. No other instrument was bloodstained. Dr Hickey described the skin of the dead body as being scraped, scratched and grimy, and the clothes as dusty and dirty, suggesting rubbing (or, of course dragging) on a dusty or dirty surface. This tended to confirm Mr Kirwan's evidence about the sounds he heard in the early morning.

Much time was spend on trying to determine the probable time of death, but it was difficult with so many facts missing, and so many assumptions to be made. When Dr Hickey arrived in Hume Street at 8.20 a.m., the internal temperature of the body was 29° centigrade — 8° below the normal 37° for a living person. Considering the air temperature and various other factors and alternatives, he placed the possible time of death between 2 a.m. and 3 a.m.; but upon another set of possibilities the time might have been between 9 p.m. and midnight on 17 April. On yet a third set of suppositions the time of death must have been much later than 9 p.m. The defence was concerned to show that death occurred as late as possible after 8 p.m., the time of the supposed appointment, and they called evidence that the time of death was probably between 4 a.m. and 4.35 a.m. Whether the jury paid much attention to these speculations is doubtful, considering all the other evidence there was before them.

Numerous fibres and hairs had been collected by the Gardaí from Nurse Cadden's room and from the clothing of the dead woman and had been microscopically examined. As human hairs do not serve to establish identity, all that could be said of them was that some hairs found in the accused's room and on the deceased's clothing were similar. This suggested that she had been in Nurse Cadden's room, but was not conclusive. The fibres were similar to fibres found on the deceased's coat, which suggested the same thing but again it was not conclusive. But here the defence came up with a surprise, for during the trial Dr Stanley Earle, their pathologist, collected samples of loose hairs and fibres at random from the footpath between Nos 10 and 19 Hume Street, and from a sweeping brush in the house in Ely Place where the deceased woman had lodged for two or three nights. Many of the hairs — although collected six months after the prosecution's specimens — were similar to them!

When the prosecution's case had closed, Mr Wood applied to have the case withdrawn from the jury for lack of evidence, and on a legal ground, but the Judge refused the application. So Mr Wood called one or two witnesses in addition to those mentioned, and also Mr Stanley Siev, Nurse Cadden's solicitor. He proved that he had sought the services of several gynaecologists to advise the defence on the medical aspects of the case but none would agree to act. So the jury heard medical evidence from the prosecution only, and the accused's lawyers had no means of testing that evidence which may or may not have been a handicap. Nurse Cadden did not give evidence.

Mr Wood had made his speech to the jury when the prosecution case ended, a magnificent six-hour effort. So Mr Hartnett spoke now, and closed the case for the defence. He was as good as he could be with such a difficult case. He reminded the jury that the syringe had been free of the disinfectant smell — a good point, but of course Nurse Cadden might have washed it. Who, he asked, owned the scarf which was around the dead woman's neck? Not the accused, and not the deceased, so far as the proof had gone. Who then? Who, but the person who had performed the

145

abortion? And the red umbrella had a fingerprint on the handle, not of either the accused or the deceased. Whose fingerprint could it be but that of the real abortionist?

When Mr Ryan was making his closing speech he misquoted the witness Patrick Rigney. When he had finished, Mr Hartnett stood up.

> Mr Hartness: I respectfully ask your lordship to discharge the jury, on the ground that Mr Ryan, in the course of his address to the jury, stated in reference to the witness Patrick Rigney, 'He had been man enough to say that the woman he saw was the accused woman in the dock.'
>
> Judge: He didn't say it, Mr Hartnett.
>
> Mr Hartness: Mr Ryan didn't say it, my lord?
>
> Judge: No.
>
> Mr Hartnett: Well, I jotted it down in my notebook.
>
> Judge: I saw you writing.
>
> Mr Hartnett: Will you tell, my lord, what he did say?
>
> Judge: Mr Ryan said that Mr Rigney said that was that woman, and that woman was the murderer.
>
> Mr Hartnett: I ask you to discharge the jury.
>
> Judge: I will, of course, make it right.
>
> Mr Hartnett: You say even if he did say it, it does not matter? That is your lordship's ruling?
>
> Judge: Yes.

Probably the judge was right, and it did not matter, but the fact is that Mr Rigney did not say what Mr Ryan quoted him as saying. However, the Judge must have forgotten to correct the error, because he did not refer to the matter at all in his charge to the jury.

Mr Wood had criticised Mr Rigney's evidence and pointed out an error he had made, which was the 'glint of the glasses'. This was erroneous because at 6.25 a.m. the sun was not shining in Hume Street — it did not reach there until 8.30 a.m. — so he could not have seen the glint. Had Mr Rigney also made a mistake about the colour of the woman's hair in the basement. It was possible, of course. Mr Wood asked the jury to consider why Mr Rigney had not spoken to this woman. Why did he not ask her 'What's happened up here?' or something of the kind? After all, the woman lying in the street might only have been ill, or drunk, or unconscious. But Mr Rigney had said he wanted to get away as quickly as he could, and the jury must have realised that he was shocked or alarmed, and therefore unlikely to behave with normal coolness.

Of Mrs Farrelly's evidence, which Mr Wood asked the jury to reject, he remarked that if the morning noises stopped when Mr Moran was due to descend the stairs, he must have stubbed his toe on a dead body and not noticed it. But if what Mr Gleeson saw was the body at 5.04 a.m. then what Mrs Farrelly heard at 5.45 a.m. must have been sweeping, or brushing, or washing of the linoleum.

The jury were out only an hour and returned with a verdict of guilty. The Judge then asked Mary Anne Cadden the customary question: had she anything to say why sentence of death should not be passed upon her? Her reply, forcefully spoken, was remarkable, indeed unique, for a prisoner about to hear the dread sentence of death. 'You will never do it,' she said 'This is not my country. I am reporting this to the President of my country. This is the third time I am convicted in this country falsely. And I will report it, and I will see about it at a later date. Thank you. Only for my counsel I would say something you would not like to hear.'

The judge sentenced her then to be hanged on 27 November, and when he had finished she spoke again, still full of fight. 'Well, I am not a Catholic. Take that now.'

As the sentence was being passed, women in the packed gallery of the Court sobbed loudly. Outside, feelings were rather different. A large crowd had gathered when the jury retired, and as soon as the verdict was known, several shouted 'Hang her!'

She appealed, and amongst several grounds argued was Mr Wood's objection at the trial to the proposed question to Mr Rigney about having seen the woman in Hume Street since. Mr Wood argued that the mere mention of the question by the prosecution suggested that the witness could identify that woman as the woman in the dock, and it was therefore seriously prejudicial to the accused. But the incident, and the trial judge's question which followed and to which Mr Wood had also objected, was held by the Court of Criminal Appeal to be unobjectionable. The appeal failed, but Mary Anne Cadden's prophecy ('You will never do it') proved to be right. She was not executed. Her solicitor lodged a petition with the Government pleading for clemency, and on the 4 January 1957 her sentence was commuted to penal servitude for life. No woman had been executed in Ireland since 1925, and Nurse Cadden may have thought she could safely assume she would not hang. Yet she showed great spirit as she stood in the dock waiting to be told she would die.

Life imprisonment for Mary Anne Cadden proved to be short. In August 1958 she was transferred from Mountjoy Prison to the

Central Criminal Mental Hospital at Dundrum, County Dublin, where she died suddenly on 29 April 1959.

The case against Nurse Cadden was so strong that a conviction was almost a certainty, despite heroic efforts by her counsel. But they had a special difficulty to deal with, and probably no advocacy could get over it: their client was notorious in the city of Dublin as a criminal offender, and if the jury had had any doubts about the case, there was a serious danger that her reputation would resolve those doubts against her. An incident early on in the trial very nearly brought her reputation out into the open. When a Garda witness was being examined by Mr Bell about a telephone conversation Nurse Cadden had had while the witness was searching the room, he was asked:

Q. Did she then replace the receiver?
A. She did, my lord.
Q. Did you notice anything about her manner on that occasion?
A. She appeared to be quite normal.

The second question seems pointless, and if Mr Bell knew the answer which was coming, irrelevant. The next question came from the Judge:

Judge:
Q. Had you known her before that?
A. Not to see, my lord.

The Judge's question was necessary, as it tested the 'quite normal' description given by the Garda, for if he had not known the woman his assessment of her normality might be worthless. The answer should have been 'No', but the words 'not to see' implied a knowledge of a kind other than visual i.e. knowledge by reputation, and that, coming from a policeman, could mean only one thing. When Mr Bell had finished his examination, Mr Hartnett asked that the jury be sent out as he had an application to make. The Judge complied, and Mr Hartnett requested the Judge to discharge the jury on the ground indicated, meaning that the witness had by implication given evidence of the accused's bad character in violation of the rule which forbids the prosecution to do this save in exceptional cases. The evidence had not, of course, come from

148

a question by the prosecution, but nevertheless had come from a prosecution witness. The Judge refused Mr Hartnett's request.

Judge: I don't think so at all. The Garda's evidence was that she appeared to be normal, and in the circumstances acted as a normal person would, and that she talked normally.
Mr Hartnett: 'I do not know her to see', my lord?
Judge: I won't discharge the jury.

Perhaps the jury did not attach to the Garda's answer the meaning Mr Hartnett contended it had, but it was a reminder of the bad reputation of the woman in the dock and of the effect it might have on the jury. So Mr Wood and Mr Hartnett decided to take the bull by the horns, and bring out her former convictions, and appeal to the jury to try her, not on her reputation, but strictly on the proved facts of the case before them.

Mary Anne Cadden was a woman of strong personality and temper, and was frequently 'in flames' as she called it when people or events crossed her. Her notoriety began with her being charged in 1939, with another woman, with conspiracy to abandon a child aged about six weeks, and of abandoning the child so as to cause it unnecessary suffering or injury to its health. This offence is a misdemeanour, for which the maximum prison sentence is two years, but it is also punishable with a fine instead of imprisonment. Clearly the offence, even at its worst, is not considered by the legislature to be a grave one, but for some unknown reason the Dublin newspapers gave the case great prominence and treated it as a *cause célèbre*.

At the time, Nurse Cadden was running the nursing home in Rathmines, and as she took in maternity cases the affair took on a special significance. The gossips of Dublin got busy, and soon the most extraordinary stories were circulating about unwanted babies having been buried in the garden of the nursing home, and even of Gardaí having dug up infant bones and corpses. It was all untrue but added to the notoriety which was enlarged yet again by the refusal of the District Justice, before whom the depositions were taken, to give bail to the two accused. In the public mind, this was a further proof of the enormity of the crime. So, each time the Court took depositions, Nurse Cadden and her fellow defendant were brought to Court in a closed police van, stared at by the curious when they emerged, and photographed on many of these occasions by the press. The case was becoming more sensational than a sensational murder trial.

Then the two women, who should have been given bail, discovered after several weeks of this unnecessary custody that their incarceration was even being prolonged, because congestion of work in the Court was delaying the hearings. So they applied to the High Court for bail, succeeded, and were released until the trial. This was taken in the Central Criminal Court in May 1939 and attracted renewed public attention. The evidence included the fact that the baby was found abandoned on the grass at the roadside in Dunshaughlin, County Meath, a place where it must have been (and was) spotted quickly, so that the danger to its health was minimised. In the vicinity, a short time before the baby was found, a red sports car driven by a flaxen-haired woman was observed, and as Nurse Cadden's hair was that colour and she owned such a car, there was not much difficulty in identifying her. She dyed her hair black for the trial, but everyone knew its true colour. She was convicted of the two offences, and sentenced to twelve months' imprisonment concurrently on each conviction. Her co-defendant faded out of the news, but by 12 May 1939, the day the trial ended, Mary Anne Cadden was the best known woman in Ireland, and the notoriety never left her.

Her next appearance in the headlines was on her conviction by the Central Criminal Court on 30 April 1945 on a charge of unlawfully using an instrument to procure a miscarriage, for which she was sentenced to five years penal servitude. Hers was one of several convictions during the period 1942 to 1945 for this offence which came about as a result of the travel restrictions imposed by Britain on persons coming from Ireland, during that part of the war. For years, pregnant Irish girls who could afford to had gone to England to have back street abortions performed, but now they could not travel and the trade in Dublin in illegal operations, then of small proportions, rapidly enlarged. One manifestation of this trade was a ring consisting of a contact man, a doctor to whom he passed on the girls to have their pregnancies confirmed, and the abortionist, all three exacting a fee for their services. The police broke up that particular ring, and the three received severe sentences.

Another abortionist who worked alone was convicted and given fifteen years penal servitude, a stiff sentence. He appealed on a point of law, had the conviction set aside and obtained a new trial at which he was again convicted but his sentence this time was seven years.

Several other persons were convicted, and many were never caught. Nurse Cadden was not one of the latter, for the police might have been expected to keep their eye on a woman with her reputation.

Thus, when in 1956 the body of a woman killed by an illegal operation was found in the street two doors from where the notorious Nurse Cadden lived, the Dublin whispering gallery, as Mr Wood called it in his speech, came to life and decided before any more facts were known that Mary Anne Cadden had killed her. And in order to give the jury a full picture of his client, Mr Wood had Superintendent Moran recalled to the witness box, towards the end of the trial, to question him about a letter she had written threatening that if her landlord tried to have her evicted from her room, she would shoot him and 'put the butcher's knife to the handle' in his stomach. Superintendent Moran had asked her what knife she was referring to and she produced a carving knife. The letter also contained vehement references to her two convictions. Superintendent Moran then charged her with the offence of sending a letter threatening to kill

When he was in the box the first time he was asked about Nurse Cadden's truculent manner, and her tongue.

Q. I don't suppose she said 'Hello, Superintendent Moran'?
A. No.
Q. She is very offensive to you?
A. Occasionally.
Q. And she was offensive that day?
A. Not alone to me, but to other Guards.
Q. And to the public too?
A. Yes.
Q. Anyone who crosses her path?
A. Yes, including solicitors.
Q. And Counsel?
A. Yes.

And during the interview about the knife she had been as abusive as ever.

By coming out into the open about their client Counsel were able to appeal to the jury's sense of fairness, and put pressure on them to consider only the evidence of the crime. 'I am sure', said Mr Wood, 'some of you have come in here to defend a woman already convicted in half the public houses of Dublin?' He warned them not to be prejudiced against her because of the particular

151

crime she was charged with. 'If someone else were the criminal,' said Mr Wood, 'then in putting the body so near to Nurse Cadden's, he had chosen the safest place in Dublin,' — a graphic point! One can hardly be surprised that with her reputation no gynaecologist would come to Court, and risk the damage of having his name associated with her.

The jury must have wondered, as readers of this story will, how Nurse Cadden had transported the body from her room to the street. She was in her sixties, suffered from arthritis, and was not in robust health. It is inconceivable that she could have moved the body unaided, down two narrow and winding flights of stairs, along the hall, down the three steps from hall door to street and then along the pavement to No. 15. Who, then, helped her? A man? A woman? Two people?

The tying of the dead woman's legs above the knees could have had a dual purpose: to prevent a flow of blood from the vagina on to the stairs and floors — there was a little blood from the vagina on the pavement underneath the body — and to assist in the carrying of the body down the stairs, i.e. with legs tied together the person holding the legs could more easily do his or her share of the carrying. But who was, or were, Nurse Cadden's assistants? She never told, which is strange, for by telling, she might have been able to divide the blame, or even better, divert it from herself to the other. Was she being loyal? It seems unlikely. Perhaps her helpers had fled and she knew that if they could not be traced she would have been disbelieved anyway, and so thought she might as well keep silent. Or possibly they were anonymous like her other callers, including the unfortunate woman she had killed.

One last question: If Mary Anne Cadden had been a respectable midwife of good reputation, would she have been convicted?

8.

Danse Macabre

(Attorney-General v. Edward Ball, 1936)

ON Tuesday morning 18 February 1936, shortly before nine o'clock, James Rafferty was delivering newspapers in Corbawn Lane, Shankill, County Dublin. Shankill is a village on the east coast, about ten miles from Dublin city and two miles from the well-known seaside resort of Bray. Corbawn Lane is a quiet road about three-quarters of a mile long, leading directly to the sea, along which are several detached houses standing in their own grounds well back from the road. It is dark there, even in daylight, for the road is bordered with tall trees which meet overhead.

About half-way down, the road rises to cross the railway from Dublin to Bray; about a hundred and fifty yards from the shore there is a barrier to prevent the passage of cars, and from there the road becomes a mere footpath sloping to the sea. In 1936 the path passed under an arched stone bridge, now demolished, which once carried the railway line to Bray. Then it widened out on to an open space or platform of earth with a drop of about fourteen feet to the shore below. Today the ground is badly broken up from the action of the sea, but in 1936 the surface was level and easy to walk on. In the summer the place attracts bathers and picnic parties; in the winter, and at night, it is deserted save for occasional couples in cars. It is an eerie place at night, especially when the lights higher up the road go off at about half-past eleven.

Rafferty's deliveries included the last house, and as he turned in at the gate he noticed at the barrier a small stationary car facing towards the sea. He spoke to Mr Margetson, the occupier of the house, and the two went down to look at it. The latter had seen the car shortly after midnight the night before as he turned into his gate, and observed that the driver's door was open. He did not examine the car then, merely noting its unusual position.

It was a two-door baby Austin, and the front was jammed up against the right-hand side of the barrier. The sunshine roof was open and the driver's door ajar, and inside on the floor there was a bloodstained towel and a piece of bloodstained blotting-paper. Drops of blood could be seen on the back seat. An envelope and some papers in the pocket bore the name of Mrs Vera Ball of Booterstown, a south Dublin suburb on the coast. Rafferty left Margetson at the car and strolled down as far as the sea, but noticed nothing strange. Presently Margetson departed and reported what he had seen to the Garda Station at Shankill. Thus began the investigations into a remarkable crime.

The Gardaí arrived quickly and examined car and scene closely. The car was jammed so tight against the barrier that it took six of them to remove it. Their search yielded further signs of blood — on a wheel and tyre, and on the ground beneath. Clearly something was amiss and two Gardaí set off for Booterstown to inquire.

The car belonged to Mrs Lavinia, or Vera, Ball, aged fifty-five, the wife of a well-known Dublin physician. They had lived apart since 1927; of the marriage there had been two children, both boys; in 1936 Edward, the younger, was nineteen and a half. Edward Ball was an agreeable, personable young man, well liked, and intelligent. He had no occupation but was interested in the stage. He had been living in a flat in Dublin but had come to stay in his mother's house on 13 February, and was living there when the car was discovered.

The house, No. 23 St Helen's Road, Booterstown, is important in the story; it was a small semi-detached modern house standing a short way back from the footpath, with a front and back garden, two living-rooms, kitchen, and out-offices downstairs, and three bedrooms upstairs, The upper rooms were off a small landing at the top of a narrow flight of stairs from the hall; the living-rooms were off the hall, which led directly through a door into the kitchen. There was a small garage attached to the side of the house. The house was comfortably furnished, as Mrs Ball was a woman of means, and supplemented her private income by a spare-time occupation.

It was about 12.30 p.m. when the Gardaí arrived at St Helen's Road. Ball was not in, nor was his mother, and apparently she had not slept in the house the night before. They spoke for a while to the maid, Lily Kelly, noticing that the dining-room table was set for three. Mrs Ball was expecting friends to lunch. The Gardaí left after a while, and returned at 6.30 p.m., Chief Superintendent Reynolds now being one of the party. Ball was there, but his mother was still missing and there was no trace of her whereabouts. Chief Superintendent Reynolds told him he was inquiring about his mother's movements and apparent disappearance. Ball was perfectly calm and collected, and readily answered questions. He had last seen her at about 7.45 the previous evening when she had left he house alone in the car, saying that she would probably stay the night with a woman friend who lived not far away, or with her sister, who also lived near. He had opened the garage door and front garden gate and closed them when she had gone; he explained that it was quite usual for his mother to stay out at night with one or other of her friends.

He was asked further questions and said his father, whom he had seen that afternoon, had told him that the car had been found near Shankill and that there were bloodstains in it. He asked where exactly the car had been found, and Reynolds told him, saying that there was quite a lot of blood in it, and in addition a bloodstained towel. Ball commented on hearing this: 'I wonder would there be more blood on it than if a person had cut their hand or had an accident.' He said he knew his mother was expecting visitors to lunch on that day, and she had told him not to be in — a normal request, as she would wish to be alone with her friends. He asked if she had stayed with either of the two ladies mentioned, and was told not; he then suggested she might have stayed with another friend near Bray, and was told she had not been there either, which he said was very strange. He could offer no suggestion as to where she might be; she had been perfectly normal when leaving and had been busy in the afternoon with the preparations for the luncheon party. He mentioned having broken a cup accidentally the evening before, which had upset his mother, who was a very highly strung, excitable woman, but they had only had a few words about it and the incident was then forgotten.

Ball was asked about his own movements on the previous evening, the 17th, and said he had been at home all night, reading till ten-thirty or eleven, when he went to bed. When Lily Kelly arrived in the morning she told him his mother was not in her room and the car was not in the garage, and he had explained where she was for the night. He described Mrs Ball's clothes on her departure: a dark red dress, a blue-and-white check belted coat, a blue hat, and brown shoes. Reynolds interrupted the interview at this point and went into the kitchen, where he found a pair of man's brown shoes, sodden with water and covered with fresh mud; then he went up to

Ball's bedroom, leaving him downstairs, and found a wet newspaper of the day before wrapped around some wet and bloodstained linen. He put the parcel back where he had found it, returned to Ball, and suggested that as his mother's bedroom was locked she might be inside, and that the door should be forced. Ball agreed, and they went upstairs; no key to the door could be found, Ball explaining that his mother usually locked the door when she went out and took the key with her. The door was then forced.

The room was in darkness with drawn curtains and the atmosphere was close; when the light came on it was seen that a portable electric fire was burning, which had obviously been on for many hours. The room was small, about thirteen feet by eleven feet, and the electric fire was near the bed, placed so as to dry a large wet stain on the carpet. The bed was made and had not been slept in; a hot-water bottle lay on it and there was dirty water in the washbasin; Mrs Ball's slippers were lying untidily on the floor. The wardrobe was opened, and Reynolds asked the maid to see if the red dress was missing; she found it, and Ball said that his mother was wearing a different one. The maid then pointed out a second red dress and said that Mrs Ball had only two of that colour. The same thing occurred with the shoes; there were two pairs of brown shoes in the wardrobe, and Mrs Ball had no others. The maid said a rug was missing from the bedroom, which Ball stated had been there the previous evening at 6.30 when he came up for his mother's spectacles. The maid remarked that the bed-clothes, though tidy, were arranged differently from the way she had left them the previous evening. Reynolds asked if any of Mrs Ball's coats was missing, and the maid, after finding two coats in the wardrobe, said no. Ball said she had not worn either of those, but a blue-and-white check coat with a belt, which however, according to the maid, was used by Mrs Ball as a cushion in the car to save her clothes.

They returned downstairs, and Reynolds asked Ball how he had spent the previous day. He explained that he had been in Dublin doing business for his mother, returned at about 5.15 p.m., and after having supper with her stayed in for the rest of the evening as already related. His relations with his mother he described as 'only suffering each other'. She was highly strung and temperamental, frequently had fits of depression, and was upset by trifles, but they were fond of each other. Asked if she had suicidal tendencies he was emphatic that she had not. 'A great fighter, with all her troubles,' was how he put it; she had never, he affirmed, expressed any intention of suicide, or said she was tired of life.

156

On the following day, Wednesday the 19th, Ball was again interviewed, this time by Superintendent Dunleavy. He was asked why he had not reported his mother's disappearance to the Gardaí and said he didn't know and that he could not understand her disappearance, though, if he had thought of it, the answer was that the Gardaí knew she had disappeared before he did, and were already investigating. Dunleavy asked him at what hour his mother had left the house, and this time he said 8.30.

He described where he had been on the 18th. He had gone into Dublin after breakfast, where he was interviewed for a job; then he went to an office and did some business for his mother; he had lunch in a café; called at his former flat for letters; went to the theatre where he sometimes did small parts; and 'knocked around town' till between 5 and 6 p.m., when he called at his father's house; then he came home. This account of his movements was incomplete; he suppressed the fact that he had made two calls — important ones.

He was asked this question: 'When you left the house on Tuesday morning did you bring a suitcase with you?' and answered: 'No, who told you that?' Dunleavy said he had heard it, and in fact his information was correct. During most of the interview Ball kept his hands either folded or in his pockets, but Dunleavy noticed that they were cut. Ball allowed the cuts to be examined; one on the right thumb he said he had got when cutting bread. As he was right-handed this couldn't have been correct, and when this was pointed out he said he had been 'fooling about' with a friend, and was holding the bread-knife with his left hand. A scratch on the back of the right hand was caused, he said, when looking for golf balls in the gorse on the previous Sunday; a bruise on the left middle finger he had got at a friend's house — then he corrected that and said he had caught it in a door in a restaurant. He could not say how he had got a cut on the left finger; it had been dressed at a chemist's on Tuesday.

They then went up to his bedroom, and found a vest, coat, and trousers, all very wet and bloodstained. Ball said he had last worn them two weeks before, but when their condition was pointed out said he might have worn them on Monday; the same happened when wet socks were found. The bloodstains and mud he could not explain. The newspaper parcel was produced and contained a towel, a handkerchief and collar of his, and a table-cloth, all bloodstained, and again he could not explain why. He was asked what shoes he wore on Monday and produced a dry pair, but when this was queried, he got the wet pair from the kitchen, which on closer examination showed sand mixed with the mud. Two other articles found in the bedroom proved to be important: a visiting-card of a Mr Tanham, and a bottle of patent stain remover. There was also a note from his mother which was as follows:

> I want you to understand that if you stay here to-night I am going to Mrs Allen. You did the usual dirty trick, coming in at 12 o'clock last night; it has upset me. I am three hours late for my work, but what can I expect?

He explained that she objected to his coming home late at night, hence the complaint in the note.

When the Gardaí checked on Ball's movements on Tuesday, the two important calls he had not mentioned came to light. One was to a shop where he had bought the stain remover; the other was to a friend's wife in whose flat he had left the suitcase, telling her it contained soiled clothes, and that he would call back for it in a few days. He told her the same story about his mother staying for the night with a friend, on account of his being in the house. He looked sleepy and yawned a lot during this conversation, but otherwise was perfectly normal.

This lady told the Gardaí that Ball had come to her flat on the 13th, saying that as his co-tenant was leaving he had given up the flat they shared. He could not pay the whole rent, he said, out of his allowances — £1 a week from his mother, and £1 10s. from his father — and would have to go to live in St Helen's Road. He had slept on a couch in a flat on the 11th, and on the 12th had surreptitiously stayed at the flat he had rented, for which he still had a spare key, but could not do so after that. He had had no food on the 13th, so she gave him breakfast. His mother, she said, called the next day and Ball and she had a quarrel in her presence. Mrs Ball said she would not stay in St Helen's Road as long as he slept there, but he could have his meals in the house. He was, unfortunately, in her charge, she said, till he was twenty-one. Ball had complained earlier to this friend that his mother had opened and read his letters — a thing he could not forgive in anybody.

Sergeant Heeney took the suitcase on the 19th, and it was opened in Ball's presence. It contained bed-clothes, towels, two shirts, a lady's coat, and an underslip, all extensively bloodstained. Ball admitted he had put all these things into the case; the bed-clothes, he said, were from his mother's bed, the shirts were his own, and the black coat was his mother's. The house had meantime been carefully examined, and there was blood almost everywhere. More than nineteen articles in Mrs Ball's bedroom were blood-stained or had drops of blood on them; the carpet was soaked. Bed-head, hair mattress, frame, dressing-table, bedlamp, hot-water bottle, hand mirror, and various other objects were all stained. The threshold of Ball's room showed five bloodstains; the landing and stair carpets, the wallpaper on the stairs, the kitchen curtains, and a basin in the kitchen also bore signs of blood. Outside, the path, the garage floor, and the chain for securing the garage door had the same tell-tale marks. The final discovery was when Ball produced, from a laundry basket hidden in the attic, the pillow from his mother's bed and the missing rug, both bloodstained.

On the 21st he was arrested, and charged with murdering his mother. In answer he said, 'I do not feel like saying anything at the moment.' He was at the time injured, as will be recounted later, and was not in a fit condition to say very much, but he asked, as he had done once or twice before, if his mother's body had been recovered yet, and was told it had not. His answers to Reynolds and Dunleavy had been recorded in a written statement; on the day before his arrest he made a second and much longer statement, which will be referred to in due course.

The Trial

The trial aroused enormous public interest, and many were un-able to get in to the Court, waiting hopefully outside during the six days the case was at hearing, one of these days being Ball's twentieth birthday. The trial began on 18 May 1936, the late Mr Justice Henry Hanna, K.C., presiding. For the prosecution were Mr Martin Maguire, S.C. (later Mr Justice Martin Maguire, of the Supreme Court) and Mr Kevin Haugh (later Mr Justice Haugh, S.C., of the High Court), Mr John M. Fitzgerald, K.C., and Mr Seán Hooper defended.

When Ball was called on to plead, he seemed almost cheerful, and answered 'Not guilty' with perfect calm. As the jury were being called, two were excused duty, one saying he had known Mrs Ball, and the other that he was a patient of Dr Ball's. The evidence then began and the events already described were proved. Next, the jury heard of the relations between mother and son.

A maid who had formerly worked for Mrs Ball described a morning in 1935 when Ball was living in St Helen's Road. As she

159

walked up the road she could hear screams coming from Mrs Ball's bedroom, and when she got upstairs Ball was in the room and his mother was in bed, hysterical. She screamed at the witness to take him out of the room and keep him away from her all day. He left, saying he did not wish to torment her. A week later there was another scene, this time in the kitchen, during which Mrs Ball threatened him with an electric iron. He said nothing and went out of the kitchen; later there were more angry words. Mrs Ball was frequently hysterical with the witness too, shouting unnecessarily at her. In September 1935, on a Saturday, there was another quarrel, and Mrs Ball told her son he must leave on the following Monday, and she would give him an allowance of £1 a week. When tempers had cooled he said he was sorry, putting his arm around her shoulders, but she shook him off. There were many occasions of angry words, always from Mrs Ball, who accused her son of laziness and told him to get a job. As another witness put it, she used to lash him with her tongue. He had never answered back or threatened her.

Mrs Ball's secretary told the same story, and said the quarrels had a very disturbing effect on her employer, who was highly strung. She, too, had never heard Edward threaten her; only once had he answered her back, saying, 'Ah! Mother, do stop!' She heard her more than once ordering him out of a room, and he always obeyed. Lily Kelly also gave evidence of quarrels, and, like the other two witnesses, had never heard Ball answer back or threaten her. Several of Mrs Ball's women friends, however, painted a different picture, saying that she was a cheerful normal woman, and that they had often seen signs of affection between mother and son, but she was inclined to be irritable in his company. Other witnesses told the Court that in November 1935 Mrs Ball had had a nervous breakdown and was in a nursing-home until December, when she again went back to live at Booterstown. Ball returned to live in the house with her on 13 February and she said she did not want him, and that he could not stay.

The events of the 17th were then narrated. The secretary said she worked with Mrs Ball until the afternoon, She and her employer and Ball had lunch together in the house, and Mrs Ball was cheerful and amicable. The two women left in the car at about 4 p.m. and went in to Dublin on business, after which they parted, Mrs Ball returning to Booterstown at about 5.15 p.m., when she changed her shoes and put on slippers. Lily Kelly was there, and Mrs Ball had bought parcels of food and other necessaries for the

160

luncheon party next day. She said mother and son were friendly all day, and she left at 6 p.m. having, as usual, put a hot-water bottle into Mrs Ball's bed. Ball was then in the house. Richard Mates, gardener and odd-job man, related that at about 6 p.m. he chopped some firewood with a hatchet which was always kept in an outhouse. He put it into a tea-chest in the outhouse when he had finished, spoke to Mrs Ball, and then left.

The time was now five past six and the house contained only mother and son. At about 7.10 a postman came up the road and saw that No. 23, for which he had a registered letter, was in darkness. He passed on, and about ten minutes later, noticing a light in the garage, rang; after a few minutes Ball opened the hall door and signed for the letter. The two spoke, and Ball seemed perfectly normal. The postman had often before delivered registered letters at that house, and Mrs Ball always took them. At about 8.30 the occupier of the adjoining house, Mr Gregory, saw someone very like Ball on the front path of No. 23, opening the garden gates. It was then raining and continued to rain for several hours. Nothing unusual was heard that evening by the occupiers on either side of No. 23, from which raised voices had often been heard before. At midnight the occupier of No. 21 was out in his front porch and saw that the curtains in Mrs Ball's room were drawn, and that the light was on, visible through a chink.

At 1 a.m. a motorist driving to Dublin was signalled at the top of Corbawn Lane, where it joins the Dublin-Bray Road, by a young man wanting a lift. It was Ball, who asked to be brought in to Ballsbridge, a suburb nearer to Dublin than Booterstown. The motorist put him down at Ailesbury Road, where he said he was staying. They exchanged names, the motorist, Mr Tanham, giving his visiting-card, and Ball saying his name was Winter or Winton, that he was from Tunbridge Wells, and was staying in Ireland for a short while. He was next seen at 7.30 a.m., when another postman called at the house with registered letters, for which Ball signed. He was then in pyjamas.

Lily Kelly described arriving at 8.30 a.m. on the 18th; the hall door key was not under the mat as usual, and she came in by the side door, which, contrary to custom, was unlocked. The kitchen floor was covered with water and there was water also on the stair carpet; a broken cup lay on the draining-board. When she went to Mrs Ball's room to call her it was locked, but that was usual when Ball was staying there. There was no answer to her knock, and she spoke to Ball, who was in his bedroom, asking where his mother

161

was. He said she had stayed the night with a friend, and would be back in time for the luncheon party at 1 o'clock. She wanted to know who had spilled the water and he said he did not know, but thought he might have spilt what was on the stairs. After breakfast he came down ready to go out, wearing a different suit from the day before. He asked her to clean his shoes, but she couldn't as they were so wet. Ball took a suitcase when he was leaving, and his hat, which she noticed was wet. As he was going he said, 'Goodbye. I hope you enjoy the party,' referring to the luncheon. During the morning a card arrived from one of the guests saying she would be unable to come; the other arrived at 1 o'clock, but went away when she was told Mrs Ball was not at home.

Ball came back about 6 o'clock, without the suitcase. Lily Kelly told him his mother had not returned and that detectives had called, to whom she had mentioned the suitcase. He asked her why, saying that they would come to all sorts of conclusions about it. He also said it was a terrible thing that he was the last person to see his mother alive. She was asked in her evidence about the hatchet, which she said she had often used, and that it was missing on the 18th. She had looked everywhere for it. A Garda had found the hatchet a day or two later in a search of the outhouse and garden. He told the Court of finding bloodstains on the flower bed and the path that led to the shed where Mates had put the hatchet on the 17th; it was not, however, in the chest but in a box underneath it, and there were bloodstains on the blade.

The Gardaí had traced some motorists who were in Corbawn Lane on the 17th, and two of these gave evidence. One had driven his car up to the barrier at about 9.45 p.m., and there was no other car there then. Ten minutes later a small saloon drew up behind his — it was the baby Austin — and about twenty minutes after that a third car came and stopped behind it. The third car did not stay long, and the driver gave what turned out to be gruesome evidence, for he saw a man in the back of the small saloon with his arm around someone whom he could not see. The man was, in fact, Ball. The first motorist left at about 11.45 p.m., and the small saloon car then appeared to be empty.

The reader may be excused if he has not noticed an important omission in the prosecution's case so far. There was much evidence of blood, and of attempts by Ball to conceal bloodstained articles, and there were his false statements. It was all very suspicious, of course, but it was not evidence of murder. The body had never been found, despite the most exhaustive search by the Gardaí, who had dragged the sea, and dug wherever they thought it might be concealed. Even the military had joined in with aircraft.

But, contrary to popular belief, a body is not an essential proof in a murder trial; what was missing from the prosecution's case was evidence of death, which is an essential proof. Ball, the last person to see his mother alive, had in his first written statement only said she had disappeared, which did not mean necessarily that she was dead; the blood could have been due to violence, or even a serious accident. But he had, as already narrated, made a second statement, and it contained the evidence of death, and upon it and certain other evidence the case for murder rested. The defence did their best to keep out this statement, but the objections were overruled, and so the jury heard Ball's second story. It was an astonishing one. Just before he began his statement to Superintendent O'Reilly, Ball had taken from his shoe a key, which he handed to the Superintendent. It was the key to his mother's bedroom.

He started with Thursday, the 13th, and explained why he had come to live at St Helen's Road; he mentioned the note from his mother which she had left for him on the 14th and not, as might have been supposed, on the 17th. On the 14th she was upset and depressed, not wanting him to stay, and asking him to go to his father or find another flat. He told her his father didn't want him and that he could not afford a flat on his total allowances of £2 10s. a week. Despite this talk they were friendly, and the succeeding days passed without incident.

On Monday, after the maid and gardener had left, the two had supper together at about 6.15 p.m. She was worried about certain details to do with the luncheon party, upset about a cup which he had accidentally broken, and she was also depressed. She talked of her failure in life and in marriage, and of her fear that he too would be a failure. She said life was hopeless and that she wished she was dead; but he sympathised with her, and she brightened a little. After the meal she became distraught again and wept a lot. She was about to go upstairs when she said, 'I want you to promise me something. I want you to promise me that you will do all you can to prevent people thinking I am a coward.' Despite her distress, he did not think the request was of significance, or seriously meant. She went upstairs then and he cleared the table, and waited for her to come down. After about twenty minutes or so — it was now about 7 p.m. — she was still upstairs, and he went to see what was delaying her.

He knocked at the bedroom door, got no reply, and opened it. The light was on, and to his horror his mother was lying on the bed with blood streaming from her neck. She was on her back, arms by her side, and her neck was cut on the right side in more than one place; her cheek was also cut. There was a double-edged razor-blade beside her right hand on the bed, and the bed-clothes covered her as far as her waist; sheets and pillow were covered with blood. He felt her heart, and there was no sign of life, and, remembering her last words to him, he was aghast. His first impulse was to get help, but then he felt he must conceal the fact of her suicide.

After that, he said, he worked 'like a machine'. The body could not be concealed in the house, so he decided to put it into the car. He removed his jacket, lifted her under the arms, and pulled her out of bed; she fell on the floor, and a lot of blood spilled on the carpet. He grabbed a towel to staunch the bleeding, and removed the black coatee she was wearing. Then he lifted her so that the head and upper part of the body were resting on his shoulders, and carried her down, through the hall and kitchen, and into the garage. He opened the passenger door of the car and put the body into the back. Then he went upstairs, changed his shirt and collar, locked her bedroom door, and took the key.

Downstairs again, he put on a hat, opened the garage door and garden gates, and tried to start the car. He had not driven for some years and did not know how to get it going, so he pushed it on to the road, knocking a wing against the gate-post, a fact which was confirmed afterwards by traces of green paint found on the wing. He got the engine going finally, and drove in by the coast towards Dublin; after a mile or two he turned inland and joined the Bray Road, went to Shankill, and down Corbawn Lane. He stopped the car at the barrier, which he had not expected to meet, got out, and walked down to the sea, came back, sat in the car again for a long time — at least an hour, he said, but it was nearer two — till the other cars had left. He was then alone at the barrier, and the hour was midnight.

The macabre and horrific nature of this adventure is heightened when one realises just what Ball had done, and recalls the surroundings. He had spent nearly four hours in a small car alongside the dead body of his mother and, if the motorist behind him was right, had sat for some of the time with his arm around the body. Then, the surroundings: the pitch darkness; the heavy rain; the utter solitude; the midnight hour; the overhanging trees; the lonely sea ahead; and the blood. The profound silence alone must have been unnerving; perhaps there was a faint sound from the waves breaking on the shore. There would be no light save from the head-lamps, and it is unlikely he used them: he needed darkness for the final stage of his fearful undertaking.

He went on to describe getting out of the car and studying the barrier. To its right was a narrow footpath, and to the right of that was a sloping bank of earth and vegetation. He decided that the car could be got through the opening and, as he didn't know how to reverse, pushed it back a little. Then he got in and drove towards the narrow space, but failed to get through, and the car stuck fast between bank and barrier. Had he been a more skilful driver, he could undoubtedly have got through by running the right-hand wheels up on the lower part of the bank; if this had succeeded, he could then have been well on the way to the perfect murder — if murder it was. For, if he could have got the car down to the fourteen-foot drop and put it into the sea after the body, by the time the car was discovered all traces of blood would have been washed away, and the body would have been taken out to sea. He could have counted on perhaps twenty-four hours before someone chanced to go down to the beach in daylight in the cold February weather, and even then they might not have noticed the car in the water, whereas at the barrier the discovery of the car next morning was inevitable. So, if he had got the car through, all he needed to do then was to clean up properly in St Helen's Road. After that he might have been safe.

However, the car stuck and he took out his mother's body and pulled it down the pathway to the sea. The imagination boggles at this feat in the eerie surroundings, but Ball did it. He said he was not sure how he held her, but it was by her legs at one stage and her arms at another. At the sea he waded in up to his ankles and left the body in the water, getting some sand into one of his cuts as he did so, which hurt him. He did not cast the body over the fourteen-foot drop, but must have scrambled with it over a rough and broken surface down to shore level — in itself a difficult feat even in daylight. He dropped the razor-blade into the water also, having brought it, wrapped in newspaper, from the bedroom.

165

It was proved at the trial that the tide was out at the time, high water having been at 7 p.m., and was due to turn at 1 a.m., but it had been a neap tide, which meant that low water was four-and-a-half feet above normal, making it easier for him to dispose of the body. Ball then came back to the car and opened the door and sunshine roof — to get rid of the smell of blood, as he said. Then he walked back to the main road, where he got the lift from the motorist. When he reached home he started 'frantically' to clean up, removing bloodstains from kitchen and garage with hot water. He tried to wash the blood from the bedroom carpet, but failed, as it had soaked through to the floor-boards, and he put on the electric fire to dry it up. The he packed the bloodstained bed-clothes and other things into the suitcase, put clean sheets and pillow on his mother's bed, and after having switched off the light, locked the room. He went to bed then — it was 4.30 a.m. — and two hours later got up, without having slept. He hid the rug and pillow in the laundry basket, tried to remove bloodstains from the stair carpet, and went back to bed again, till the maid came at 8.45 a.m. At the end of the statement he was asked about the hatchet and said he knew nothing about it.

———————

How much of Ball's story was true? All of it, from the moment when he hoisted his mother's body on to his back and set out on his nightmare journey. The route from bedroom to garage was marked with blood; there was some in the car and more at the barrier. From barrier to sea there was a trail, marked by minute evidence discovered after a close scrutiny by Gardaí: tiny tufts of the dead woman's hair, a hair-pin with a strand of hair attached, small fragments of red fabric similar to that in the garment belonging to Mrs Ball, blood, and a red-stained stone. Ball's trouser-ends were stained with sea-water and blood; his shoes were soaked with sea-water and covered with sand and mud, and his other clothing, as related, was extensively bloodstained. The surface of the lane showed no scoring or mark made by the dragging of the body, but that was explained by an experiment conducted by two muscular Gardaí. One pulled the other, who lay inert, along the grisly route, an operation which took eight minutes; the inert one was wearing shoes, and his heels left only a light trail which a few hours of rain would easily have washed away. As Mrs Ball's slippers were at home, her feet must have been unshod, and therefore left no trail.

166

So, that part of the story was corroborated. Was the story of the suicide true? No, said the prosecution, and this was one of the two points of controversy at the trial. Although the body was missing, there was a lot of other evidence: Ball's statement of the manner of death, the hair found in Corbawn Lane and more hair found on the coatee — all proved to be Mrs Ball's from a comparison with hairs on her hair-brush — and the bloodstained bedroom carpet. From these facts, and from experiments conducted by the State Pathologist, Dr John McGrath, the prosecution were able to advance the theory of murder by violence.

The carpet was a vital piece of evidence, and was brought into Court for the jury to see. The staining was such that about three to four pints of blood must have spilled on it, whereas the bed-clothes showed only about a tenth or a fifth of a pint. The extensive bleeding on the floor, said the pathologist, suggested that Mrs Ball had died there, and not on the bed, unless she had either been placed on it afterwards, or had struggled to it with her last gasp. The latter was a remote possibility, as her strength would have been exhausted, and she could not have pulled up the bed-clothes, as Ball said he had seen them.

Microscopic examination of the hair tufts showed that they had been either cut or chopped, and Dr McGrath's experiments on other hair with a razor-blade, and with a hatchet, showed that chopping had been more likely. He considered it would have been very difficult for the dead woman to have cut her throat with the razor-blade, a difficult feat, only one in twenty attempts at which ever succeeded. She would have had to make several strong and deter-mined cuts through the side of the neck to the depth of half an inch, through the jugular vein, for there had been no arterial bleeding, as was shown by the absence of any sign of spurting blood in the room. The hair could not have been cut or chopped if the wound had been on the side of the neck, unless Mrs Ball had with one hand held out her hair to offer the necessary resistance, a highly unlikely possibility.

Death, in his opinion, had not been caused by bleeding. If it had, the post-mortem bleeding could not have been so extensive as appeared from the blood on the towel, for most of the blood would have left the body before it was put into the car. He thought the hair was cut, or chopped, by the edge of the hatchet meeting the skull at the back of the head and neck — he had experiment-ed with a hatchet on a corpse — and that post-mortem bleeding had come from one of the large blood-vessels and not from the

167

skull. The hatchet bloodstains were slight and had been wiped, not washed, and from this he was able to show, by experiment with another hatchet and some blood, that the quantity of blood originally on the hatchet in St Helen's Road was small. This was to be expected, he said, as lethal weapons rarely showed substantial quantities of blood.

The prosecution, of course, contended that disposal of the body could not have achieved Ball's alleged purpose, namely concealment of his mother's suicide, for if the body was never found suicide would be assumed, and if it was found the injuries Ball said he saw would show, beyond doubt, that it was suicide. The disposal could only be for one purpose: to conceal murder. As for his alleged fondness for his mother, he could never have treated her dead body so callously if that were true. 'Was there a single tear from Ball for his mother's death?' asked Mr Maguire as he opened the case, and answered the question by saying that he could find nothing in the nature of regret in the evidence. What was the motive for murder? Money, said the prosecution, for Ball was a beneficiary under his mother's will and was unable to live on the allowances he was receiving from his parents.

The jury now heard of something which had occurred on 21 February at St Helen's Road. Ball had not yet been arrested, but was being closely watched; at about 1.30 p.m. he was writing letters and told a Garda he wished to go upstairs to the lavatory. The two went up and Ball tried to lock himself inside the lavatory, but was prevented by the Garda. While he waited outside the Garda heard a suspicious noise, opened the door, and saw Ball's heels disappearing through the window. He ran down and found him lying on the ground below, dazed and concussed.

He did not seem to know what had happened, and several times asked for his father and mother. He was brought inside, put to bed, and later removed to hospital, where he was found to have fractured a vertebra in his neck. Two letters sticking out of his jacket pocket were taken possession of by a Garda, one addressed to Dr Ball and the other to the Coroner and both dated of that day. To his father he wrote that he would never see him again, apologised for any trouble he had caused, and expressed affection, and said he had loved his mother and she had loved him. After some directions for the disposal of his personal effects, he concluded:

168

'The events of the last few days have been unbearable and I claim the right to take my own life.' To the Coroner he said he had no wish to live after the recent nerve-racking events, and that he was going to join his mother, whom he loved.

Ball's attempt to end his life failed, for his injuries were not serious and he soon recovered. It was his second attempt; the jury heard later from the defence of the first one. But he had spoken of suicide in January 1936. His former co-tenant told the Court that Ball was moody and easily depressed and upset, and had threatened to kill himself by taking a quantity of aspirin tablets. Although Ball had spoken seriously, the witness treated the matter jocularly, and said he would only make himself sick. Another witness, however — the caretaker of the flat — described Ball quite differently and said he was light-hearted and cheerful, often sang, and never showed any sign of depression.

The prosecution ended with expert evidence from the Dublin Harbour Master, on the effect of the tides on a floating body put into the sea at Shankill. His opinion was that at low water it would be carried out clear of Dublin Bay and would set towards the Welsh coast; even if it drifted south after entering the sea, it would still set towards Wales, and in any case would almost certainly be carried out to sea from the Bay. He also mentioned the possibility of a passing steamer severing the body, in which case it would sink immediately. This opinion was confirmed by an experiment carried out by the Gardaí, who had put seven oildrums attached to crates into the sea at Corbawn Lane. Three floated out a short way and were washed back to the shore; the other four went out to sea, and two were recovered, one from the coast at Wicklow about twenty miles to the south, and the other six weeks later from Ramsay Island in Wales. The other two were never recovered.

The Defence

It was now Mr Fitzgerald's turn, and after applying unsuccessfully to have the case withdrawn from the jury he opened the defence. It was in two parts: first, of course, that Mrs Ball had committed suicide, and secondly, if the jury did not accept suicide, that Ball was insane. He spoke at length on the suicide, saying that Mrs Ball was a most likely subject for it, specially that night, as she had been contemplating the ruin of her life and her marriage, and her attempts, as he said, to ruin her son's life. The 'queer, mad, excitable lady' he called her. While Mr Fitzgerald was speaking, Ball wept more than once.

Ball did not give evidence, and the first witness was Dr Dockeray, a pathologist, who disagreed with Dr McGrath on four matters. He told of a case where hair cut with a razor looked as if it had been cut with a blunt instrument, but agreed that that was exceptional. He thought it quite possible that Mrs Ball had cut her throat with a razor-blade. The Judge produced one at this point and handed it down to the witness, asking if he thought she could have cut her throat with it and bled so profusely on the carpet, and he reiterated his opinion. After all, she might have been the successful one in twenty. He said it was quite possible that she had got to the bed after losing half her life's blood on the carpet, and that she could have covered herself with the bedclothes. He instanced cases where suicides had, after exsanguination, performed quite remarkable feats of strength considering their condition, but he admitted that it was unlikely, though possible, that she would have taken the blade to the bed with her. He had to agree that the evidence was compatible with her having been struck down by violence, and that the hairs could have been cut with a hatchet. He disagreed that the amount of blood shown to have been on the hatchet before wiping was consistent with its use; if it was the weapon, it should have had more blood originally.

The defence called two doctors on the insanity issue. One, a well-known Dublin psychiatrist, had seen Ball in hospital and considered he was mentally abnormal, gravely so, had a foolish and immature outlook, and was irrational. He seemed not to understand the seriousness of being charged with murdering his mother, and appeared indifferent to her death. He was suffering from dementia praecox — congenital adolescent insanity — in a grave monomaniacal or paranoidal form. The other doctor, a London psychiatrist, had seen Ball in 1932, when he was consulted by Dr Ball about him, and gave evidence to the same effect. Ball, he said, was weak-minded and morally deficient, and spoke readily and cheerfully about suicide, the seriousness of which he did not seem to appreciate. The prison doctor was called by the prosecution to rebut this evidence, and said he had seen no sign of insanity in Ball, but that his history confirmed that he was a case of adolescent instability.

Dr Ball now gave evidence, and when he came to the box his son buried his face in his hands and wept. He had an unhappy story to tell; he married in 1902, and in 1903, at the birth of their first child, he noticed signs of mental instability in his wife. He was asked to describe her, and paused. 'I don't like saying anything against her,' he said. The Judge said he understood, but that the evidence had to be given. Dr Ball then said that the signs of mental disorder had gradually got worse with time. She had been extremely neurotic, had had several nervous breakdowns, suffered from sustained periods of depression, and would remain completely silent for days, speaking to no one. At other times she would nag and complain for days at a stretch. Her behaviour to him was extraordinary. She insulted him in the presence of his patients, and met patients at the door, advising them not to consult him as he was useless as a doctor. She told her friends terrible lies about him, and several times had induced people to telephone him to go to the country for visits to non-existent patients.

In 1927 he had been forced to part from her and they had lived separately ever since. He took Edward, sent him to an English public school, and kept him for holidays. He would not allow the boy to be with his mother, whose attitude to their son was similar to her attitude to him: violent and nagging at one moment, and the opposite a moment later. Her temper was uncontrollable and violent, and he was convinced she had suicidal tendencies, for there were two cases of suicide in her family and one of insanity. She had frequently stolen things from him — she was a kleptomaniac. When he heard from detectives on the 18th that she was missing, he thought it was another trick of hers to persecute him.

He told the jury about his son's first attempt at suicide, at the age of thirteen. He had been called one night and found the boy in a distressed condition, having taken either twenty-five or fifty aspirin tablets, he could not say which. Dr Ball had used a stomach pump, and no harm was done. He had no idea why his son had tried to kill himself; that evening they had been the best of friends.

The problem of a career for Edward was very difficult, for he had no aptitude for study and no ambition, talking of almost every conceivable occupation, many of which were wholly unsuitable. Dr Ball's wife was complaining at this time that he was depriving the boy of mother-love, so he allowed her to take him during school holidays. But she showed no sense of responsibility or control over him and allowed him to idle about, regardless of the future. Edward was now wholly indifferent as to what his future was to be. He had had leanings towards the stage, and his mother wanted him to be trained in a leading London academy. Dr Ball refused his consent, as he considered the stage a most unsuitable occupation, since the avoidance of an exciting atmosphere was imperative in view of Edward's mental condition, about which he had sought medical advice. Mrs Ball then encouraged the boy to train in a Dublin theatre. At one time Dr Ball had considered placing him under restraint, but his wife would not hear of it. The boy had never expressed ill-will towards his mother, complaining only of her nagging.

Dr Ball had last spoken to his wife about six months before her death. They corresponded occasionally, when necessary, and once in the street she had handed him a letter saying she feared everybody, and the future, and had a presentiment of an approaching tragedy which she hoped would not involve the boy. The letter, said Dr Ball, was typical of her neurotic disposition.

Mrs Ball's personal physician, a woman, was the last witness. She said the dead woman was extremely excitable, nervous, and subject to frequent fits of depression, and that worry might lead to her suicide. She confirmed Dr Ball's statement that his wife was a kleptomaniac, for she had more than once missed money from her handbag when Mrs Ball was present. She had watched, and three times saw her actually taking money.

The summing up was not unfavourable and showed that Ball's unhappy life and homelessness had aroused the Judge's sympathy. 'Most pathetic', he called his plight when he had to give up the co-tenancy of his flat and was without a home, unwanted by his mother, and by his father too. Of the suicide story, the Judge remarked that the description of Mrs Ball on her bed with the razor-blade beside her was very convincing, and was either true or the invention of a very powerful imagination. As to his falsehoods, the jury had to decide whether he had lied in his own interest or in his mother's. In his favour, said the Judge, was the fact that his second statement was made within forty-eight hours of the death, when, for all he knew, the body might have been found at any moment. The summing-up finished with a reference to the duality of Mrs Ball's nature, her charm and good humour with her friends, and her neurosis and irritability when with son or husband. The Judge thought that if her mind became unbalanced she might well have committed suicide.

The jury retired at 12.30 p.m. to consider which of the three possible verdicts they would bring in: not guilty, guilty, or guilty

172

but insane. They had no easy task, and after four hours came back requesting the recall of some witnesses. The foreman asked Lily Kelly if she had ever seen Mrs Ball using a razor-blade, and was told not. A police witness was asked if any safety razor or blades were in Ball's room. The hairdresser was asked to say how long Mrs Ball's hair was, and answered that it reached to her elbow. It looked as if the jury were examining the suicide story with some care, and Ball brightened a little as he listened to the questions.

They retired again and took another hour, and at 5.20 came back. Ball studied their faces closely as they filed into the jury box, and the tension in Court was extreme as the registrar stood up and inquired if they were agreed on their verdict. The foreman nodded and handed over the issue paper; it was given to the Judge, who broke the silence by announcing that the jury had found Ball guilty, but insane. He had hardly finished speaking when a girl burst into loud sobbing, and had to be helped out. She had been in Court all through the trial and had been seen smiling at Ball each day. He seemed startled by the result and stared at the Judge for a moment with his hands clasped. Then he heard the Judge's direction that he be detained during the pleasure of the Governor-General and went down from the dock with the warders, one hand to his head.

Ball was, perhaps, fortunate in the verdict, though the medical evidence and his family history were ample justification of the finding of insanity. His youth too must have helped him, and despite his terrible crime the jury, like the Judge, may have felt sympathy because of his unhappy life.

But what really happened in St Helen's Road that night? A sudden loss of the control Ball had always shown in quarrels with his mother — a brainstorm? One wonders, because if the hatchet was the weapon, it had to be fetched from outside, which would take a couple of minutes at least — time enough for him to cool down and reflect upon what he was contemplating, unless he was in the grip of uncontrollable forces. He had certainly cooled down afterwards, for the disposal of the body, the concealment of the bloodstained clothing, and his first story to the police showed no want of coolness or intelligence.

Was it a planned murder executed with the weapon in readiness? The use of a hatchet may have been in Ball's mind beforehand,

173

for in November 1935 the theatre with which he was associated played a dramatised version of Dostoevsky's novel, *Crime and Punishment*. In the novel, an old pawnbroker and her sister are murdered with an axe; the murder was not staged, but was of course, part of the plot. Ball did not appear in the play, but his co-tenant had a part in it.

Or was it really a case of suicide? Only the sea could have told, and it never did.

9.

The Man With Eight Aliases
(The People v. James H. Lehman, 1944, 1945)

HE was a likeable person, a good and persuasive talker who, without boasting, subtly gave the impression that he was of more consequence than appeared. He charmed almost everyone he met, especially women, who found him very attractive and whose company he enjoyed. His appearance helped: he was tall, good looking, wore a dark moustache, and occasionally glasses.

His real name is still not known. When he first joined the Canadian Army he was calling himself William Martin; in 1939 he took the name James Herbert Lehman, but he had used others in between, among them James Richman and James Hiames.

According to his own evidence, James Lehman was born in Montreal in 1899, educated in Pennsylvania, and in 1916 joined the Canadian Army, from which he was discharged, so he said, as unfit from brain fever; but this is unlikely, as he joined the American Army in 1917 and was discharged on medical grounds with a disability pension of sixty-two dollars a month. Back again in civil life he held various jobs, and in 1925 took a diploma in a law school in Philadelphia. He married in 1933; three years later his wife divorced him. In 1939 he rejoined the Canadian Army, as a private, and was posted to Britain and stationed at Aldershot in 1940. There he met Margaret Hayden from Ireland, who worked in the NAAFI canteen, and they married in February 1940. At Christmas she became ill, and when he could not get leave to visit her he absented himself without leave, and was a deserter until 7 February, when he surrendered himself, and was sentenced to ninety days detention. He had injured his back while on manoeuvres, and in January 1942 was discharged unfit from the Canadian Army. He served in the Home Guard in England for a while after that. It was certainly true that he was married to Margaret Hayden; in August 1943 she brought their two children to live in Ireland. All four lived at his wife's home in County Kildare until

October, when he was referred to a British Military Pensioners' Hospital in Dublin for treatment for his back. His wife and children joined him when he left hospital in early December; at first they lived in a small hotel, but soon moved to furnished rooms nearby belonging to the owner of the hotel. By Christmas Lehman was destitute, and had to sell some of his personal belongings, and it was only owing to the generosity of the hotelier that his family had any Christmas dinner. The hotelier's wife later described Mrs Lehman, who was then pregnant, as an unhappy little person, quiet and unassuming; Lehman, in his talkative way, had told her his marriage was unhappy — 'a war marriage' — one of his few truthful statements. In January 1944 he decamped, owing a substantial bill, moving family to furnished rooms in Leinster Road, Rathmines, a south Dublin suburb. They had a bedroom at the top of the house and a kitchen on the floor below with a sink on the landing.

He had to set about making a living, and he very soon succeeded in charming about £225 from people he had met since coming to Dublin, with which he opened a shop for baby foods in Ranelagh, not far from Leinster Road. He employed three women assistants, one of whom was a Miss Finucane. The business lasted for about a month and the stock had then to be sold off, but Lehman kept the premises and, using the trade name 'Leigh' opened a retail coffee business. His idea of commerce was rudimentary in the extreme, for a shop selling only coffee in a small Dublin suburb could not possibly have survived for long. It was failing by the second week in March, and Lehman started to look for another shop, this time in Dun Laoghaire, the well-known coastal resort outside Dublin city.

During his stay in the Military Hospital, Lehman became friendly with one of the staff, Nurse McCaigue. He told her about his married life, and how he had recently discovered that his marriage was void: his wife, he said, was already married to a man named Stokes when she went through the form of marriage with him. He spoke slightingly of her and said they were separated, and that she had gone back to England, and only returned to Ireland when he was in hospital.

After Lehman left hospital he and Nurse McCaigue met occasionally and she introduced him to some of her friends. He never told her that he was living with his wife, but after a short time Nurse McCaigue said she wished to end the friendship. Lehman seemed annoyed at this, but soon afterwards told her (untruthfully) that he had bought an expensive ring. Why, she asked, had he bought it — they were no more than friends? He said he had been deceived once before, but this time knew he had met a decent girl. Later she learned he was starting in business, with wonderful prospects as described by him. He suggested she should resign from her hospital post, and offered her the position of supervisor when, as he intended, he had opened a chain of shops. He promised her the use of his car for her work, though he did not own one; he said he had bought and sold at a profit a similar shop elsewhere in the city, which was also untrue. She put up £25 for a share in the business.

He talked later of his wife and said that she — whom he called Mrs Stokes — and her husband were now living in Dublin, and that he had heard she was in hospital as a result of an overdose of aspirins. It was no concern of his, he said, Stokes could look after her. Lehman spoke also of his future and said he needed someone to look after him, and proposed at one stage that his and Nurse McCaigue's shares in the shop be amalgamated. But she was somewhat more realistic than he; she said she would have to know more about him before that could be considered. He offered to bring her to see the Stokeses, who would confirm that he was telling the truth, but this bluff was never called.

Lehman gave Miss Finucane an equally false account of business. When she answered his advertisement offering employment, he said he was the manager of the shop owned by a firm with a chain of shops in America and England which was opening a branch in Ireland for the first time. She could not afford the £50 security he asked for, but she gave him £40 and he said he would ask the 'directors' to accept it. What was to be secured is not clear. Later, evidently forgetting his story about the 'directors', he told her Nurse McCaigue was the real owner of the business and had invested £300 in it. He intended to marry her, he said, probably in June. He described the ring, saying that it cost £300, and repeated the story about his wife and her real husband Stokes. He added that his wife was unbalanced, and that he had been pressed to marry her by the Canadian Army authorities, who insisted on this after he and some 'fellow officers' had been on a drinking bout. He concealed from Miss Finucane that he was in fact living with his wife. At about this time he mentioned she was taking poison, and was ill. Some of his pretences were extraordinary. One day his wife and Mrs O'Callaghan, his landlady, came into the shop, and he told Miss Finucane that the latter, whom in fact he saw daily, was a stranger to him; he said that the other woman, who was in fact his wife, was his 'ex-lady-love'; later he referred to her as the only person he had ever hated.

Early in March, Lehman called on a chemist he knew with a shop near Leinster Road. The chemist inquired how the coffee business — then on its last legs — was going, and Lehman said it was going very well. He wanted, he said, to get some cyanide to test the bottled coffee for sugar, as he was anxious that his stock should be of the best quality and not contain any impurities. The chemist asked what the test was, and Lehman explained that a small portion of cyanide, mixed with coffee and water, would show the sugar content. The chemist had no cyanide in stock, but a few days later sold him a crystal of cyanide weighing about 150 grains. The fatal dose is anything from about 2 to 5 grains. Lehman brought the cyanide to his shop, and in the presence of the assistants flaked it into powder on to a sheet of paper and then transferred it to a small bottle. He explained to the girls that it was an acid for testing bottled coffee, a deadly poison, and he took great care to clean the scissors used in the flaking operation. When one of the girls asked if the poison was hard to get he said yes, but 'there are ways'.

On Sunday 19 March Mrs Lehman, whose confinement was now imminent, was up and about as usual, quite well save for a cold. That evening at about 7.20 p.m. Mrs O'Callaghan was in her rooms downstairs when she heard a sound overhead; she went out to the landing and noticed immediately a strong and unusual smell, which she could not describe; it seemed to come from above. She went back to her rooms, and presently Lehman came down with a box which she had lent him. She inquired for Mrs Lehman, and he said she had been feeling giddy; if she wasn't better next morning he would get a nurse and doctor. He went up again, and in five minutes came running down and met her. He was agitated. 'Come quickly! My wife is terribly ill! I brought in some rum for her and she must have taken it.' Mrs O'Callaghan went up, and as she came near the bedroom door heard Mrs Lehman groaning, and found her unconscious in her night clothes. Her face was blue and her forehead clammy. She asked Lehman if his wife had taken any 'dope', meaning aspirin, in the rum; he said he didn't know. He was very distressed, running up and down the room and crying. She went for assistance, and presently an ambulance came. By now Mrs Lehman was purple in the face and deeply unconscious. One of the ambulance men said, when Lehman told him his wife had been in that condition for some hours, that they should have been called much sooner; Lehman said he had tried several of the doctors in the district, but had failed to get one.

On the way to the hospital he asked the driver if she was bad. 'Bad enough,' said the man, and unfortunately proved right, for Mrs Lehman was dead on admission to hospital, as was her baby. When Lehman was told by the doctor that she was dead, he wept and became distressed, and almost dazed. One of his sisters-in-law who worked in the hospital asked what had happened. What had her sister taken? Lehman said she had been having dizzy spells.

While he was out Mrs O'Callaghan again noticed the peculiar smell in the bedroom. She could not identify it, but it was, in fact, almost certainly the smell of bitter almonds, which is the characteristic odour of prussic acid. In the sink on the landing the smell was so strong as to make her gasp, but the kitchenette was free of it. She looked in the bedroom and kitchenette for a bottle, cup, or glass, but could find none.

Lehman returned at 9.30 and told her his wife was dead. He seemed distressed and wept, and said more than once, 'Poor Peg! — I knew she had something on her mind.' He may have thought this sounded convincing, but in fact it was a damaging remark, for it implied suicide by poisoning; yet at the hospital he had been told that the cause of death was not known. He talked for a while longer with Mrs O'Callaghan, mentioning an earlier 'attack' which his wife had had at her own home. Mrs O'Callaghan inquired what the doctor had said about that attack, and he told her his wife had recovered quickly and he had not called a doctor.

Miss Finucane called at Leinster Road later that night, in response to a note from Lehman, and he told her his wife had died. She asked, 'Was it the result of poison?' and he said, 'I am afraid so.' Had he any idea what the poison was? He thought it might have been aspirin. A few days earlier he had told one of the assistants that his wife was taking 'something' again, and on the 17th had said

179

to Miss Finucane that she was rather 'low'. Next morning Miss Finucane called again, at his request, to make some telephone calls for him. They looked through Mrs Lehman's handbag and burnt a few letters, and then went to a public telephone box nearby, where he asked her to ring Nurse McCaigue. The message was somewhat cryptically phrased: 'I am speaking for a friend of yours. There has been a death in the family.' And she was asked to meet Lehman that afternoon. Nurse McCaigue kept the appointment, but Lehman did not, as he was detained at the hospital.

Later that day he called on the chemist and wept when he told him the sad news. The chemist sympathised and asked if Mrs Lehman had been ill. The day before, Lehman said, adding, 'Anyway, she was always taking something and didn't want children.' While he was out, Mrs O'Callaghan went up to the kitchenette and found an empty bottle in a conspicuous place; it had not been there the night before.

That night Sergeant Sheppard of the Gardaí saw Lehman at Leinster Road and told him he was making inquiries and that the doctors were not satisfied about the cause of death. They had suggested that Mrs Lehman might have taken poison or some other irritant. Lehman said, 'She got no poison here,' another damaging remark. The Sergeant searched the rooms and found no drinking-vessels in the bedroom, but the rum bottle was in the kitchenette with a small quantity of rum left in it. Asked what had happened to his wife, Lehman mentioned an influenza attack at Christmas, and that she had a bad cold on the 18th and took some rum with cero-calcium tablets. He described how he had gone out on the 19th at about 3.30 p.m., done some errands, and returned two hours later; Mrs Lehman was then crooning the children to sleep. An hour afterwards he went up to the bedroom again and found her ill.

After the funeral Lehman had another talk with Miss Finucane. She asked him if there would be any further police inquiries — he thought there would. Then he made a rash request: he wished her to tell the police that she knew nothing about his private life, nor whether he was married or single. She protested, 'I cannot and won't tell lies to the police,' and asked, 'What about those acids you were working at in the shop?' He answered, 'I got rid of those a long time ago, and anyway you know nothing about them.'

A day later, when Lehman and his sister-in-law were packing things at Leinster Road, he took his wife's overcoat from the back of the bedroom door and searched it. In a pocket he found a bottle and a crucifix; he began to weep, apparently upset at the find, and wondered why the objects were there. The bottle contained some drops of moisture, and he gave it to his sister-in-law, saying it should go to the Coroner; then he took it back from her. The bottle was, in fact, the one which had contained the flaked cyanide. He mentioned the find to Mrs O' Callaghan later, and added another article — a letter from his wife which he called 'terrible', and said he had burned it for the children's sake.

On the 23rd he called to see Nurse McCaigue. One wonders what kind of reception he thought he would get; in fact it was cool, to say the least, for she had found out the lies he had told about his wife. When he asked her if she had heard about Mrs Stokes's death, she said she knew about Mrs *Lehman's* death. She asked, 'Where is Stokes?' Lehman said, 'If only I could lay my hands on him!' which he may have thought sounded plausible. When Nurse McCaigue expressed surprise that Lehman had gone to the hospital, since he was not the dead woman's husband, his answer was: 'I did no more than anyone else would have done.' She then ended the interview and said their friendship was finished.

Next day he told Miss Finucane that all was over between Nurse McCaigue and himself, and after some further talk left the shop, saying he would be back later. He did not reappear, and she then heard from him by letter dated 29 March, from County Kildare.

DEAR ANNA,

Kevin [*his son*] is very ill, therefore my absence. Will be back on Monday.

Please close the shop or do with it whatever you should like or think best. I am terribly sorry. Will call at your residence when I get back.

Sincerely

JIM

He did not turn up on the Monday, and she closed the shop, disposing of some of the fittings for cash, thus getting back some of her £40, but not all. She next saw him in Court.

Lehman stayed for some days with his wife's people, and of course mentioned the events of the 19th; his story agreed substantially with what he had told Sergeant Sheppard, except for his departure time from the house, which he said was 4.30, and his return, which he placed at 7.30. He also mentioned that his wife did not want to have her baby, said she had had dizzy spells, and that she tried to bring on an abortion by taking some pills given to her by a woman friend. He invented some details; that the dead baby was black — an extraordinary fantasy — and that Inspector Reynolds of the Gardaí had said the bottle in his wife's coat contained foreign poison.

The Gardaí had asked him to call at the Store Street barracks in Dublin, but he had not come; they wanted to see him, however, so he went to Ballytore barracks, near his wife's home, on 2 April. There he made a statement in the presence of Inspector Reynolds and two detectives; it was a very long document, and took over twelve hours to record, with intervals for food, and consisted largely of his life story. The events of the 19th, and other matters which will later be referred to, were included, and he again gave his departure time from the house as 4.30, but could not fix the time of his return. He described the errands he had done while out; he had called at the shop, examined some accounts there, written and posted letters, made some purchases, and had then returned home.

On the 7th, Good Friday, he came to Dublin with his son, leaving behind him an unpaid bill for car hire. He placed the boy in a convent, the younger child having been left in his mother-in-law's care, and then called on Mrs O'Callaghan. As they talked, he asked if she had seen the newspapers, which were featuring his wife's death. She said yes. He remarked, 'Would you not think I had done it?' When he left, he said he was going to stay with his brother-in-law in County Dublin, but he never arrived there. He disappeared.

On Saturday evening 8 April, James McCaigue, an American airman, arrived in Monaghan town from Belfast (he said), and booked into the Oriel Hotel. Monaghan is about eighty miles north-west of Dublin, close to the border between Eire and Northern Ireland, and at that time American servicemen stationed in Northern Ireland occasionally came to stay in the Eire border towns. McCaigue, an agreeable, friendly individual, clean shaven and fairly tall, said he was on sick leave and would be staying a few days. His name was well known in the district, and he claimed relationship with families of that name in various parts of the county. In his chatty way he showed a ring and a lady's wrist-watch to the manageress; they were, he told her, mascots given to him by a war widow to bring him luck when flying.

Next day he left, saying he was going to Belfast and would be back on Friday. But he returned on Wednesday evening, saying that he had got an extension of sick leave. When he was asked to sign the hotel register afresh, he asked, as he was in a hurry to go upstairs, if the manageress would sign for him. She did. He mentioned later that he had forgotten to bring his identity papers to Belfast, and when she asked how he had crossed the border without them, explained that the officials knew him too well to object.

He spoke to a young woman staying in the hotel, and told her he had been born near the town, and was taken to America when only nine months old. He became quite friendly with her and presented her with the ring he had shown the manageress. Another young woman living in the town who lunched daily at the hotel found him equally agreeable; they went to the cinema together, and he gave her some small gifts. He spoke of his life in the Canadian Air Force — obviously a slip of the tongue. He was no less popular in the bars in the town, where he called himself 'Captain Lehman', and struck up various acquaintanceships, telling about his experiences as a bomber pilot and a rear-gunner in a Flying Fortress in raids over Germany and France. He explained that he was now 'grounded' owing to age, and feared he would not fly again. His health, and the good luck in the air which he attributed to his mascots, were toasted more than once. One evening a stranger joined the airman's group and, when introduced, asked to see his identity documents, and was shown an identity card of some sort.

The charming airman who had made such an odd slip of the tongue was, of course, Lehman, who had promoted himself since his disappearance, though only in the bars. He was still McCaigue in the hotel. How long he thought he could maintain a dual identity in a small country town we can only guess, but it was not for long. He was short of money, and when he tried to borrow ten shillings, someone remarked that he had plenty of money in his mouth — a reference to two gold-filled false teeth. He had been drinking quite a lot in the few days of liberty left to him, and it may be wondered how, being so short of money, he was able to give presents. The answer is quite simple: the articles had belonged to his dead wife.

The 'expert tale-teller', as junior prosecuting counsel called him at his trial, had told the truth about going to Belfast. On 12 April, at a recruiting office there, he had applied for enlistment in the Royal Air Force. On the application form he called himself James Joseph Feeley, of the Oriel, Monaghan, using the name of a man who had stayed in the hotel just before his arrival. He told the recruiting officer that he was born in London, was a cook, and had come to Ireland in 1938 with his sister, who had bought a farm near Castleblayney, Monaghan. As he could not produce either a birth certificate or identity papers, which he said were in Monaghan, his application was deferred. The recruiting officer thought him much more intelligent than the average recruit, and said he looked as if he had been drinking heavily.

On the morning of the 14th, Friday, he rang down and asked for breakfast to be served in his room. He may have felt that the trail was growing hot, and not wished to show himself downstairs; he was right, for, unknown to him, he had been shadowed by a detective the day before. While his meal was being prepared, the Gardaí arrived; he was in bed, and they asked his name. 'James McCaigue,' he answered. 'I am an American airman and am now grounded.' By now his gold fillings had disappeared. When he was asked for his identity card he said it was kept at headquarters in Belfast. He was arrested, brought to the Garda Station in the town, and given breakfast and a newspaper to read while his suitcase was being searched.

He had been quite alert, intelligent, and normal in every way, but in half an hour became drowsy and seemingly deaf. This must have been an unconvincing performance, for one of the detectives decided to test it. He spoke to him from behind in a whisper. 'Did you get your cigarettes all right, Lehman?', which made him jump up and say, with no sign of drowsiness, 'Yes, sir, I got them all right.' That was at eleven o'clock; later, still insisting that he was McCaigue, he continued sleepy and deaf.The newspaper that he was reading while he got so suddenly drowsy contained his photograph, and an announcement that the Gardaí wished to interview him. He was asked if he recognised the photograph, and said, 'I never saw the man.' But his attempts to deny his identity were futile. The missing gold-filled teeth were found in his pocket; he said he had never been in Dublin, but two Dublin tram tickets were found in another pocket. He persisted, nevertheless, that he was McCaigue, said that he had never been married, and had no son.

He said nothing in reply when he was brought to Dublin and charged with the murder of his wife. But though his pretence had failed he still managed to give the impression that he did not know his whereabouts, and several witnesses said that during the taking of depositions he seemed a changed man, dazed and stupid. That, however, might have been from a realisation of his peril.

Murder trials always attract large crowds, and Lehman's was no exception. Whether it was because the victim was a woman, or because even in the dock women found him interesting, is a matter of surmise, but day after day women filled the galleries and formed long, hopeful queues outside the Court. Inside, Mr Justice Martin Maguire, S.C., presided, Mr George Murnaghan, S.C. (later Mr Justice Murnaghan, of the High Court) and Mr Felix Sherry prosecuted, and Mr Charles Casey, S.C. (later Mr Justice Casey, of the High Court), and Mr Desmond Bell defended. The trial began on 16 October 1944 and took nine days. The defence was: suicide.

There was little controversy as the prosecution witnesses told the story already narrated; the defence tried to make Miss Finucane and Nurse McCaigue admit that damaging incidents and conversations with Lehman had never taken place. But they remained unshaken. The medical evidence was that Mrs Lehman had died from cyanide poisoning, but the quantity consumed could not be estimated. The doctors explained that prussic acid itself causes almost instant death; the action of cyanide is slower, and depends for its speed on the quantity of hydrochloric acid in the stomach, for the prussic acid in the cyanide is released by the stomach acid acting on it.

Much depended on the possible speed of the action; the State pathologist said that a minute or two only, depending on the quantity consumed, would elapse before the sufferer lost the power to make voluntary movements; but Dr Dockeray, another leading pathologist, said five minutes might elapse, and that after taking the poison Mrs Lehman might have been able to wash out a cup. She had, in fact, lived about fifty-five minutes from the time Mrs O'Callaghan went upstairs. During the cross examination the case of Rasputin was cited: he had taken a number of chocolate cakes and some wine, both heavily doctored with what his murderers believed was cyanide, and suffered no ill effects whatever. The trouble about this story is that it has been suggested that the substance in the food was not cyanide at all, but a harmless substitute supplied by a suspicious chemist — either that or Rasputin must have been supernatural! The doctors agreed that the sudden withdrawal of morphia from an addict — which Lehman was going to swear his wife had been — would produce depression and mental instability and that pregnant women were subject to fits of instability.

When the prosecution came to prove Lehman's long statement to Inspector Reynolds, the defence objected and the jury were sent to their room. Mr Casey then told the Judge that Lehman had been suffering from amnesia — 'a black-out' — when he made the statement, and for some time before and afterwards: if this was true, the statement was not voluntary and so not admissible. Lehman then came down from the dock to prove this, and said he had had a complete loss of memory from about 28 March until the middle of July when he found himself in Mountjoy Prison, where, incidentally, he had been since arrest. This meant that he could not remember making the statement, nor being in Monaghan, nor being in Belfast. In the course of a close cross-examination he told of finding a valedictory letter from his wife in her ration book, in which she said she was going to take poison. That was while he was at her home after the death and was the last thing he could recall, and the suggestion was that the shock of this letter had caused amnesia. When Inspector Reynolds and the other Gardaí gave evidence that Lehman was perfectly normal on 2 April, the Judge, wholly unconvinced by his story, ruled that the statement was admissible and the jury came back to Court.

The statement was then put in and Inspector Reynolds repeated his evidence that on 2 April Lehman was normal and intelligent in every way, and that he seemed dull and stupid in Monaghan barracks. The jury, of course, heard about the whispered remark to Lehman and his reaction to it, and Reynolds said that Lehman claimed not to recognise him or the other two officers, with whom he had spent over twelve hours in Ballytore. When reminded of that occasion he had made no reply. Reynolds asked Lehman if he objected to coming to Dublin, and his answer was, 'No, so long as you don't bring me back to camp,' an authentic touch if Lehman was not acting, and a fairly plausible one if he was.

The prosecution ended their proofs then, and Mr Casey applied to have the case withdrawn from the jury on the ground that it had not been shown that Mrs Lehman had not committed suicide. The Judge refused the application, and so Lehman came for the second time to the witness-box.

The Defence

He began his evidence by an account of his early life and army career, as already narrated. Then he was asked about his wife; he

186

said she was a morphia addict and that in December she threatened that if he could not get supplies for her she would bring about a miscarriage. He tried to get morphia, failed, and when he returned found that his wife was vomiting from taking aspirins in whiskey to satisfy her cravings. He had met an army officer, whom he named, and this man came to their rooms and gave her two injections of morphia.

He then explained his purchase of cyanide. When he started selling coffee, he read an article in the *American News Weekly* describing a method of testing coffee for the purpose of making the bottled article from coffee beans, which disclosed the proportions of sugar and saccharine in bottled coffees. It required a solution of synthetic uric acid and sodium cyanide; he obtained the latter from the chemist and flaked it as already described; he bought the uric acid in a chemist's shop in the city, the name of which he did not know. He brought the powder home, and, after talking with some medical students whom he met in a public-house, carried out the experiment. His wife assisted him, he said, and he told her the cyanide was a deadly poison. He made three or four experiments, but without result, and found he was using too much coffee, and by then he had very little cyanide left, as he had already lost some through the breakage of the bottle in his pocket after leaving the chemist.

At this point the Judge asked him to describe the experiments in detail, so he explained that he had boiled some ground coffee in a saucepan and put it into a jam jar, and added the two acids. There was no reaction whatever, which is not surprising, since the experiments were intended to discover sugar and saccharine reactions in bottled coffee, not ground coffee. However, he went on to say that he discovered his proportions of coffee and cyanide were wrong, and thinking he might be using the wrong acids, consulted some medical students, who confirmed his view as to the proportions. That was all he said about the experiments; they had, seemingly, never been repeated or followed up in any way.

He was then brought to the 19th. That morning, he said, his wife was feeling dizzy, and suffering from a bad cold she had had all the week; after lunch she asked him to bring home some coffee when he was out. Lehman now introduced an entirely new incident into his movements on that afternoon, saying that he went to the flat of a young widow, his next-door neighbour at the shop, and had tea there with her and her children. He got to her flat at about 4 p.m., and left about 7 p.m., getting home about 7.30. This visit was not mentioned in his statement, nor had he disclosed it to anyone to whom he had recounted his movements on that afternoon.

He described finding his wife ill, and the arrival of the ambulance men, and had to explain why he had said his wife was ill for some hours. He said it seemed like hours to him. His remark, 'I am afraid so', in reply to Miss Finucane's question 'Was it the result of poison?' also required an explanation. She had been pressed in cross-examination to say that she had said 'poisoning', and not 'poison', but would not agree, although she had used the former word in her deposition; there was a distinction, of course. But, whichever word she used, Lehman's remark, if made, was very damaging, since he did not know that night, nor did the doctors, what his wife had died from. However, contrary to expectation, there was no explanation; Lehman simply said that he did not discuss his wife's death with Miss Finucane, and that poison was never mentioned that night.

Next day, he said, he tidied up the bedroom and removed a cup and spoon from the bedroom mantelpiece to the kitchenette; it will be recalled that Mrs O'Callaghan had seen no drinking vessel in the bedroom the night before. Then Miss Finucane called. He dealt with her account of what took place by denying that she phoned Nurse McCaigue; he admitted going to the telephone kiosk with her but said that it was to phone his solicitor. He denied opening his wife's handbag in her presence; he also denied that after the funeral he had asked her to say she knew nothing about him; that she had asked him about the acids; and that she had refused to lie to the police. How far the jury could have believed Lehman's denials is very doubtful, but he made many more. He said he did not tell Sergeant Sheppard 'she got no poison here'; he contradicted Miss Finucane's evidence that he had said he was free to marry again, and that his wife had 'taken something' and was admitted to hospital; that he had expressed hatred of his wife or ever called her his 'ex-lady-love'; what he had said was, jocularly, 'ex girl-friend'.

He then dealt with his wife's former marriage, and said he had received a letter from her while she was at her parents' home and he was at the hospital, telling him that she had been already married to a man named Stokes at the time of her marriage to him. After she came to Dublin she introduced him to a man named Larry Dorset, whom he met a second time in the street later on; he learned on 29 March, when he found the letter from his dead wife, that Dorset was in fact really Stokes.

He contradicted his sister-in-law's evidence about the bottle he found in his wife's overcoat; she had said he kept it; he swore that he gave it to her for the Coroner. He said he showed it to a priest, whose advice he sought about its disposal, and then gave it back to her; the bottle had, he said, contained the cyanide, and had been kept in a linen-closet at Leinster Road.

He then came to the events preceding his loss of memory, and recounted what he had said in the jury's absence about finding his wife's letter in her ration book. As the letter was lost, he reconstructed it from memory. She had asked for his forgiveness for what she was about to do, said that she could not live without morphia, was taking the rest of the acid left over after the coffee tests, and would put the bottle in her coat pocket, so that if the poison failed he would never know. She referred to the future care of the children and ended by saying that her real husband's true name was Dorset L. Stokes. Lehman said the letter so upset him that he took four morphine tablets and some codeine, went to see a priest, took some whiskey in a public-house, and remembered no more until the middle of July. He was then taken through his statement, and said it contained many errors and inaccuracies and false statements, but he had no recollection of making the statement. It also, unfortunately, contained several truly recounted incidents and details which, presumably, could only have been furnished by a man with a normal mind. And if he had lost his memory on 29 March he could hardly have said to Mrs O'Callaghan on 7 April, 'Would you not think I had done it?'

A damaging part of the statement concerned the coffee tests, and was wholly at variance with his evidence. In the statement he related that the tests were carried out, not by him, but by a man named Dorset, a baby-food manufacturer, who had told him two of the acids to buy, had provided the equipment for the tests, and had himself provided one of the acids. These tests were carried out in the shop with Lehman merely looking on, and produced no result. Lehman now swore that this man's name was not Dorset, but D'Arcy, and that he had not carried out the tests, and had never been in the shop, and had never bought any of the acids.

But the statement contained an even more damaging passage. After mentioning that he had discussed Dorset's tests with his wife, though not in detail, he had said that he did not think she knew he had bought acids, and was definite that she did not know where the acids were stored, which was in a cabinet in the shop; he had further said he had no idea how his wife could have obtained

189

poison, and knew of no reason why she should have taken it, that they had always been very happy together and were very united. If this part of his statement was true, the suicide theory was nonsense, and must lead to the inference that Lehman had murdered her. He now swore that his statement that she did not know where the acids were stored was untrue, and that he had in fact discussed the tests in detail with her. He did not contradict the remainder of this part of his statement.

After a few more questions, Mr Casey finished, and the cross-examination began.

Mr Murnaghan first asked was the coffee business virtually finished in March, and Lehman agreed. Then it was suggested that, if so, the tests were pointless. Lehman didn't answer at first, but then said the business still existed and there was still some stock, and he hoped to make money by manufacturing his own coffee. Asked how in his state of destitution he could have done this, he said he had not given the matter full thought, but there was always a possibility of raising money with which to carry on. The following then occurred:

Q. And was it on that possibility you were thinking of testing the coffee?

A. I did not give it any idea at the time.

Q. I put it to you that there is no reality in this story about the testing of coffee — that there was no necessity to test the coffee. What necessity was there to test the coffee at all?

A. No answer.

Judge: It is put to you that there was no reality in reference to your proposed test of the coffee — do you understand that?

A. No answer.

Mr Murnaghan: I put it to you that in the week before your wife died there was no question of testing the coffee, because there was no coffee to test, that your business had gone?

A. No, the business had not gone. The shop was still running, and still had stock.

Q. It was on the verge of collapse.

A. Yes.

Q. The wolf was at the door?

A. He may have been.

Q. Do you still say in that situation that there is any reality in your story of your testing the coffee?

A. There is every reality because I had attempted to test it.

Q. What was the reality?

A. That I had made an attempt to test the coffee, for the purpose of entering into the manufacture of bottle coffee from the coffee beans.

Q. What were you going to manufacture?

A. It was my object to test coffee for the purpose of finding the potentialities of the manufacture of coffee and its possibilities.

Q. Again I put it to you that there is no reality in it. Where were you going to start the manufacture of bottle coffee in your circumstances?

A. At that time I had given it no thought, it was a little premature yet.

Q. And this was something up in the air, was that the position?

A. No answer.

Q. What experience had you, if any, as a chemist?

A. None.

Q. Or as a doctor?

A. None.

Q. How did you think you were going to get any result from the experiment?

A. I was only going by the advice of certain medical students.

Then he was asked to give the names of any of the medical students, but could not, nor their addresses, nor locate the chemist where he had bought the uric acid. He had said O'Connell Street, but did not know on which side of the street, nor could he place the shop in relation to well-known Dublin landmarks such as Nelson Pillar and O'Connell Bridge. He could not even describe the shop in any way.

The next topic was his army pension, which he said was assigned to a mortgage corporation and was overdrawn, though he could not say by how much. As the prosecution were suggesting that there was no pension, and that Lehman had invented it to give himself an air of substance, Mr Murnaghan then put the following:

Q. I put it to you that you have no pension from the American Army at all? What do you say to that?

A. I have.

Q. Because I put it to you further that you are an American Army deserter?

Mr Casey: I object to this attack upon the witness. He is not entitled to attack the character of the witness.

191

Judge: I will allow the question. I don't think it is an attack on the character of the witness at all. These explanations were introduced by the witness himself.

Q. You told my lord and the jury you were discharged from the American Army on account of brain fever?
A. No, I did not tell you that.
Q. I beg your pardon. You told us you were discharged from the American Army and had a pension?
A. Yes.
Q. I put it to you that you deserted the American Army on 19 September 1917?
A. No, that is incorrect because I was in hospital at that date in Gettysburg, Pennsylvania.
Q. How long were you there, then?
A. I cannot say, but I was there a little time.
Q. You told us, speaking of the American Army, that you joined it in the name of — what?
A. I don't believe I said it.
Q. Well, tell us now, if you did not?
A. What is your question?
Q. Under what name were you known in the American Army?
A. Martin.
Q. What is your full name?
A. William.
Q. When did you cease to use that name?
A. I don't remember that.
Q. What name did you use after William Martin?
A. I don't remember that.
Q. Well, if I told you, would you remember?
A. Perhaps.
Q. Did you ever use the name Hiames?
A. Yes, that is the name attached to the family that I was adopted to once.
Q. What Christian name did you use?
A. James.
Q. Your previous Christian name was William.
A. No, not the previous, the subsequent.
Q. When did you say you used that name?
A. When I was living with the Dutch family.
Q. I put it to you that you used that name in the year 1926?
A. I may have, but not to my knowledge.

192

Q. Did you use the name Richman?
A. Yes, James Richman.
Q. When?
A. Most of my life.
Q. Why?

Mr Casey objected also to the last question, and it was disallowed. Mr Murnaghan then continued.

Q. You told my lord and the jury you used the name of James Richman?
A. Yes.
Q. Did you, on getting married, use that name?
A. I did.
Q. Whom did you marry and use that name?
A. Ruby Dora Engreen.
Q. Did you ever live at the International Villas, Minnesota?
A. No, I have been there, but I never lived there.
Q. How did you come to take the name James Herbert Lehman.
A. I cannot answer that.

Although these questions showed Lehman in a very unfavourable light, as it turned out they proved a blessing in disguise.

When he was asked about his wife's health he was in trouble again, for he could not remember if she had been 'in great form', as Mrs O'Callaghan said, the night before her death, but said she had been depressed a few days before. As he had not told the hospital doctor, when asked about her previous illnesses, that she was a morphia addict, nor of her illness when deprived of the drug and her depression, his evidence on this looked very thin. His explanation of the omission was that he thought it unnecessary to mention these matters to the doctor.

He had to answer many questions abut his wife's consumption of morphia. They both took it daily, he said, he to ease the pain in his back, but he could not say what doses each took, which, if true, meant that they daily risked poisoning themselves. He was very vague when asked where he got the drug, and mentioned the anonymous medical students again, and seamen, also anonymous, on the Dublin-Lisbon boats. He said he had not asked for nor received any morphia when in the military hospital, which was odd if he was an addict. Then Counsel inquired where he had got the drug when living in England, and he said at military hospitals and factory dispensaries, but refused to name any individual who had supplied him. His answers were hopeless when he was required to place the public-houses where he used to meet the students; he couldn't name one, or say where it was, except vaguely. When he tried to describe how to get to one of them, and mentioned a lane off a Dublin street, he couldn't say whether one turned right or left at the end of the lane. However, he said the lounge was square and the seats upholstered in red.

He said he was happily married, but was not sure if he had told his landlady in December that his marriage was a failure, and could not explain the inconsistency. He was closely questioned about his wife's letter telling him of Stokes. He thought he had destroyed it, and when it was suggested that the letter was very important, gave the absurd answer that he didn't think so, as he didn't believe what she wrote. This led to the following:

Q. You were telling us before lunch that you didn't believe what you say you saw in this letter about your wife being married before, to Stokes?

A. Yes.

Q. At any time, if you received the letter, did you change your opinion as to whether or not your wife was previously married?

A. Yes, I did.

Q. When?

A. On the 29th March.

Q. Was that the day you say you received the other letter?

A. Yes.

Q. And was it because of this letter you changed your opinion?

A. Yes, to a great extent.

Q. Was there anything else?

A. I cannot say just now.

Q. May my lord and the jury take it that before the 29th March you thought your wife had not been married before?

A. No. I thought the letter was only for the purpose of me securing a home in Dublin.

Q. Does it mean that up to the 29th March everything was all right, that she had not been married before?

A. No, I cannot say.

Q. Did you think she was married before — before the 29th March.

A. I was not sure.

Q. Did you suspect it?

A. I am not sure of that.

Q. What were your views, opinions, or ideas on the subject before your wife died?

A. Well, I was not sure. I thought is had been only an excuse for me to bring them to town.

Q. If you thought it was an excuse, did you dismiss it from your mind, or what did you do?

A. No, I don't know; I cannot answer; I don't know for sure.

Q. Do you realise that you are the only person who can tell the jury what was in your mind?

A. Yes, I realise that.

Q. You told a number of people during the period between Christmas and March that your wife was married before to a man called Stokes?

A. No, I am not sure of that. You know that from the depositions.

Q. You say that Mrs O'Callaghan has told the truth in her evidence?

A. I said I accepted her evidence.

Q. You realise that she has sworn that on the night after you came back from the Rotunda Hospital you told her that your wife had something on her mind; that she had been married before?

A. Yes, I heard that, but I don't remember saying it.

Q. Do you accept as a fact that when Mrs O'Callaghan swore it, you did, in fact, say it?

A. Well, I am quite positive I must have said it or Mrs O'Callaghan would not have said it.

Q. Will you explain, if you said it, why you said it?

A. I cannot explain it.

Q. At that date, as far as you knew, it was not a true statement?

A. I cannot say that for sure.

Q. Had you any information on 18th March which would lead you to know that it is a true statement your wife had been married before?

A. I had nothing definite.

Q. Nothing more than the letter which you disbelieved?

A. That is right.

These answers were bad enough, but what made them worse was, he had told the Gardaí that the letter had simply asked him to find a home in Dublin for his family. He had said nothing to them about the alleged bigamy.

Larry Dorset, or Stokes, whom the prosecution suggested was mythical, was next dealt with, and once again Lehman was vague. He did not know the man's address, could not recall what they had spoken of at their two meetings, and had not tried to trace him, but, surprisingly, said that he had seen him in Court a few days earlier. He had immediately sent for his solicitor to tell him, but Stokes had not been traced. He had to admit to some lies; for instance, the story about pressure being put on him to marry was false; so were the statement that his wife was unbalanced, and the story of the purchase of the £300 ring.

His suppression of the visit on Sunday to the young widow had to be explained; the reason he gave for not telling his brother-in-law about it was that it might be misunderstood; he could furnish no reason for not telling Sergeant Sheppard. He had to say what he had told this lady about his marriage and stated, after some hedging, that he told her his wife and children lived in Leinster Road; he didn't know if he had said his wife was previously married; he thought he might have.

Sheppard's visit gave rise to further questions; Lehman had undoubtedly failed to tell him that the cyanide was still at Leinster Road. If by now Lehman was not utterly discredited, his explanation that he didn't think of the cyanide when Sheppard was there, and his alleged inability to remember saying 'she got no poison here', must have completed the process. His account of that conversation was that Sheppard asked was there any poison in the dresser drawer, and he answered, 'I don't think so', which could hardly have deceived a child. He admitted not showing the cup and spoon from the bedroom to Sheppard, although it had occurred to him that his wife had taken 'something'. During these questions it emerged that there was codeine, as well as the cyanide, in the linen closet. He had not told either Mrs O'Callaghan or Nurse McCaigue of finding the cyanide bottle, although he had suspected poisoning when he found it, and could not explain this omission.

The cross-examination ended with the following:

Q. Have you at all times for years past worn a moustache?
A. Not all times, but for the last three or four years.
Q. And for the last three or four years you have worn a moustache?
A. Not altogether. I shaved it off at various times, but I have no idea when.
Q. No approximate idea, whether two or four years?

196

A. No.
Q. Or where you were at the time?
A. No.
Q. Did you shave it off since you came from England?
A. I cannot say that.
Q. Can you give any satisfactory story about yourself?
A. I can't give the dates on which I shaved my moustache.

The widow corroborated Lehman's evidence of the visit to her flat, and his arrival and departure times, but unfortunately had told the Gardaí, in a statement, that she did not see him that day, and she could not satisfactorily explain the discrepancy. She contradicted his account of what he had told her of his marriage; according to her, Lehman said his solicitor advised him that he need not seek a separation, as his wife was already married, and had not said he was living with her. His son, he told her, was being cared for by someone else. She had shown some interest in Lehman, for she had visited him nearly every day while he was awaiting trial.

The defence next called two doctors, one of whom said that cyanide could be used as a reagent for measuring sugar in bottled coffee. The other, Dr Lee-Parker, a neurologist and mental specialist, dealt with Lehman's flight, which it was important, if at all possible, to present in a favourable light. He began by describing Lehman as a pathological liar — meaning one who was unstable at an early age and incapable of telling the truth. This was probably less damaging than it seems, for by now the jury knew Lehman was a liar, anyway. The doctor then said that a shock caused by discovery of a wife's suicide, followed by the consumption of morphine, could cause over three months' loss of memory, and that in such a state the sufferer could perform normal actions and present a normal appearance. He called the loss of memory condition a 'fuge', or hysterical flight. This was, perhaps, better than nothing, but unfortunately it was based on a case history supplied by a pathological liar. His evidence finished with another morsel of help to the defence; pregnant women were more liable, he said, to mental breakdown than others, though he would not expect one in a healthy young married woman whose circumstances were reasonably happy. As Mrs Lehman's circumstances were not conspicuously happy, the suicide theory was still open, though by now very shaky.

The evidence ended then, and the jury retired. They took from 3 p.m. to 5 p.m., with a short interruption for further directions from the Judge, and then came back with a verdict of guilty. Lehman made no answer to the usual question whether he had anything to say why sentence of death should not be passed.

He appealed and — an unusual indulgence — was allowed to be present, and so had the almost unique experience of hearing his own murder appeal succeed. Two grounds were argued, but the Court dealt only with one, namely that the questions about his alleged army desertion and use of aliases were inadmissible. The Court held they were inadmissible, and considered that they tended to prejudice Lehman in the jury's eyes, and 'the Court is not able to say that if the inadmissible questions had been omitted a reasonable jury after a proper summing-up must have convicted the accused on the rest of the evidence', and ordered a re-trial. So, on 15 January 1945, Lehman got a second chance, this time before Mr Justice Overend, K.C., and a different jury. The same Counsel appeared.

The first trial and the appeal had, of course, been reported in the papers, and most Dubliners knew all about the case, so Mr Casey asked the Judge to question each juror, before being sworn, as to whether he had formed any opinion about the case. When the Judge refused this application Mr Casey asked permission to administer the question himself, but this was also refused, the accused being left to his ordinary right to challenge five jurors without showing cause, and as many more as he could show cause for.

The prosecution's case ran on almost identical lines with the first trial, but there were a few variations in the evidence. Miss Finucane did not this time quote her refusal to tell lies to the police, which was possibly a crumb of help to the defence. Sergeant Sheppard, anticipating Lehman's story about the letter in the ration book, said that Lehman had flicked through the pages of the book in his presence, and he saw no letter. And the hotelier's wife mentioned that, in December, Lehman had asked her for a hat-pin which his wife wished to use. She did not at first understand, but then 'it dawned on me' and she asked 'who will look after her?', and he said, 'I will'. All this referred to an attempt to induce a miscarriage, and it corroborated Lehman's statement to the Gardaí that his wife did not want to have her baby.

The defence ran differently, however. They called no evidence, thus gaining the right to address the jury last, and depriving them of the spectacle of Lehman under cross-examination, and of the evidence that he was a pathological liar; and, of course, they heard nothing to suggest that he was an army deserter, nor that he had used aliases, nor of the young widow and his interest in her. Against these advantages his alleged loss of memory, his coffee test, and his wife's letters about suicide and bigamy were never proved, but as the first jury had not believed Lehman on these matters, it was unlikely that the second would, so perhaps no harm was done. Furthermore, none of the damaging evidence was denied, but once again it probably made no difference; and the flight was unexplained. Finally, there remained Lehman's statement that his wife did not know where the acids were kept, and did not even know he had bought any.

So, when the jury retired, he might have had a better chance, though he was unfortunate that by then there were only eleven of them, one having become ill; one juror can cause a disagreement, which gives a prisoner another chance. But the second jury, though taking half an hour longer, reached the same verdict and so Lehman was sentenced to death for the second time. When he was asked the usual question, he answered, 'I am satisfied that on my second trial there has been a small degree of fairness. I am innocent and my conscience is clear.' As Judge Overend was speaking the words of sentence he became visibly moved, and faltered — then he went on: 'and may the Lord have mercy on your soul.' Several people in the packed galleries wept, and many blessed themselves. Lehman appealed again, but this time without success, and he was executed on 19 March 1945, the first anniversary of his wife's death.

Was he guilty? The real question is: was he proved guilty? — for a criminal trial is not an inquiry into guilt, but into legal proof of guilt, a very different matter. He should only have been convicted the second time if it was proved beyond a reasonable doubt that Mrs Lehman did not take the poison herself. As accident may be ruled out, did she in fact commit suicide? This raises three questions.

First, had she the means? Yes, if she knew the cyanide was in the house. If she didn't, then, as already remarked, Lehman murdered her; if she did know, she could have committed suicide. The only evidence the second jury had on this point was Lehman's statement that she didn't know that he had any acids, and definitely did not know where they were stored. But this was a very odd statement indeed for Lehman to make if he was guilty; one would have expected him, when being questioned at Ballytore, to provide every possible evidence of suicide, and the statement clearly did the reverse. So, if the suicide letter, the finding of the bottle, the alleged illnesses of his wife, the 'something on her mind', and her former use of poison were all part of an elaborate build-up to cover murder, why did he throw it all away by that statement? He could not have been so stupid as not to see that he was putting the rope around his neck by saying that his wife knew nothing of the poison. It is one of the puzzles in the case, created by Lehman's endless falsehoods. But there was surely some truth somewhere in the maze of lies, for even a pathological liar will tell the truth occasionally.

Second, had she the motive for suicide? By March 1944 she could have had no illusions about Lehman, and what her future with him was likely to be. From August to early December he had not supported her and her children; they lived at her own home. By Christmas he was destitute, and it was her second experience of destitution with him, for while in the army in England he had left her penniless and she was supported by her sister. In March destitution was again her lot, two businesses having failed and a substantial sum of money lost with them. What future could she have seen for herself and her children with Lehman? She knew also he had little or no interest in her; she may have also known of his interest in Nurse McCaigue and the young widow; and she was unwillingly pregnant. Was it, then, so very unlikely that in a fit of depression she would want to end her life?

Lastly, could she have taken poison, removed the drinking vessel from the bedroom, and got back to bed before the drug deprived her of volition? She had about four or five minutes in which to do it, which was ample. The defence had a strong point here, namely the powerful smell from the sink on the lower landing. This was the smell of prussic acid, released from the cyanide, according to the doctors, by the action of hydrochloric acid — a very rare thing to find in a domestic sink. Lehman's Counsel argued that Mrs Lehman may have come downstairs after taking the poison, vomited in the sink, washed the cup, and gone up again, and suggested that the smell could be caused by the vomit. The Court called on the prosecution to reply on this point, but held that it was a jury question, and the jury had found against

Lehman on the evidence. There is, incidentally, a further possibility in support of suicide, which is that Lehman was toying with the idea of murder, but had not got to the point when his wife killed herself.

His motive for the murder is far from convincing. Was it his interest in Nurse McCaigue? That was the only motive the second jury could have considered, but one wonders if he was prepared to risk his neck — for his course of preparation was careless in the extreme — on the off-chance that she would marry him. She never said at the trial that she had given him any reason to think she would. He had been twice married, and if he was tired of his second wife one would expect that, with a war on, and an escape route open into either the American or British Army, he would simply have deserted her. That would have been in keeping with his character.

But, although of course neither jury knew this, he had a criminal record, consisting of three previous convictions. One was in 1919, under the name of William Martin, for robbery in Ohio, for which he was sent to a reformatory; the next was in Minnesota in 1936, for grand larceny, his name then being James Edward James, and the sentence was a long term of imprisonment; the third was in Aldershot in 1941 for eleven offences of obtaining goods and money by false pretences, mostly worthless cheques; the sentences were six months hard labour for each offence, running concurrently.

Here are the eight names Lehman used:

William Martin
James Edward James
James Richman
James Hiames
James Herbert Lehman
Leigh (his trade name)
James McCaigue
James Joseph Feeley

We will never know his real name.

201

10.

The Malahide Mystery

(Attorney-General v. Henry McCabe, 1926)

A HOUSE in flames, and six dead bodies lying on the lawn! This dreadful happening on 31 March 1926 at Malahide, a village near Dublin, is still remembered there. The house was La Mancha, standing on its own grounds just off the main road to Dublin. The bodies were those of the owners, Peter and Joseph McDonnell, brothers, their sisters Annie and Alice, and the servants James Clarke and Mary McGowan, all wiped out in one awful stroke. Their bodies had been found in the burning house and taken out one by one; the fire brigade tried in vain to save the building which, by the afternoon when the fire was at last extinguished, was almost gutted.

How had this ghastly tragedy occurred? Let us go back a little and hear something of the ill-starred family. The McDonnell brothers were retired merchants, bachelors who had sold their business in Ballygar, Galway, eight years before and bought La Mancha, where they lived with their unmarried sisters. They were well-liked in the district. Peter McDonnell was a keen golfer, and a member of the Malahide Golf Club. There is plenty of golf in that part of County Dublin, for just across the estuary from the Malahide Club is the Island Golf Club, a fine eighteen-hole, wind-swept course, with Portmarnock three miles away. Joseph McDonnell was an agreeable, quiet person, fond of a game of cards and a social evening; Annie and Alice were intelligent cultivated women, especially Alice, who was fond of travel and played the piano. The servants were James Clarke, highly esteemed by his employers and more friend than servant, and Mary McGowan the maid. There was a third servant Henry McCabe, a gardener who lived nearby with his wife and family. He was a small quiet man.

The house was a two-storeyed building with a basement; there were five bedrooms upstairs, a morning-room, dining-room and drawing-room on the hall floor, and a kitchen and servants' quarters in the basement. The house had two entrances: a hall door at the top of a flight of stone steps from a gravelled drive, and a side entrance which is important to the story. It had a porch with three steps down to a strong outer door; through this there was a short passage, and then an inner door of lighter construction, beyond which was another passage leading to the kitchen. Off this passage were Clarke's bedroom, a storeroom, and a stairway leading to the hall floor. There were two avenues to the property, both from the Dublin–Malahide road, and a footpath from the road to Swords, a nearby village. One avenue, with a lodge at the gate, led to the house, the other was to the farmland, some thirty acres in extent. Behind the house were two yards containing farm buildings which were closed off by wicket gates set in walls attached to the house.

———————

On Wednesday 31 March at 8.30 a.m. Harry McCabe, a son of the gardener, called at the Garda Station at Malahide, which is about a mile from the house, and told Sergeant Kenny there was something wrong at La Mancha, and that his father was outside. The Sergeant went out and learnt from McCabe that the house was on fire. He immediately called for two other Guards, and all four went to La Mancha, where they found smoke pouring from the chimneys and drifting from the windows and doors. All the windows had drawn blinds and shutters closed and were bolted from within, except for the scullery window in the basement, through which it could be seen that the basement stairs were in flames. Sergeant Kenny knocked loudly at the hall door and rang, and made as much noise as he could to attract the attention of the household: he couldn't know that all six were dead inside. He then sent for the Dublin Fire Brigade, broke a window, tore down the blinds, and burst the shutters, but fire and smoke kept him from getting in.

The Sergeant asked McCabe which were the family bedrooms, and McCabe pointed to the window over the hall door, and later to two other windows. Someone — not McCabe — got a ladder, and a Garda went up, broke in a window and its shutters and got in. He reappeared, shouted that there was nobody in that room, and tried two more rooms in the same way. Still no one was found. Someone then suggested that possibly the occupants were at Mass, and a messenger was sent off to the church to look. Just then McCabe told Sergeant Kenny that the inner door had been forced open, and that 'there must be some foul play'. He went with McCabe to the porch, found the outer door open, and the inner door half open, and lying in the passage inside the inner door a staple, a piece of broken wood, and a lock receiver which had been attached to the inside of the inner door. Also in the passage were a can of paraffin oil and a candlestick. The basement stairs were burning, but the fire had not spread to any other part of the basement.

By now many people had come to the house, and someone reported seeing a body in Clarke's room. The bars on the window were forced open and the Sergeant and others went in. Clarke's body was lying on the floor near the window, clad in underclothing only, and there was a large wound on the side of the head, with dried blood on it. The body was brought out and laid on the lawn. Someone told McCabe of the find, and he came running from the front of the house. When he saw the body he said that it looked like murder, and he ran away with a fearful cry. If this was acting, it may have been convincing, but McCabe had omitted to show surprise that the man who was thought to be away, was in fact dead in the house. McCabe's cry was relied on by the defence at the trial, as evidence of his horror and distress at finding Clarke dead, and possibly murdered. The prosecution, however, suggested that the true interpretation was that McCabe was horrified to find that Clarke's body was untouched by fire, contrary to his expectations, as the basement fire had not spread to Clarke's room.

At 9.15 the fire brigade arrived, and a fireman kicked in the hall door, which was now well ablaze and collapsed. In the dining-room they found the naked body of Peter McDonnell lying face down on the floor with two undergarments thrown over him. There was a strong smell of paraffin in the room, which, however, was not on fire, though the kitchen below could be seen through a two-foot-square hole that had burned right through the floor near the body. This body was removed to the lawn.

The fire brigade did their best, but it was impossible to save the building. The fire had got a good grip before they arrived, and the roof collapsed as they drove up the avenue. The upstairs rooms were now dangerous to work in, but before they collapsed the bodies of the women — Alice and Annie McDonnell, and Mary McGowan — were found in one of the bedrooms. There were now five bodies on the lawn. The last to be found was Joseph McDonnell's, in another bedroom, lying face upwards on the floor.

It was soon obvious that the house was not in the grip of a single fire, but that there were separate fires in the hall and each of the ground-floor rooms. These were easily put out, but the fire in the hall seriously damaged the remainder of the upper part of the building. By 1 p.m. the fire was practically extinguished, but only a gutted house was left.

The disaster gave rise to great speculation. How had it occurred? McCabe was interviewed by the reporters, of course, but he had no theory to offer. One Dublin daily said the affair 'had unnerved him', and was of the opinion that '. . . Providence decreed that Henry McCabe didn't perish in the building'. This was because Clarke was said to be away, and usually when this was the case McCabe slept in the house, though for some reason not this time. One theory, said to be put forward by the Gardaí was that Peter McDonnell had become insane during the night, slain the household, and then set the building on fire. It was thought that the murder weapon was a poker found in the dining-room near Peter's body, and said to bear traces of brain matter. These were interesting speculations, but they were soon forgotten, and the poker was never mentioned again. On the following day, 2 April, the newspapers carried an entirely different message, reporting, apparently on reliable authority, that 'developments of a sensational character were possible in the near future'.

By 4 o'clock on the 31st the bodies had been removed to Malahide for the inquest, the public had departed, and the Gardaí were investigating. Their task was not easy, because the ruin of the building and the amount of water seriously interfered with detective work. Some furniture had been brought out on the lawn during the fire by willing helpers, of whom, however, McCabe was not one. He had spent most of his time standing around hands in pockets, looking on, a strange attitude for the only survivor of the household. The pockets were those of a pair of grey tweed trousers which he wore the whole of that day and the next day. He had not been wholly idle, however, for to one bystander he had said, bringing him to the inner door, 'This is the place where they must have broken in,' and had produced from somewhere the can and candlestick. This man had asked where the oil used to set fire to the place had come from, and McCabe showed him a small shed in which there was a barrel of oil — the house was lit with oil-lamps.

To another man, Daniel McCann, who asked where Jim Clarke was, McCabe said he had gone away on the previous Saturday evening to the country to look after some land the McDonnells had bought.

Next day, while the inquest was being held, he told a stupid lie to McCann. He said, 'I forgot to tell the Sergeant that Clarke was bad friends with his brother over fifteen acres of ground,' which was presumably an attempt to suggest a motive for Clarke's murder. McCann answered that it was still not too late to tell the Sergeant, and McCabe said he didn't like to tell him too much. Then, drawing attention to a man standing in a group nearby, he added, 'I am talking, and maybe this is a CID man.' The man was McCann's nephew, and had nothing to do with the police, but McCabe didn't know that.

On the day of the fire McCabe also spoke to a young man named Theodore McKenna, whose father had once employed him. McCabe said it was an awful affair, and that he had come to the house early that morning to milk the cows, as Clarke was away. He was surprised he had not been asked to stay the night as was usual when Clarke was absent. The night before, he said, Joseph McDonnell had been very ill, and he had stayed up late speaking to him at the kitchen fire, where he had been paid his wages. McCabe also said that he had spent the rest of the night at a wake. Then he mentioned a safe which the McDonnells had in the storeroom, brought from Ballygar and at first buried by Clarke and himself, by direction of the family, in the garden near the back door, but later dug up and brought into the house. He also spoke to Sergeant Mooney of the Gardaí, saying that when he left the night before 'they were all right'. A few minutes later, before the bodies were found, he said to another bystander, named Murphy, 'Could they be all gone?' — meaning dead.

Next day, 1 April, Superintendent O'Halloran interviewed McCabe at the barracks. The interview was not necessarily significant, for McCabe was the only person who was likely to be able to throw much light on this dark affair. But even at this stage he was under suspicion.

He was asked about the McDonnell family and when he had last seen them, for the police knew now that none of the household had been seen since Monday. He said he saw Annie on Monday at midday, when she had asked him to kill a chicken. Joseph told him, he said, that both Annie and Peter got ill that day and had gone to bed. He saw Alice the same day a few times in the kitchen, and saw Mary McGowan up to 5 p.m., when she was in her usual health.

He described the various members of the family. Alice, he said, was known locally as mad Alice, and at times would appear in the garden, screeching and hysterical; Peter, according to him, was often very abnormal in manner, behaving like a schoolboy, and Joseph never spoke to anyone, even at meals, or so he had been told by former servants employed in the house.

He spoke of the evening before the fire, and said he had sat in the kitchen with Joseph McDonnell reading the papers until 8 o'clock, when he left to attend the wake, where he stayed all night. In the morning he left there at 7.45 and went home; half an hour later he went to La Mancha, and on arrival at the lodge saw smoke coming from the chimneys and the bathroom window. He ran up, found the big yard gate open, went to the inner porch door, which had been burst open, and saw the broken lock lying in the passage. He went in as far as he could, found the stairs on fire, and shouted but heard no one. Then he ran to the Garda Station to report, meeting his son on the way and sending him ahead.

The Gardaí were of course trying to find some explanation of the extraordinary tragedy, and lunacy could explain it. McCabe must have been thinking that too, for he was saying that three of the McDonnells were very peculiar: Alice seemed to be a madwoman, Peter wasn't much better at times, and Joseph was morose and very unsociable. But if McCabe thought his story would put the police on to a false trail he was wrong, for all that he said about them was wholly false. It will be noticed that he said nothing about Joseph McDonnell's illness on Tuesday night, which he had mentioned to McKenna.

After the statement was completed they went to La Mancha, where McCabe demonstrated how the inner door had looked the morning before when he arrived, and where he had seen the staple, piece of wood, and lock receiver. Presently the two men separated, the Superintendent going to the storeroom where the safe was, and about ten minutes later McCabe reappeared, and took from his trousers' pocket a bunch of keys. 'Here are some keys that I found,' he said, handing them with some burnt pennies to the Superintendent. He explained that he had got the keys upstairs in Peter's bedroom, in the pocket of a pair of grey trousers, and the coppers in a tin box in the same room. The keys fitted the safe, which the Superintendent opened. It contained no money, which seemed to surprise McCabe. 'Surely there must be some,' he said. But there wasn't. The safe contained only papers.

McCabe had made several mistakes since reporting the fire, but the production of the keys was probably his most serious, for of course it raised questions. How did he know which was Peter's room? and why did he, among the various articles in that room, search only a pair of trousers, and find the keys which happened to fit the safe which the police were just then examining? The fact was that at that moment he was wearing the trousers which he said were in Peter's bedroom, and had worn them the day before, and they were part of a suit belonging to the dead man.

The basement of the house was still intact save for the stairs and there were still parts of the bedrooms undamaged, or at least holding together, and the police searched thoroughly. In the kitchen range they found a dish of cooked food, and in the oven two unused bread puddings, suggesting that a meal had been interrupted. The ashes in the kitchen grate contained buckles, safety-pins, portions of corsets, some charred fabrics, hooks and eyes, and buckles of men's braces. Obviously a quantity of clothing had been burnt there. In two of the bedrooms they discovered many bloodstained garments, some also stained with paraffin oil, among them bloodstained shirts with cuff-links still in the sleeves, ripped up as though removed from the wearer, and a woman's blouse similarly ripped. In one room there was a small sum of money, and in Peter McDonnell's room, which was the least damaged, a wardrobe and chest of drawers containing clothes, including the coat and waistcoat which matched the trousers McCabe was wearing. In McCabe's house were found six pairs of trousers he did not own and a pair of bloodstained boots.

It was now 9 April, and time for another talk with McCabe. He was interviewed by Chief Superintendent Leahy, and made another long statement. He mentioned the burial of a wooden box in the grounds by order of his employers, which remained buried for about three years, and was said by Peter McDonnell to contain insurance papers and books. It was also supposed to contain 'treasure'. He and Clarke opened the burial-place after three years, by order of their employers, and the box was taken into the house, and he never saw it afterwards. He said he had heard from a neighbour, about three weeks before the fire, that the house was advertised for sale, and he went to the public library, where he read the advertisement. He told Clarke about it that day, and after that noticed that he was very peculiar and always talking to himself.

He was questioned about his wages, and said he received thirty-five shillings every Saturday and took it all home to his wife; she occasionally gave him a shilling out of it. This did not happen on Saturday 27th, but he had had a shilling in his possession, of which he spent sevenpence in a public-house on Monday 29th. He was then asked some questions based on information the police had, though he did not know this. He denied telling Mrs O'Reilly, who lived in the lodge, that Annie was sick on Monday and had sent him to Dublin on an errand. On the Tuesday, he said, the only people he spoke to at La Mancha were Joseph McDonnell, a rate collector named Lambert, and two children who called selling tickets for a fête. He was asked again about Tuesday evening, and said Joseph McDonnell was reading the newspaper when he left — presumably, he said, that day's *Irish Independent*, but he did not see the paper come that day, and nobody gave it to him to give to Joseph McDonnell.

The Gardaí were far from satisfied about his story of the finding of the keys and he could not explain why he looked for keys only in the bedroom, nor why he had not brought down other articles as well as the pennies to Superintendent O'Halloran. He was interviewed again the next day and asked further questions about the keys. He described the colour of the trousers, which he said was light grey, and explained that he was only looking at the clothes in the wardrobe when he heard the rattle of keys.

Two days later he was arrested, and charged with murder of the six dead people, and with arson.

The Trial
The Case for the Prosecution

The trial began on 8 November 1926, and took six days. Public interest was intense and each day the courtroom was packed, whilst outside many stood, unable to get in. The trial Judge was Mr Justice John O'Byrne, K.C., a former Attorney-General, and said at the time to be the youngest Judge in Ireland or England. For the prosecution Mr William Carrigan, K.C., a veteran of many criminal trials, Mr Dudley White, K.C., and Mr Charles H. Bewley, K.C., a recent 'silk' appeared. Against this array of talent and experience Mr Alec Lynn, of the Junior Bar, fought alone.

209

McCabe was indicted separately for the murder of each of the six, but the trial proceeded on one charge only, the murder of Peter McDonnell. However, he might as well have been tried for the six, because the evidence of all the deaths was given, and indeed it would have been impossible to confine the facts to the murder of Peter McDonnell, so mixed up with it were the other murders. Mr Carrigan's opening speech foreshadowed the sensational developments the newspapers had spoken of in April. He told the jury that they might have to consider whether the crime was the work of an outside gang, or of one man, but after that the gang was forgotten. The one man, he said, must have been a member of the household circle, meaning McCabe, and the motive was either robbery, or disappointment at the prospective loss of his employment.

Sergeant Kenny described how he and the other Gardaí found the house on fire, and the discovery of the bodies. His statement that McCabe did nothing to help was contested, the point being made that he could not know as he did not have McCabe continuously under observation. One of the questions put to him in cross-examination showed that McCabe realised he would have to explain his production of the keys. The Sergeant was asked had he not sent McCabe to Peter McDonnell's bedroom to look for them; he denied this, and was corroborated by Superintendent O'Halloran, who said that the keys had never been mentioned until McCabe produced them.

Witness after witness who knew the McDonnell family well made nonsense of McCabe's description of their peculiarities and showed that they were perfectly normal, intelligent people. There was an attempt in cross-examination to suggest that Peter was not normal because two years earlier, at the funeral of his sister Margaret, when the coffin was being brought out from the church, he had started 'keening', an old Irish custom of lamentation by cries over the dead. The custom is still observed in parts of the West of Ireland and in County Kerry, but the witness who was asked about this did not think it showed abnormality or eccentricity, nor would anyone else who knew of the custom. As for Alice, all that emerged was that she was rather reserved in the street and not inclined to greet acquaintances. Otherwise she was perfectly normal and the description of her as 'Mad Alice' was shown to be an invention. No single witness, including former servants of the family, who spoke of them with affection and respect, had ever heard her so called.

The defence tried but failed to exclude McCabe's statements, as the evidence showed that each statement was voluntary and had been read over to him, and he had acknowledged their accuracy before signing. Superintendent O'Halloran and an expert witness described the condition of the inner door, which McCabe had said was 'burst open' when he arrived at La Mancha on the 31st. There was no mark or other sign on the door to show it had been forced in from the outside; very little pressure was needed to do this, and the lock and staple could not have been so dislodged. It was obvious that the force had been applied from within, and the prosecution suggested that McCabe had damaged the door so as to lay a false trail. The Judge directed the door to be brought into court, and the jury spent some time examining it.

There was a minor sensation when arsenic was mentioned in cross-examination. The Superintendent agreed that the Gardaí had tried to trace purchases of the poison by McCabe, but had failed. He also agreed that at first the Gardaí had thought the crime was the work of a gang, but not for long. There was, obviously, no gang. It was important to establish the time when the fires had begun, but the fire-brigade chief could only say that the fire in one room had been started six or seven hours before 8.30 a.m., or possibly longer. The fires had spread slowly, because the windows and shutters were closed. As McCabe was seen in the vicinity of the house at about 10 p.m. on the Tuesday, he could have started the fires between then and 11.30, when it was proved he arrived at the wake.

The prosecution called various witnesses to show when the victims had last been seen. Clarke called in and had a word with Mrs O'Reilly at the lodge at about 9.20 p.m. on Friday before going up to the house. Nobody except McCabe had seen him afterwards. Annie McDonnell and Mary McGowan were both seen on Sunday, but never again, the latter at about 9 a.m. on her way to Mass, the former in the village at about 1 p.m., when she spoke to a friend and was very agitated, indeed almost in tears, over Clarke's departure. She said he had left 'in a huff' on Saturday, because of the forthcoming sale. The defence scored a point here, for the friend agreed that Annie seemed to be upset out of all proportion to the event of Clarke's departure, and Mr Lynn got her to admit that something more that his mere departure, almost something sinister, seemed to be distressing her. The defence suggested on this evidence that perhaps Clarke had been done away with by one of the family, and that Annie knew or feared something. Alice was with her dressmaker in the village on Monday afternoon at 3.30, and said she was in a hurry to get home, as Annie was sick. After she left no one saw her again. Joseph and Peter were last seen on Monday morning, coming home from Mass.

So none of the six was seen alive after Monday, and as the story unfolded it seemed certain that all six were dead by Tuesday, if not by Monday evening. But the medical witnesses could only fix the times of death of two of the six, Peter McDonnell and Clarke, because the other four bodies were so affected with heat that the onset of rigor mortis could not even be guessed at.

Each of the three men had died from a fractured skull, from blows delivered from behind with a heavy blunt instrument. Clarke's body was untouched by fire, and the pathologist's opinion was that he had been dead on Monday, or even earlier and that he could have died as early as Saturday. Peter McDonnell had died on Tuesday or possibly Monday, but had not been dead as long as Clarke. No cause of death could be given for any of the three women owing to the severe mutilation of their bodies by the fire. All six bodies contained arsenic and all except Clarke's in such quantities that each of the five must have been ill. McCabe had said that both Peter and Annie vomited on the Monday, and Alice had said that Annie was ill that day.

There was nothing much to be done with this evidence in cross-examination, but the pathologist agreed that Clarke's head injury could have been caused by a blow from a golf club. This was the ghost of Peter the golfer rising again, but it was soon laid, as the evidence was that the blow could equally well have been caused by any other blunt instrument.

Mrs O'Reilly filled in the picture of events on Monday. Among the objects found in the kitchen was a piece of ham, still wrapped and tied with string. The grocer who supplied it said that it was ordered on the previous Friday, and delivered to Mrs O'Reilly on Monday afternoon. At about 4.30 p.m. she went up to the house bringing the parcel, and a can for water which she usually got from a pump in the yard. When she tried to open the wicket gate it was locked, an unprecedented occurrence in day-time. She went to the hall door, knocked and rang several times, but got no reply. She waited a few minutes, tried the other wicket gate, but it too was locked, also without precedent. She looked through the dining-room window, but could see no one, returned to the hall door, lifted the nearest window and put the parcel inside. She went back to the gate lodge about ten to five, and a few minutes later McCabe came into the avenue from the main road. She asked him what was wrong at the house. 'Were you up there?' he asked. 'I was,' she answered, 'and I could get no reply. What's wrong, Harry? Tell Miss McDonnell that I left in the parcel through the window on the left of the hall door.' McCabe said 'They are all sick.' She asked who were sick, and McCabe said that Mary McGowan was, and had had to go to bed early that morning, thus contradicting his statement that he saw her up to 5 p.m. in her usual health. Peter, he said, was ill at midday.

Mrs O'Reilly said, 'I saw Peter at Mass this morning,' and McCabe replied, 'He got sick in the yard and vomited at 12 o'clock. Annie came out to me at 1 o'clock to kill a chicken and got sick in the yard also. She was going to Dublin and wasn't able, so she sent me.'

'Were you in town?' she asked.

'Yes. I went in on the two and came back on the four train.'

She asked where was Jim Clarke and said she hadn't seen him the day before, Sunday. McCabe said he was away.

'Since when?'

'Since Saturday.'

'He was in on Friday with me and said nothing about going.'

McCabe made no reply to this and went towards the house.

Then she dealt with Tuesday morning. McCabe came down to the lodge from the house at about eleven o'clock, and asked was she going to the village, as he wanted tobacco. She wasn't going, so she promised to try to get someone else to do the message. He gave her a shilling for the tobacco. She told the Court she had a standing arrangement with Peter McDonnell that if he was not at early Mass she would buy the daily paper and he would call to her for it. He had not been at Mass, nor had he come to the lodge, as he did every Tuesday for bread, so she gave McCabe the paper — the *Irish Independent* — and asked him to give it to Peter. McCabe told her she need not come up to the house with the tobacco but he would come down for it — a significant request, said the prosecution, for McCabe needed privacy that day. Mrs O'Reilly said that in all the years he had worked at La Mancha he had never before asked her to do a message. At one o'clock McCabe returned, and as she had not got the tobacco she gave him back the shilling, and he said he would get it himself during the dinner hour. He did not mention the illnesses of the family nor, curiously, did she ask him.

None of this was challenged in cross-examination, except the day of McCabe's request for tobacco, which was suggested to be Monday, but Mrs O'Reilly was positive it was Tuesday, which was confirmed for her by the newspaper purchase and Peter's non-appearance for the bread.

The prosecution then came to Tuesday afternoon. A Mr Lambert, rate collector, called at about 2.30 p.m. to collect the water rate, usually paid by Peter McDonnell. When he got to the house, everything, he said, was 'silent as the tomb'. The dogs were not about; the blinds were drawn in the dining-room and the drawing-room; nobody was to be seen. He knocked and rang several times, got no answer, went to the side of the house, but as he still saw nobody, he returned to the front steps and knocked again. He was about to try the side again when he saw McCabe standing close to him, but didn't see where he had come from. He told him he had been knocking and ringing and could get no reply, and McCabe said Peter was ill and in bed. Mr Lambert apologised to him. 'My God, had I known there was anybody ill in the place I wouldn't have come near the house at all,' and in Court he added, as if he had done something unforgivable, 'My lord, I would not go near the place if there was a dog or a cat sick in the house. I was very sorry for what I had done.' His concern over the trifle must have caused a few smiles in the grim trial atmosphere. He said he gave McCabe the demand note — found afterwards in a drawer in the kitchen — and left. At about 5 o'clock, on his way home he passed the avenue and saw no smoke coming from the chimneys, nor any sign of life. As he said, 'About 5 o'clock the people have their tea, and you usually see smoke.' He was a chatty witness.

Two children, Mary and Seamus Wall, completed the picture of the silent house. They were selling tickets for the Malahide Fête. Calling between 5 and 6 o'clock, on the way up to the house they sold a ticket to Mrs O'Reilly. At the house nobody was about; they knocked repeatedly, but got no response. Then McCabe appeared from the left-hand side, and asked what they wanted. Mary explained, and McCabe said he had not got his money with him, and went round to the side to get some. The boy gave him the book, and after a while McCabe returned and said he would take three tickets, one for himself and the others for Joe and Miss Alice. He gave half a crown, got a shilling change and the tickets, which were found afterwards with the rates notice. Mary Wall noticed that McCabe was wearing grey trousers. The remaining evidence as to Tuesday concerned McCabe's movements. He was seen by one man at about 8.15 p.m. near La Mancha, carrying a milk-can, and by another at about 9.40 p.m., going towards the village about two hundred yards from La Mancha.

So far, the notice had not been touched, and the prosecution now called a man named Willoughby, who said McCabe told him he was expecting to be 'knocked off' by the McDonnells, and asked if there was any work available where he was employed. As a motive for murder and arson, the coming loss of employment seemed very slender. And the robbery motive was thin, too, for none of the loot was ever traced to McCabe or found in his possession, apart from some clothing. The McDonnells were believed by McCabe, and by repute generally, to be wealthy, but no evidence was given to show that the valuables in the household had been stolen instead of being destroyed in the fire. That was left to inference. These valuables were described by a former maid, Sheila Reilly, who said that the McDonnell women owned diamond and sapphire rings, brooches, and the like, which were never locked up, but kept in jewel-cases and open presses. The men had gold watches, chains, and tie-pins, and one wore a gold ring, and money was kept loose in the house.

This witness flatly denied having ever told McCabe that Joseph was not on speaking terms with the others; she had never known such a thing. During her time there — she left in 1924 — the yard gates and the inner porch door were invariably locked at night, and unlocked first thing in the morning. McCabe always came in through one of the wicket gates, and never had occasion to go further into the house than the kitchen. She was asked in cross-examination if McCabe, so far as she was aware, could know in which rooms the various members of the family slept. She could not say, as she she had seen him only in the kitchen. The question was designed to refute the prosecution's suggestion that he had deliberately misled Sergeant Kenny as to the location of these rooms, so as to give more time for the fire to gain a grip, but the witness added that she only knew the various bedrooms from working upstairs. So McCabe's knowledge of Peter McDonnell's bedroom again looked peculiar. How did he know it was not Joseph's bedroom unless he had been there, and in the other bedrooms, before the 1st April?

The Gardaí had taken the grey trousers from McCabe, and these were identified as Peter McDonnell's, and matched with the coat and waistcoat of the suit. Then Garda Hayden gave evidence of an incident concerning the trousers. When McCabe was in the barracks under arrest, he said to the Garda, 'It is all up with me now. I am going to Mountjoy [prison] in the morning. It is all over the pants I have on me. Will you be able to get out and tell my wife to say that I got the pants some time ago, in a parcel that the McDonnells sent me, and tell her to keep it quiet?' This was a most incautious request, for McCabe must have realised, if he thought of the matter at all, that the Garda would be bound to report the conversation to his superiors. The cross-examination did not seriously challenge this evidence, although McCabe was going to give a very different account of the incident.

The prosecution closed their case with two more witnesses. One was Clarke's brother John, who said that there had never been any dispute between himself and the deceased, and that they were good friends always. The other, Daniel McCann, described a curious incident. On 2 April, the day of the funeral, he met McCabe in the village and in conversation asked him if he thought Joe did it [the murder]. McCabe said, 'Nonsense, not at all.' Just then the cortège was seen approaching, and McCann said he was going to the funeral and inquired if McCabe was. McCabe said no, and left him to walk down the street.

The Defence

On Thursday afternoon, the fourth day of the trial, McCabe began his evidence under Mr Lynn's questioning. His narrative started with Saturday 27th, when he arrived for work at 9 o'clock, and at midday Peter McDonnell gave him his wages, which he sent home to his wife. At about 2 o'clock, he said, Clarke asked him to go to the public library in the village to look at the newspaper advertisement of the sale of La Mancha; they had heard something about this from a neighbour earlier in the week. He told Clarke he had no time to go and went on working. This made nonsense of his former statement of how, three weeks before the fire, he had read the advertisement and told Clarke about it, and of Clarke's reactions. If that was true, Clarke wouldn't have asked him to go to the library on 27 March, since he already knew about the advertisement.

Later, he said, at about 3.30 p.m. he saw Clarke crossing the yard, towards a barn, and never saw him alive again. At about 4.30 Joseph McDonnell told him Clarke had gone to Dublin, and might or might not be back by the last train, and said no more. McCabe had now contradicted what he had told McCann on 31 March, that Clarke had gone to the country to see about some land for the McDonnells.

He said he was asked by Joseph to stay and milk the cows and to wait until the last train came in. He left the house at midnight, and as Clarke was not back he was told to come early on Sunday.

Next morning (Sunday) Mary McGowan admitted him through the wicket gate and he worked as usual, and she gave him his tea that evening, and went to the chapel at about 7.30 p.m.; at that time Annie, Alice, and Peter were there. Joseph told him to come early next morning to milk, and he then went home.

On Monday, he said, he arrived at 8.50 a.m., meeting Joseph and Peter on the avenue, did some work, and was called by Alice to breakfast, Mary McGowan being there then. He worked as usual, and during the morning went down to Mrs O'Reilly for tobacco, and returned later to collect the shilling from her. She, it will be recalled, was positive that this occurred on Tuesday. Annie called him at 2.30 p.m. — he had said twelve noon in two of his statements — and asked him to kill a chicken which he did — a dead chicken was in fact found hanging in a shed. She told him she was in a hurry to go to Dublin, and went into the kitchen, where he heard her vomiting (he had told Mrs O'Reilly that this happened in the yard). After he had killed the chicken he went into the kitchen to return a knife Annie had given him, and Mary McGowan was there washing clothes. He went back into the yard, where he saw Peter McDonnell, and worked on in the garden till about 5 p.m. This was his evidence then:

Q. Up to what time did you work in the garden?
A. Roughly about 5 o'clock.
Q. What did you do then?
A. I went into the house and got some water.
Q. Whom did you see when you got the water?
A. I saw Joe McDonnell.
Q. Did you speak to him?
A. I spoke to him and I said. 'I wish Mary was here to take the clothes out of the sink, as I can't get the bucket under the tap.'
Q. By Mary you referred to Mary McGowan?
A. Yes.
Q. Did he answer?
A. Yes, he said Mary was not well.
Q. Did he say anything about the other people?
A. In fact, he said they were all a bit sick.
Q. Did you answer anything?
A. Yes, I said it was very sad.
Q. Did Mr Joe McDonnell say anything to that?
A. Yes, he said: 'They are not bad. I think it is only their dinner has upset them.'

217

Q. Did you have dinner that day with the McDonnell family?
A. I did.
Q. Judge: About what hour?
A. It would be about 1.45 p.m.
Q. Judge: Did you take it in the kitchen?
A. I did, my lord.
Q. Judge: Did anybody else have dinner with you?
A. Yes, Mary McGowan.

Another contradiction occurs here, for his statement said he last saw Mary McGowan up to 5 o'clock, and in her usual health. Now he swears that at roughly 5 o'clock she is not there and he is told she is ill.

Mrs O'Reilly had said that at 4.30 she got no reply when she knocked, but according to McCabe's evidence Joseph and he were there then, and so was Mary McGowan if his statement was true — he saw her 'up to about 5 o'clock'. One of the three, therefore, should have answered the door. Yet Mrs O'Reilly was quite positive that McCabe came in from the road and told her he had just been to Dublin, and her evidence had not been challenged. But McCabe was going to deny that he had said this. He went on to say that he went to the village at about 5 p.m. and had a drink in Hogan's public-house, as he was feeling sick, and came back at 5.30 when Mrs O'Reilly told him about leaving the parcel and finding no one at the house. He said he told her he thought they were unwell — another inconsistency, since he knew Joseph was not ill. The judge asked was anything else said, and he was positive that that was all.

He said he went into the kitchen for his tea about 6 o'clock, having been called by Joseph. Nobody was in the kitchen, not even Joseph; he just heard Joseph calling him. After tea he worked till about 7.15 and returned to the kitchen, where Joseph was now sitting by the fire. McCabe sat on the other side of the fire, and both read, and talked a little, about the Grand National and cattle prices. The sick people were not mentioned, which is astonishing. It was very hard, said McCabe, to get an answer out of Joseph, who was known to be a quiet person. 'I was very much like themselves. They were not like other gentlemen I worked for at other places. In La Mancha it wasn't "Mr Joe" and "Mr Peter"; it was "Joe" and "Peter", and "Harry" and "Jim".' This was, presumably, to give colour to the unusual picture of employer and servant chatting by the fire. He left at about 8 o'clock, saying that he wished Clarke was back. Joseph said, 'Have a look round and you might see him.' If

Joseph said this he was being very off-hand about his servant, who had only gone to Dublin, nine miles away, and was due back on the evening he left.

On Tuesday, the critical day, he said he arrived at La Mancha at about five minutes to nine, found the gate bolted on the inside, and after a few minutes Joseph came and opened it. They said nothing to each other apart from greetings — still not a word about the sick household. There was no one in the kitchen, and he worked as usual, being called by Joseph at about 9.45 for breakfast. He said he heard steps overhead as if someone was walking in the hall. At this stage of the day he might as well have been, on his story, in a house of the dead, and probably was, for even Joseph was not in view, though McCabe said he called him again at 1.30 for his dinner. In the afternoon Joseph was in the yard, he said, 'just standing there'. McCabe's version of his meeting Lambert and the Wall children suggested two coincidences — that he happened to go out to the front of he house as each was there, and not in response to their knocks. His account of what he said to Lambert was, 'I think Mr Peter is ill. But Joe is up in the yard.' Lambert, he said, was in a hurry and gave him the demand note, which he handed to Joseph immediately.

His tea on Tuesday evening was prepared and served to him by Joseph — the fourth of such meals, if he was to be believed — but he said nothing of food being prepared for the invalids, nor of anything else being done for them — no doctor, no servant to replace Mary McGowan, no attention of any kind. And McCabe did not inquire how the sick ones were, if his story was true. But of course it could not have been. He described Tuesday evening after tea in exactly the same way as Monday; he and Joseph sat in front of the fire, and talked of the same topics as the night before. The scene was indeed identical. He said he left at about 8 p.m., though he had told McKenna he stayed up very late with Joseph, and when going asked again about Clarke, and was told, 'Have a look around Malahide and you might see him.' He went to the railway station, he said, after going home, thinking that Clarke might come, and returned home about 10 o'clock. There he was told that a neighbour was dying, and he went to the house at about 11 p.m. where he stayed all night, as several witnesses proved and the prosecution accepted. His evidence as to events from then until his arrival at the Garda Station tallied with his statement, save for two contradictions: he said the inner door was half open, not 'burst open', and he saw no object lying in the passage.

219

His account of the finding of the keys was that, when going through the house with Sergeant Kenny, they came across a ladder placed where the staircase to the bedrooms had been. Kenny said, 'McCabe, you are a lighter man than I am. Go up that ladder and see if you can find any photographs; or if you can get any keys, bring them back to me'; he did as he was told, and found the keys and pennies as already recounted. How the jury could be expected to believe this story we can only guess, for McCabe was saying that he had, in effect, been employed to assist the Gardaí in their investigations, and to search an upstairs room; and this at a time when he was under suspicion, though he didn't know it, and the house was full of Gardaí and the public was being kept out.

He had to give his version of the conversation with Garda Hayden about the trousers. He said Hayden came into the barracks, walked over to him and asked how he was, expressing some surprise at his change of garments, for he was no longer wearing the grey trousers, which had been taken by the Gardaí. McCabe told him he had been charged, and Hayden said, 'Good Heavens! I did not expect that.' McCabe said, 'They are making a lot of fuss over the trousers I was wearing; one would think it was a crime to accept a present from their employers.' Hayden asked did his wife know, and he said not, and that he didn't want any of his children to know about it, and 'if you see her will you tell her to keep it quiet'. He explained to the Court, 'I was referring to the arrest and that she should keep it quiet from the young children. I was not referring to the trousers.'

Before the cross-examination, he was again asked when he had last seen Peter and Annie, and he changed the times again, this time saying he saw Peter last at about one o'clock, and Annie about twelve or half-past.

Mr Carrigan began by asking McCabe if the inner door was 'burst open' when he arrived. 'It was open,' he said, and was reminded that he had said 'burst open' in his statement. He was asked the question again, and didn't answer, but then said he had told the police that the door might have been burst in. That was the first pitfall. He denied having shown the inner door and lock to Sergeant Kenny and saying, 'There must be some foul play,' and said that someone else had shown these things to the Sergeant. Again he was referred to the statement, and asked when he had seen the lock lying in the passage. He said, 'I did not notice the lock at the time. I did not look for anything like that,' which was another contradiction of his statement.

He had to resort to further denials. He said he did not tell Sergeant Mooney that the family was 'all right' the night before the fire; what he had said was 'everything' was all right. This, he agreed, meant both house and occupants, and then had to explain whether he had thought the occupants would be at Mass when their house was on fire. He said he hadn't known what to think, and denied asking Murphy if they could all be 'gone' (dead). He put himself into a hopeless tangle by saying, in answer to further questions, that when no one answered his shouts, he had no fears for the occupants, and did not think it was a case of murder.

One wonders if he can have had any idea of the meaning of this evidence, for according to his story on Tuesday night he left the house with five people alive, four of whom were ill, either in bed or confined upstairs; on Wednesday he found the house in flames, and must have thought the invalids were in mortal danger, and, as Joseph was not about, that he too might have been in peril. Yet he said he had no fears for them!

He could not explain his absence from the funeral. When asked the reason, he said it was because he had been busy at the time getting a pump mended in the village, a pump belonging to La Mancha. When he realised the absurdity of this answer, he changed his ground, and said the real reason was that he didn't know the time of the funeral. Then he had to explain why he, the sole survivor of La Mancha, didn't know this, and said that he had inquired but could not discover it. Yet he had to agree that McCann had said the funeral was coming down the street as they talked. He tried to get out of that admission by saying that McCann was wrong; the funeral wasn't coming then.

He was then asked why he had described Alice, Peter, and Joseph as being very peculiar, and was again in difficulties. He agreed that the family were perfectly normal, except that Alice sometimes came into the garden singing after washing her hair, but that was no answer to the question. All he could say then was that the words used in the statements were not his, but his questioners'; and that the statements did not represent what he had said. The police officers had sworn that they read out the statements to McCabe before he signed, and that he had agreed they were accurate and correct, but he denied this, and said he had just signed without knowing their contents.

Clarke's absence was then dealt with. No preparations were made for his departure that he knew of, and he was not asked to stay in the house, as was the custom formerly. He agreed that Clarke

221

suddenly disappeared, in effect, and was wearing his working clothes when he saw him last, crossing the yard towards a shed. He had not discussed Clarke's absence with Mary McGowan, nor with anybody else, which was strange to say the least.

The rest of his evidence consisted principally of denials. He denied having told Mrs O'Reilly that 'they were all sick', that Peter had vomited in the yard, and that he himself had been in Dublin. His statement that he last saw Mary McGowan up to 5 o'clock on Monday was a mistake; it should have been 2.30 or so. Asked to say how he was free to go out for a drink during his working day, he said that whenever he or Clarke wanted to go out they did not need permission, for the McDonnells were not strict. If this was true, of course, he could also have gone out to buy tobacco, and need not have asked Mrs O'Reilly to do it. He was positive that on Monday, not Tuesday, he went down to the lodge for the tobacco and got the paper. As to Lambert, he did not hear him knocking and ringing because he was in the vinery at the time.

The last topic was the keys. He could not reconcile his statement — 'There was no particular reason why I looked for the keys' — with his evidence that Sergeant Kenny had sent him up the ladder to look for them. He tried to suggest that he had told Superintendent O'Halloran about it, but that the Superintendent had left it out of the statement.

When McCabe returned to the dock there was a serious omission from his evidence. He had not been asked by either counsel how he had come by Peter McDonnell's trousers, and so this vital matter was left to inference, and there could only be one inference, for McCabe's suggestion to Garda Hayden that they were a gift was not evidence.

The defence now produced what seemed at first to be a trump card. Two women swore that on Tuesday 30th, soon after 8 p.m., they met Joseph McDonnell near La Mancha, walking towards Malahide. He greeted them — 'Good night, ladies' — and they returned his greeting. They had seen McCabe a few minutes earlier, near the station. But they did not tell anyone of this incident, although they had heard next morning of the tragedy. One of the women was McCabe's next-door neighbour, and could not explain why, when the police were at her house digging the garden and doing likewise at McCabe's (they were searching for the spoils of La Mancha), she did not tell them about meeting Joseph. The Judge questioned her, and she agreed the information was important, but it did not occur to her to tell the police about it.

When the defence had finished, the Judge recalled Lambert and Sheila Reilly. Lambert was asked if McCabe had mentioned Joseph when they spoke, and was positive that he hadn't, for otherwise, he said, he would have gone into the yard and given the demand note to Joseph. 'Absolutely false,' he said of that part of McCabe's evidence. Sheila Reilly provided the finishing touch. The Judge asked her where the family usually sat at night, and she said the dining-room. She had never known Joseph to sit in the kitchen for more than a moment or two, which was to be expected, since he had a comfortable room upstairs.

The evidence was now complete, and all that remained were the speeches and the summing up. Mr Lynn did his best with a hopeless client, and a hopeless case. He suggested that Annie's agitation on the Sunday was the key to the case, and that she then knew Clarke was dead and murdered by one of her brothers. He poured scorn on the motive, saying that if McCabe had wanted to rob the place, the proper time to do it was a few years earlier, when there was a civil war in Ireland and property was being destroyed daily.

Mr Carrigan spoke at length, calling McCabe an arch-criminal and concluding with a scriptural reference to Cain and Abel, and the blood of the dead crying to be avenged.

The Judge's charge was not favourable to McCabe, but he told the jury that if they believed the two women had seen Joseph McDonnell on Tuesday night they should acquit; he did not believe them, but of course it was for the jury to believe or disbelieve. He commented upon the failure of the defence to call the publican, to corroborate McCabe's evidence that he had been in the public-house on Monday for a drink. He pointed out that McCabe had not told how he got possession of Peter McDonnell's trousers, and suggested he might have needed them because his own were in such a state from blood, or otherwise, that he was forced to wear another pair.

The jury did not take long. After fifty minutes they returned with a verdict of guilty. It was 9.05 p.m. on Saturday, and everyone engaged in the trial was showing signs of strain. McCabe had exhibited strangely little interest during the preceding days in what was going on, but in the last few hours had shown some anxiety. When he was asked had he anything to say before sentence, his answer was 'All I have to say is, God forgive them and you. I have been the victim of bribery and perjury.' He was then sentenced to death, the Judge adding amidst tense silence, 'I can hold out no hope of mercy to you in this world. I advise and implore you to spend the remainder of the time allotted to you in this world, preparing to meet your Maker.'

McCabe appealed unsuccessfully, and was executed 9 December 1926.

———————

The case is still spoken of in Dublin, and is known as the Malahide Mystery. There is not much mystery about McCabe's guilt, as this story shows, and observers at the trial say the same. But there are two mysteries. One is: what happened to the valuables? They were never traced to McCabe, nor to anyone else. The other mystery is: how did McCabe murder six people without being discovered?

The first victim must have been Clarke. He disappeared at some time between Friday evening and, at the latest, Sunday morning, for on that day Annie McDonnell spoke of his earlier departure. The only other clue to the time of Clarke's disappearance is McCabe's evidence that he last saw him walking across the yard towards a barn on Saturday afternoon. If this was true, McCabe may have followed, murdered him, and concealed his body in the straw for later removal, telling his employers that he had gone away in a huff. As Clarke was tall and big, McCabe would have had difficulty in felling him from behind, but a Malahide resident who remembers the case says it was generally believed in the village that McCabe waited until Clarke was stooping to milk a cow, and then attacked him from behind with a spanner.

How did he murder the other five? The arsenic, presumably put into the food by McCabe on Monday, is perhaps the clue to this. It seems at least likely that all were still alive on Monday up to midday, but having eaten were forced to retire to bed, and so became incapable of resisting violence. But Annie was out that afternoon at the dressmaker's, and, at least up to then, unaffected by the poison. Were the other four despatched while she was out? — and did she meet her doom on returning to La Mancha? The house was well set back from the road, and until Mrs O'Reilly came up with the parcel of ham there were no callers to interrupt McCabe at his dreadful work. Was he alarmed by her persistent knocking? It would have been easy for him to reach the road by the footpath, appear at the lodge a few minutes after her with his story of the Dublin visit and the illnesses, to allay her curiosity, and so ensure that she would not go again to the house.

———————

La Mancha remained in ruins for some years, and was then sold and all but the basement walls demolished. These still stand, but are hidden beneath earth and weeds, though the stone steps up which Sergeant Kenny and the others climbed are intact. One of the yard buildings is now used as a dwelling, and the yard is as it was in 1926, except that the wicket gates are gone. The gate lodge has also been demolished, but the entrance gates from the road are there still, and the avenues and drive are intact, though over-grown and neglected. The place has a sombre and melancholy air, brightened a little by some attractive bungalows which have been built on the ground between the site of the house and the road. As you pass along the road, you get glimpses through the trees of the rank and overgrown lawn, and the stone steps, reminders of the tragedy of 1926.

In the nearby cemetery there is another reminder. All six were buried in Margaret McDonnell's grave, and the headstone reads:

Of your charity pray for the souls of
Margaret McDonnell, late of Ballygar,
Co. Galway, who died at La Mancha, Malahide,
19th January 1924,
her sisters
Annie McDonnell
Alice McDonnell
her brothers
Joseph McDonnell
Peter McDonnell
Also their faithful servants
James Clarke
Mary McGowan
who died at La Mancha, Malahide, on or
about 31st March 1926.

R.I.P.

Mother of Sorrows intercede for them.